LANGUAGE
AS A LIVELY ART

LANGUAGE
AS A LIVELY ART

•

Ray Past

Department of English
University of Texas at El Paso

WM. C. BROWN COMPANY PUBLISHERS
Dubuque, Iowa

CONTENTS

FOREWORD

Here we have at last a lively and understandable single textbook, linguistically sound, that seeks to give the student a decent understanding of recent developments in English language study and theory and to provide some breadth of viewpoint as regards other areas of language study than the grammar itself.

This book is not erudite, but neither is it childish. In no place has the author sacrificed accuracy in order to entertain. Its easy informality is that of a knowledgeable scholar conversing with interested but uninformed persons and able, in talking, to translate the specialist's prose into terms the layman can understand. In this book will be found a content that should give to the person using it an educational experience such as he has never had before. He will look at language in a new way and see it in a new perspective. He will gain not only factual details but also an attitude that will inform all his thinking about his language the rest of his life.

University of Minnesota   Harold B. Allen

PREFACE

It is the conviction of perhaps most language teachers that language study ought to be stimulating, even exciting. Sadly, students seldom find it so. A poll on any campus—at whatever level of the educational process—would inevitably show "English" to be the least liked subject, and the "language" component of it to be primarily responsible. The student knows, perhaps accepts on faith, that grammar is somehow supposed to be "good for him" but he loathes it. Worse, he is bored by it.

This book is an effort to break through that barrier of boredom, to show the student that tedium is not a necessary concomitant of "English," and that in fact a study of our language can be lively. Further, the points are made both explicitly and implicitly throughout the text that (1) we do not need to accept as gospel statements made to us about language but can and should test such statements against our own knowledge of our own language, and (2) we can adopt an objective attitude toward language study and need not discuss it in whispers nor in the professorial prose the student has learned to dread.

The lightness of tone (and I hope the simple clarity) of this book most emphatically should not be taken as implying that the material in it is unsound or has been dealt with casually. I have treated it as honestly and as earnestly as if I had written with all the ponderous pomposity of which I have at times been guilty elsewhere.

The instructor will understand that this is an *introductory* book to modern language study and is not, therefore, comprehensive. I wrote it because I could not find a book like it for my own introductory course, my underclassmen being generally students who would find Gleason, Francis, Chomsky, *et al* pretty rough going. The book doesn't pretend to meet the needs of all students from third grade through graduate school: it is intended for the college freshman or sophomore, not for the upperclassman majoring in linguistics, much less for the really advanced student. It should also be very useful for prospective teachers, who will (whatever they teach) be teachers of language, inevitably, and could afford to know something about it. The book will not make the reader a linguist but rather will introduce him to some of the directions being taken by modern students of language, hopefully whetting his appetite for deeper exploration. To this end a bibliography of further readings is appended, and frequent mention is made throughout the book of articles, chapters of books, and occasionally entire books which the student might likely find interesting.

There is available, to accompany the book, an exercise manual designed to aid both comprehension and retention. It contains an answer section so the student can check comprehension for himself.

Because this text is not the alpha and omega of language study, the instructor will be able to find much that he can supply. Though I made every effort to make the text simple, clear and easily-understandable, and the student should have no trouble with it, there is still much beyond its limitations that the classroom instructor will want to take up. This is not only inevitable (for any but an advanced-level book on a limited topic, which this isn't) but is, I think, desirable. I still remember my frustration a number of years ago when as a result of one of those staff emergencies that occasionally occur, I suddenly found myself conducting a course in modern British drama, which I didn't consider myself particularly qualified to teach. I had a textbook that was really good. In fact I had the uncomfortable feeling that if the student read the plays with any sensitivity at all, and then read carefully the editor's critical analyses, historical backgrounds, stage histories, biographies, and so on for a disgustingly brilliant performance, drat him, there wasn't really very much left for me to add. I can modestly say that the instructor will not find that flaw in this text. However, I know of no language text that could provide him with this particular problem. In any event, the teacher will not feel that the book limits him, but will more likely find it a springboard.

ACKNOWLEDGMENTS

I tried to keep this text free from the usual scholarly apparatus of footnotes, which meant that I denied myself the privilege of pulling books down from the shelves to get someone's telling point here and someone else's juicy quotation there, for of course the result would have been footnotes. The book, then, comes primarily from my own introductory language classes and from knowledge and information locked up in my own head.

This knowledge did not, obviously, suddenly germinate itself within those limited confines, nor did I invent it. I have acquired it over the years from many sources, and many of those sources, were they to read this book, would find familiar ideas and even, perhaps, expressions. Right now I both thank them for what they taught me and offer a blanket apology to any who might think I have given insufficient recognition to their contributions. You will recognize that after a number of years' work in a field it is frequently difficult to cite the source of an idea—and sometimes very easy to assume it is one's own.

Of all the scholars to whom I am indebted I undoubtedly owe the most to those whose books I have taught from. There is no way to absorb a book thoroughly that is quite equivalent to using it as a text. Among the books that have served me in this fashion, some of them for a number of years, are the following:

Allen, Harold. *Applied English Linguistics,* Eds. 1 & 2.
Anderson, Wallace L., and Norman C. Stageberg. *Introductory Readings on Language.*
Bach, Emmon. *An Introduction to Transformational Grammars.*
Baugh, Albert C. *The History of the English Language.*

Brown, Dona Worrell, Wallace C. Brown, and Dudley Bailey. *Form in Modern English.*

Buchanan, Cynthia. *A Programed Introduction to Linguistics.*

Dean, Leonard F. and Kenneth G. Wilson. *Essays on Language and Usage.*

Francis, W. Nelson. *The Structure of American English.*

Fries, Charles C. *The Structure of English.*

Gleason, H.A., Jr. *Linguistics and English Grammar.*

Hunt, Kellog W., and Paul Stoakes. *Our Living Language,* Eds. 1 & 2.

Koutsoudas, Andreas. *On Writing Transformational Grammars.*

Roberts, Paul. *English Sentences.*

———————. *Patterns of English.*

———————. *Understanding English.*

Thomas, Owen. *Transformational Grammar and the Teacher of English.*

Other books with which I consider myself thoroughly familiar are: Bloomfield's *Language,* Chomsky's *Syntactic Structures,* Fries' *American English Grammar,* Gleason's *Introduction to Descriptive Linguistics,* Hill's *Introduction to Linguistic Structures,* Hockett's *Course in Modern Linguistics,* Marckwardt's *Introduction to the English Language,* Robert's *English Syntax,* and Whitehall's *Structural Essentials of English.*

To the authors of all these books, and to others I may have overlooked including, I give a wave of thanks. Though few of their names appear in the pages of this text, their ideas and their teachings are what it is very largely made of. Or more accurately, their thoughts and their teachings as they have been jumbled together, mashed and fermented, and even—with presumption—added to in the course of my using them—these make up what I have to say.

I have been fortunate in being able to sit at the feet of many fine language scholars and in knowing others outside the classroom, with the opportunity and privilege of discussing language matters with them. Among them would be Albert C. Baugh, the late Bagby Atwood, Rudolph Willard, Summer Ives, Sol Saporta, Samuel Martin, and the late Bernard Bloch. Among distinguished language scholars I am happy to count as friends and fortunate to be able to learn from are Archibald A. Hill, Rudolph Troike, and William Slager.

I owe a particular debt to Dr. Troike who did me the immense service of reading this text in manuscript and who offered me scores of invaluable suggestions, saving me from a number of blunders.

Another linguist whose help was invaluable was Dr. Edward Blansitt, now a colleague at The University of Texas at El Paso, who also read and critiqued the typescript. A tagmemicist by persuasion, he takes a dim view of binary IC analysis and of transformational grammar, so his patience in aiding me was particularly kind.

Professor Barnet Kottler of Purdue University also made numerous valuable suggestions, for which I thank him.

Among colleagues on my campus who have been most generous with their time and of inestimable help to me have been Professors C.L. Sonnichsen, Haldeen Braddy, Tony Stafford, Patricia Adkins and—most especially—my office-neighbor, Eleanor Cotton, who read all the m.s. and made many good suggestions.

All or any of the above-named people, whether friends, colleagues, authors of cited books—or all these things together—will find in the pages of this text traces of their contributions, and for their aid, whether voluntary or unknowing, I thank them.

I am grateful to Mrs. Sherrye Bradshaw Powers, a very young lady originally entirely innocent of "linguistics" who not only typed the entire manuscript but read it and says she understands it, bless her. I wish to thank also Miss Margarita Correa who re-typed about half the m.s. after numerous editings had reduced it to a shambles.

Finally, I owe a special thanks to two members of my own family. To my son Al, an English major with a minor in Linguistics at The University of Texas at Austin, who read my pages critically with an undergraduate's discerning eye; and to my wife Frannie, who puts up with me.

July, 1969   R.P.

CHAPTER 1

LANGUAGE: WHAT IS IT?

If you're like most people you talk a lot. Perhaps too much sometimes. Almost everybody, except hermits and Trappist monks, starts talking when he gets up in the morning and keeps at it until he hits the pillow at night. This is not to say we don't ever hush—you're probably silent at the moment you read these lines—but obviously talking is one of the things we humans do the most. Did you ever stand in the doorway at a large party and note the uproar of talk? One person raises his voice to be heard above the racket, so his neighbor has to raise his still further, until the noise approaches the unendurable. Perhaps this is, partly, why so many people have headaches on the morning after parties. Be that as it may, this constantly clattering tongue is man's most distinguishing characteristic, so much so that man is often defined as "the talking animal." Whatever the theologians may have to say, the most *obvious* thing distinguishing men and women from what we like to call lower forms of life is *speech.*

And you do all this talking unconsciously. That is, hopefully you are thinking about what you are saying, but only rarely, as when you're being interviewed for a job or dining for the first time with your fiancee's family, do you ever think about how you say it. Almost always you have the subject agreeing with the verb, the adjective placed before the noun, the words in their proper order, and the words pronounced in proper fashion—all without thinking. Of course sometimes you slip—everybody does—but nearly always you'll catch the error and correct it. For instance, did you ever create a Spoonerism? A Spoonerism, named after an English gentleman named (naturally) Spooner, who was quite famous for this error, occurs when we accidentally swap the sounds of two words. Two of his more famous

1

ones are "ears and sparrows" when he meant to say "spears and arrows," and "tons of soil" for "sons of toil." Anyhow, if you ever did make such a blunder you undoubtedly noticed it immediately and corrected it, amid the hilarity of your friends and your own embarrassment. (Spooner also is said to have asked a lady in church: "Pardon me, madam, is this pie occupewed?") Undoubtedly speakers of all languages make such slips, and considering the tremendous complexity of language, which becomes more and more apparent as we try to analyze it, it's amazing that we don't all make more of them, especially considering also how very much we talk.

Since language is so much a part of us, then, it is appropriate for us to inquire into its nature. What is it really? How does this miracle work? It really is a miracle. Some electric impulses get zipping around in your brain, charging up the little grey cells, and you come up with an idea. The idea is probably useless where it is: you want to tell somebody about it. So, zap, zap, some more electronic impulses and you take a breath and get your voice motor going. You make the proper series of sounds, which set the air in vibration. These vibrations bang up against the eardrums in your friend's head and set them to vibrating too. This vibration stirs up some other electronic impulses in his brain and presto: the idea you once were stuck with as sole proprietor now lodges in your friend's head too. It has been shared. Trying to describe just exactly what takes place during this process is very difficult and has occupied the full time of a great many distinguished scholars and scientists, and they haven't described it yet, either. But they are constantly coming up with ideas—hypotheses—and they are worthy of our attention.

Why? Simply because language is so intensely human. Let's face it, nothing interests us so much as ourselves. What do we like to talk about, hear about, read about? Ourselves, mostly. We study history, archaeology, biology, sociology, psychology, etc. etc. to learn more about ourselves. Such studies are not going to "do us any good," not unless we plan to become professional historians, archaeologists, biologists, sociologists, psychologists, etc. etc. So with the study of language. We are not interested in it because it will somehow wonderfully make us more efficient, more lovable or more plutocratic. The study of language very likely won't even make us better speakers or writers of it. But if we ask the right questions as we study language, and if we go about finding out, or working out, the answers in the proper spirit, we can learn some things about ourselves, about how we function in our daily lives: about, in short, what it is that makes us human.

With all the talking that you do, have you ever thought about exactly what language is? What is it that you do when you use it? How does it work? How does it differ from some other language? What does it have in common with some other language? How does an idea get from my brain to my friend's brain with, usually, a fair degree of precision? Or, on the other hand, when the transmission of the idea is fouled up, how did it get fouled up? Why did the communication system, which I've always taken for granted like breathing, break down?

Let's begin our probing into this matter of language with a definition of it. We must recognize that there are many definitions of "language," depending sometimes on the intended purpose, and that ours will be a tentative, imperfect, working definition. If we need to revise it later we always can. However, to get our discussion started we need a starting point. Let's try something like this:

> A language is an arbitrary system of arbitrary vocal symbols used by a human society in carrying on its affairs.

This definition certainly is not airtight. But neither is it casual, even to the stylistically clumsy repetition of "arbitrary." Each word in it has a purpose, as we shall see.

Let's consider some of the terms in this definition, one at a time and in no particular order. We'll begin with the word "vocal."

The first thing to notice is that "vocal" implies that language is speech, not writing. You might think this obvious enough but to many people it isn't. And perhaps it is natural that we think of writing rather than speech, for certainly *as a problem* writing looms much larger than speech. Consider. When did you learn to talk? You can't remember. When you project your memory back as far as you can, what are the very earliest things you can recall? Probably some stirring events that took place when you were four, or maybe three. But at this time, if you were a normal child, you were already chattering brightly away and mommy and daddy were boring their friends with repetitions of your bright sayings. You don't remember a time when you couldn't talk. Much less can you remember anything of how you learned.

But writing is a different thing. Most of us can remember our early struggles with pencil and paper. The schoolroom with model letters of the alphabet displayed above the chalkboard. The paper with the wide-ruled lines so we could get the short and the tall letters in correct proportion. The prize papers, perhaps with gold stars, pinned to the classroom bulletin board. The struggles with spelling.

One of my early school memories is of getting busted out of a spelling bee for spelling "dirt" d-u-r-t. The fact that my best friend was a boy named "Burt" was not taken into consideration at all. We can all well recall our struggles with writing. So perhaps it is not surprising that when we think of "language" (or "English") we think first of writing.

Nevertheless, language is speech. Suppose you had no speech. What would you write? It certainly seems clear that there must be a spoken language on which a writing system can be based before the writing system can be created. There are no written languages which do not represent spoken ones. This is true of classical Latin and Greek, too, which though not spoken today were once spoken. The reverse, however, is not true. You can read educated guesses that of all the languages in the world perhaps half have never been written. Are they nevertheless languages? Certainly. What else would you call them? So we see that while a spoken language can exist without a writing system, and perhaps thousands do, the opposite is not true: the written language doesn't exist without a spoken language to be based on.

Now we come, in our definition of language, to the second word that seems to demand a bit of discussion: "Symbols." The sounds we make are not things but instead stand for, or symbolize, things. Children at times understand this, as the jingle indicates: "Sticks and stones will break my bones, but names will never hurt me." There's a noticeable difference between getting called a name and getting clobbered with a rock or a stick. It is true that we often forget this and react as though the words were actually the things. It is also true that primitive peoples, including our own forebears, often treat words as though the words themselves somehow contain magical power. Hence the symbols representing "magic words" engraved on helmets and sword hilts. Hence the prohibitions in some societies against even uttering certain sacred words. (This particular prohibition is enshrined in silly enough fashion in the "mystic rites" of my own college fraternity.) Strings of sounds are not really more than strings of sounds, except as they stand for or symbolize "reality" (whatever that is).

Let us turn in our definition to the word "arbitrary" in the phrase "arbitrary vocal symbols." This implies that there is no *necessary* relationship between the sounds the speakers of Language X might use to designate a given object and the object itself. What do you call the whitish fluid we extract from cows and on which we nourish infants? You answer "milk." But that's only because you happen to speak English. In other circumstances you might have answered "leche," or "lait," or "milch," or "gala." Gala? Sure, why not? It's at least possible that in one of the world's many languages this child-sustaining substance is or has been called something like "gala." If not, why not? There's no reason why this particular series of sounds couldn't indicate, in some language, the liquid we're talking about. If our ancestors had happened to hit upon calling a hand a foot, and vice versa, none of us would be the wiser, and perhaps we would say of the person who said something particularly graceless, "He sure stuck his hand in his mouth, didn't he?" In other words, and to repeat, there is no necessary relationship between the sound and what it symbolizes. When you stop to think about it, if item X had to be symbolized by sound Y we'd all be talking the same language, a situation which clearly doesn't prevail. (Incidentally, the "gala" above is what a Greek would answer if you asked him what you call the whitish fluid that comes from cows. "Gala" is the root of our English word "galaxy," and hence the Milky Way. Now would you like to bet that milk isn't called "karonk" in some language?)

You might reasonably object that there are some words that pretty much have to sound about the same from one language to another, and you would probably be thinking of the so-called ono-matopoeic words. These are the words that supposedly actually sound like what they represent, like the "buzzzzz" of a bee or the "splash" or "plunk" when you drop a rock into a bucket of water. The bee, however, doesn't "buzz" everywhere. To the Arab he "taneens," to the Frenchman he goes "ronronne," to the Spaniard's ear he goes "zurrier," and the Turk hears a sound like "wuzultu." As for the splash, the Poles hear "plusk," Hindus "chapak," Greeks "bloum," and the Ceylonese "telikiratu." A fascinating article on this subject, from which the above examples are taken, begins:

> Wyatt trailed the stagecoach bandit to Ma Kettle's farm. He dismounted to search the barns and other buildings. He could hear only the farm noises. Old Rover came bounding through the gate, "Kulaiduratu! Wong-wong-wong! Yanbah!" In the cowshed he heard only the familiar "Mangwa, Tahoor" from Bossy. He saw something move at the top of the haystack, and was about to draw his gun when he saw Pussy's tail and heard her "Tamoo" as she swatted at a bumblebee wuzultuing around her head. . . .
> He turned toward the house. Just then Black Bart threw open the screen door and reached for his holster. But Wyatt was faster. "Mendentum! Cudal!" both guns barked. Bart fell back into the house and the door charpmakked behind him.[1]

---

1. Eugene E. Clark, "It's the Cat's Tamoo," *Foreign Service Journal,* July, 1964. Copyright ©1964, *Foreign Service Journal,* by permission.

The author remarks that if these sounds came over your TV you'd probably send it out to get it fixed, yet each of them would be recognized by the people of some country as quite appropriate to the story.

Now we need to direct our attention to that phrase in our definition of language which says it is "used by a human society." Actually there are two aspects of this phrase which we must notice. Let us consider the word "society." This implies what is certainly true, that language is a *social* phenomenon. You do not use it alone—not ordinarily or often, at least. And you could not have acquired it alone. Language is not like breathing or crawling or walking, which all infants do without instruction. Language must be learned. A baby deprived of human company would nevertheless crawl. He would not speak. True, the ability to learn a language is inborn in us, but the language itself is not. (Thus the man who declaims that he is self-made and owes society nothing obviously owes society even the words with which he is making the statement.) Language is a social phenomenon, and the very shape of the language is determined by the needs of the society which uses it. We might look briefly at the linguists' contention that each language is very nearly perfect for its speakers.

Is French better than Navajo? Is Navajo better than French? And what do we mean by "better"? It is certainly true that the resources of Navajo would be entirely inadequate for living in French culture, even if, let us imagine, the French could understand the "words." There are scads of things—and not only objects but "concepts"—in France which Navajo would have no way of expressing. How go about the refinements of *haute cuisine,* for instance? But it is just as emphatically true that French, again assuming the words could somehow be understood, would be equally inadequate on an Arizona reservation. There would be both objects and concepts which the language couldn't begin to handle. Each language suits the needs of its own culture perfectly, linguists say. A language is the best and most faithful reflection of its culture, and if the culture should develop some interest, some need, which the language can't express, the language will automatically be revised to include it. One can't exist without the other. Thus it has been wisely said that if you prefer Language X to Language Y, it simply means that you prefer Culture X to Culture Y. "Culture" in this sense is not, by the way, elevating your pinkie as you drink a cup of tea. It's a difficult concept to define clearly, but one scholar did it pretty simply by observing that the culture of a society is the way it deals with universal human problems. Man everywhere has to eat, shield himself from the elements, have kinfolk (with or without family problems), express his religious feelings, dispose of his dead, make love, deal with illness, eliminate bodily waste, etc. etc. How does a given society handle these myriad matters? The sum total is its culture.

Naturally, the things the culture conceives of as important will be emphasized in the language. Would it be easy to discuss time in a culture where the people had no clocks and watches and no concern whatsoever for scheduling events—and where, very likely, the language operates without tenses? A language without tense is very difficult for us speakers of English to imagine. A classic example of culture affecting language is the Eskimo's generous variety of words for different kinds of snow. The Eskimo understandably considers snow an important factor in his environment so he has a multiplicity of words for snow in its different conditions: dry snow, dirty snow, melting snow, hard snow, blowing snow, soft snow, snow falling in big flakes, snow in a near-sleet condition, snow crusted over, snow in more kinds and varieties than you or I could dream of. He does not, as we do, use the word "snow" with various modifiers. No, he has separate words for each variety—and has no word at all for the general substance, corresponding to our word "snow." The explanation seems to be that he doesn't need a word "snow"—his interest in it is too keen to allow mere generalities to suffice. Imagine an Eskimo peeping out of his igloo and turning to his companion and saying excitedly, "Hey, Joe! Guess what's outside! Snow!" Joe answers, "So, what else is new?" The Eskimo is not, as some older philosophers used to suggest, deficient in intelligence to the point where he is unable to generalize "snow" from the varying specific conditions of it. He doesn't need the generalization. It would do him no good, so he doesn't have it.

Henry Lee Smith in an interesting lecture series filmed for television, "Language and Linguistics," makes a parallel with our own culture. In our mechanistic civilization, where we are always building, tearing down, setting up, putting together, we have a great many devices for fastening things together, like pieces of wood. We have nails, brads, staples, spikes, screws, bolts and nuts, cleats, tacks—and we have subdivisions of these classes, like upholsterer's tacks, carpet tacks, thumb tacks—but we have no name for all these more-or-less similar items taken together. We would have to resort lamely to "fastening devices" or some such, which wouldn't quite do it either. Perhaps our inability to generalize indicates that we have a defective intelligence. So-o-o-o . . .

Back to the definition we are examining. The word "human" in the phrase "used by a human society" is simply to forestall a lot of quibbling about the communicating of porpoises, of bees, of dogs and cats and various other creatures that are sometimes asserted to have a language. Your favorite pet may be highly skillful at letting you know his wants: he's hungry, he needs to go outside, he wants to play with the chocolate-flavored rubber bone you bought him. Bees returning to the hive engage in an elaborate ritual that lets their fellows know the direction and distance of the nectar source they've just discovered. And porpoises—well, I don't know just what porpoises do but it's enough so that they are being investigated by Navy scientists with tape recorders. Anyhow, linguists remain unconvinced that other creatures have language, and we include the word "human" in our definition so as not to get into arguments about it. What we're concerned with here is the kind of communicating that people do, not how smart somebody's poodle may be.

Another word in our definition which demands some comment is "system." A language is a *system* of arbitrary vocal symbols. The sounds of speech as they issue trippingly from the tongue are not mere random sounds but are arranged, precisely, in patterns. This is true in any language. The baby babbling in his crib produces random sounds, and a great variety of them, but he is not producing language until he somehow miraculously learns the system. We don't know how he does it.

Assuming for the moment that letters *are* sounds, which we already have noted they are not, reflect on the following: *nrbu*. Try pronouncing it. It's a bit difficult, isn't it? Utterly without sense. Let's rearrange the letters and try it again: *burn*. Ah, now it's different! Now, you say, it "makes sense." Yes it does, and why didn't it before? Because the sequence of sounds was not in a recognizable order. So we see that individual speech sounds must occur in particular permissible patterns, within a given language, if they are to "mean" anything. It should go without saying that the permissible patterns vary from one language to another, and for all I know *nrbu* may be something quite intelligible in Swahili or Chichewa. It obviously isn't in English.

The system of a language, though involving the way sounds may be arranged into individual words goes far beyond that. It governs the way parts of words may be combined. What would happen if instead of *king* + *-ly* = *kingly* you put the *-ly* on the front? *Lyking*. Nonsense. The system also governs the way words may be combined into sentences. Consider this one: *Man mustache the his fire to set.*

You conclude that it doesn't mean anything. Let's change the order, though: *The man set fire to his mustache.* Now we say it has meaning, but what is the difference between the two versions? Merely word order. We have to conclude that word order is part of the system of English. In fact, word order is basic to the system of English. Contrast these two sentences:

1. Edgar killed Simon.
2. Simon killed Edgar.

The difference in meaning is vital, especially to Simon and Edgar. Note how it is accomplished: through a change in the arrangement of words. It is part of the English system to signal who did something and who had something done to him through the location of words in sentences.

Word order is not the only kind of signal that English employs. Here is another pair of sentences. Read them out loud and listen to them.

1. The boy threw his shoe at the cat.
2. The boy threw his shoes at the cat.

What is the difference in them? Of course, you say, in the first he threw only one shoe and in the second he threw more than one. You might assume he threw two because we usually think of shoes as coming in pairs, but you don't know that. He might have emptied out his closet and thrown thirty-seven of them: all you really know is that he threw more than one. But that isn't the question we're interested in, which is: How do you know he threw more than one shoe in the second sentence? (If you say "Because *shoe* has an *s* added to it in the second sentence," you're wrong. We're thinking of language as speech, remember?) You know it's more than one shoe because in the second sentence there is a "zzzz" sound added to the word "shoe." And since you speak English, and therefore understand the English-language system, you are going to interpret a "z" sound in that position as signalling "more than one." (Incidentally, to make you feel better after the trap laid for you with the "z," if it had been a *hat* the boy threw it would have been more nearly correct to say that we recognize the plural because we hear "s" added to it because the way we pronounce the letter is closer to the sound of the plural on *hats.*)

Thus, adding little sounds to words here and there is part of the English system, too. We will observe this system in some detail later.

Each language has *its own* system and each language's system is unique. Furthermore, the systems are "arbitrary," thus accounting for the first use of that word in our definition of language: "A language is an arbitrary system...."There is no reason why English *had to* develop a signal like "z" to indicate plurality. Old English (the language up to about 1100) used an "-en" also for plural, like German. This old plural still hangs on in "children," "oxen," and one or two other words. As a matter of fact, there is no reason why English has to have a signal for plurality at all—most of the world's languages do not.

As we have seen, modern English depends heavily upon word order. Not all languages do. Consider the following Russian sentence:

МУЖЧИНА УБИЛ МЕДВЕДЯ.

Muzhchína ubíl medvédya.   (Transliteration)

It means "The man killed the bear." Now look at these:

УБИЛ МУЖЧИНА МЕДВЕДЯ.

МЕДВЕДЯ УБИЛ МУЖЧИНА.

They mean "the man killed the bear" too. In Russian, word order has much less significance than in English, and in the above sentences the Russian speaker knows what got killed and who did the killing by means of word endings, or *inflections*. (The "z" on *shoe* a few paragraphs back was an inflection.)

Latin was a "highly inflected" language too, which is to say it relied more on inflectional endings to indicate the relationships among words in a construction than it did on word order. (A "construction" might be a sentence, or it might be only part of one, like a phrase: It is something "constructed" and has therefore a unity. In English we would say "the boy" is a construction, but "boy the" is not, even though "boy the" might occur in a sentence, like "I gave a *boy the* money.") Something of the flexibility enjoyed by Latin, in regard to word order, is indicated by the following example:

> Nerō basium ancillae dēdit.
> Dēdit basium ancillae Nēro.
> Basium Nēro dēdit ancillae.
> Ancillae basium Nēro dēdit.
> Nerō dēdit ancillae basium
> Basium Nēro dēdit ancillae.

Ancillae Nēro dēdit basium
Dēdit ancillae Nēro basium.

These all mean precisely the same: "Nero gave the maid a kiss." There are eight combinations written out for you, and you should be able to figure out sixteen more if you want to take the trouble. They will all mean exactly the same thing, too.

Changing "Nero gave the maid a kiss" in this fashion is impossible in English, of course, which merely is to say that the two languages have different systems. Which is better? Actually, neither. They're different, that's all. You might naturally insist that English is much easier since we don't have to learn all that clutter of inflectional endings, and I as an English speaker would be inclined to agree with you. The truth, though, is that English merely seems easier to us because we're familiar with it, and that all languages are really equally easy for those who speak them. If this wasn't true, if Cantonese, for instance, was really a great deal more difficult than English, we might expect to find on a visit to China that the children weren't able to talk fluently until they were several years older than their American contemporaries, but this simply isn't the case. They chatter equally briskly, equally young. As a matter of fact, English isn't as easy as you might think. Would you believe that if you run through all the variations of an English verb, including all the auxiliaries or "helping verbs," you will get over 800 different possibilities? Perhaps many a schoolboy, from Cathay or Malay, would despair of ever learning English if he saw our verb, with auxiliaries, laid out in all its glory.

We are forced to conclude, then, that (1) all languages have system, (2) each system is unique, (3) there is no reason why any system should be what it is: it is "arbitrary," and (4) all systems are equally easy or difficult, depending on whether you are optimistic or pessimistic by nature.

One other thing to note about our definition of language and we'll have done with it: It begins "A language is. . ." That is to say, the definition applies only to one language at a time, though it is true of each individually.

Our attempt at a definition of language is now ended: "A language is an arbitrary system of arbitrary vocal symbols used by a human society in carrying on its affairs." As you can now see, the terms of the definition—always excepting the rather clumsy conclusion—are rather carefully thought out. It is not as easy to define "language" as might at first appear. No doubt more thought and greater knowledge would refine further the definition we've been working with, but it will do for the time being.

Our definition is general enough to apply, I think, to any language at any time. It is interesting to note, though, that a *description* of a language (which is a different thing from a definition) wouldn't apply for very long, but would have to be continually revised. This is because it is a fact of linguistic life that language is constantly changing. We can demonstrate this historically, at least for languages that have a written form which enables us to gain some idea of what they were like in the dark ages before tape recorders. However, many people find it revolting to think that the process is still going on. But language doesn't remain fixed for a couple of centuries and then overnight shift into a new phase. The process is a gradual one which most of us don't notice, partly perhaps because we don't pay attention.

That English has changed over the centuries is not too difficult to demonstrate. Here is a tenth century English version of the Lord's Prayer, plus three other verses (Matthew iv, 9-16) to make the sample a little longer. (For a modern translation, see below, pp. 16 f.)

(9) Eornostlīce[1] ġebiddad[2] ēow dus Fæ der ūre þū þe eart on heofonum,
    Earnestly   pray you thus: Father our thou that art in   heaven

    sīe dīn nama gehālgod.
    be thy name made holy.

(10) Tō-cume þīn rīce. Ġeweorde dīn willa on eordan swā swā on
     Let come thy kingdom. Work thy will on earth as much as in

     heofonum.
     the heavens.

(11) Urne ġedæghwæ mlīcan hlāf sele ūs tō-dæg.
     Our   daily   loaf give us today.

(12) And forġief ūs ūre gyltas[3] swā wē forġiefad ælcum pāra   þe wid
     And forgive us our guilts as we forgive all   those that against

     ūs āgyltad.
     us make guilt.

(13) Ne ġelæd þū ūs on costnunge ac ālīes ūs of yfele.
     Nor lead thou us into temptation but deliver us from evil.

---

1. *Eornostlīce* is the forebear of our word "earnestly," obviously. The ending -līce is the source of Mod. Eng. adverb ending *-ly*. ċ = the sound commonly spelled *ch*, as in *church*.

2. The prefix *ġe-* was pronounced something like "yuh" and meant as used here that the word to which it was attached meant what it said in a stronger sense than usual. We would call it an intensifier.

3. This could be translated "sins," but "guilts" is what it says, and besides the relationship of Old. Eng. to Mod. Eng. is thus clear.

(14) Witodlīċe ġif ġē forġiefað mannum heora synna, þonne forġiefeð ēower
　　 Indeed if you forgive　　men　　their　sins　then　will forgive your

sē heofonlīca fæder[4] ēow ēowre gyltas.
heavenly　father　you　your guilts.

(15) Ġif ġē sōþlīce ne forġiefað mannum, ne ēower　fæder ne[5]　forġiefeð
　　 If you truly do not forgive men, (neither will) your Father forgive

ēowre synna.
your　sins ("you of sins").

(16) Sōðlīce þonne ġē fæsten, nellen[6] ġē wesan swylċe lēase liċetteras. Hīe
　　 Truly　when you fast,　will not you be as　if faithless feigners. They

fornimað heora ansīena, þæt hīe ætīewen
"take away" (hide) their countenances (so)　that they appear

mannum fæstende. Sōðlīce iċ secge　ēow þæt hīe onfēngon　heora
to men fasting.　Truly I say (to) you　that they receive　their

meda.
meed (reward).

Presumably the Lord's Prayer part of this, at least, is familiar to you, but it is probable that in this version it looks a little strange. So much has English changed over the course of some ten centuries. (To help you unravel it, in case you are curious, check the footnoted comments, the translation on pages 16f. below, and your own Bible.) Even with no previous study of Old English, which is most likely your condition, if you look at the above text carefully and with imagination you can see clearly that it *is* English. Some of the words have fallen into disuse and others have changed radically, but most of them are at least recognizable, especially if you play imaginatively with pronunciation. What really makes it look "foreign" is that the basic system of the language has changed a great deal in the ten centuries since then: the elaborate set of inflectional endings in Old English has almost entirely disappeared, to be replaced by a quite rigid system of word order.

---

4. Here is where the flexible word order of an inflected language gets us into trouble as we put it into Mod. Eng. To the modern eye it would look better thus: þonne ēower sē heofonlīce fæder forġiefeð ēow ēowre gyltas. (then your heavenly father will forgive you your guilts.)
The *sē* doesn't "mean" anything, but is a grammatical signal that a masculine noun is coming.

5. *ne . . . ne* is a double negative, which means "no" twice as much as a single one.

6. *nellen* is "will" and "not" together, a convenient device. Thus if we still had it we could say "I will," meaning what we always mean by it, and "I nil," meaning "I will not." This grammatical device lingers on in our expression "willy-nilly," meaning whether he wills or doesn't will.

Chaucer's English, some four centuries later than the above sample, is much easier for a modern student to read, largely because much of the modern system of English had by Chaucer's day been established. It would be too much to say that you can read Middle English, as the English of this period is called, without trouble, but it is certainly easy compared to Old English. If you have a glossary, some imagination and a bit of determination, you will find that Chaucer will become fairly easy reading after some practice. You will also discover that the effort is greatly rewarded. Here are a few lines from the Prologue to *The Canterbury Tales,* his introduction of the Prioress:

> Ther was also a Nonne, a Prioresse,
> That of hir smylying was ful symple and coy;
> Hire gretteste ooth was but by Seinte Loy;
> And she was cleped[7] madam Eglentyne.
> Ful weel she soong[8] the service dyvyne,
> Entune in hir nose ful semely,[9]
> And Frenssh she spak ful faire and fetisly,[10]
> After the schole of Stratford atte Bowe,
> For Frenssh of Parys was to hire unknowe.
> At mete[11] wel ytaught was she with alle:
> She leet no morsel from hir lippes falle,
> Ne wette hir fyngres in hir sauce depe;
> Wel koude she carie a morsel and wel kepe
> That no drope ne[12] fille upon hir brest.
> In curteisie was set ful muchel hir lest.[13]
> Hir over-lippe wyped she so clene
> That in hir coppe there was no ferthyng[14] sene
> Of grece, whan she dronken hadde hir draughte.
> Ful semely after hir mete she raughte.[15]
> And sikerly[16] she was of greet desport,[17]
> And ful plesaunt, and amyable of port,[18]

---

7. cleped = called, named

8. soong = past tense of sing, *sang*

9. semely = seemly; i.e., pleasingly

10. fetisly = handsomely

11. mete = meat. In older use, "meat" meant food generally.

12. ne = a negative following the verb to make it negative in spades. Something like "That no drop never fell upon her breast."

13. lest = lust, used in the sense of "desire" or "will." Thus, a reading like: "Her desire was set very much on being courteous." Nevill Coghill (*The Penguin Classics*) translates the line: For courtliness she had a special zest. (She liked to be courteous.)

14. ferthyng = farthing; i.e., not the tiniest bit (literally, one-fourth)

15. raughte = reached. Why not? Teach—taught; reach—raught.

16. sikerly = surely.

17. desport = amusement, sport.

18. port = bearing. Still used in this sense, though not often.

And peyned hire to countrefete cheere
Of court,[19] and to been estatlich[20] of manere,
And to ben holden digne[21] of reverence.

Certainly, with the little assistance provided you by the few foot-noted comments, you can read that. But equally certain, it isn't the English you are used to, and the differences are not merely matters of odd-looking spellings. There are vocabulary differences, distinc-tions in the meaning of some words that appear familiar but seem to be oddly used, variations in inflections, and revisions in a number of constructions—not to mention the many changes in pronunciation which must be deduced if this poem is to be read, as it must be, with regular rhythm and with rhyme.

Let us look briefly at the English of a couple centuries later than *The Canterbury Tales,* in this case a passage from Shakespeare's *Ham-let.* These lines are from Act I, Scene iv, in which Hamlet is discuss-ing the lusty drinking habits of the Danes while he and Horatio await the re-appearance of the ghost of Hamlet's father:

Hor.   Is it a custom?
Ham. Ay, marry, is't;
But to my mind, though I am native here
And to the manner born, it is a custom
More honour'd in the breach than the observance.[22]
This heavy-headed revel east and west
Makes us traduc'd and tax'd[23] of other nations;
They clepe[24] us drunkards, and with swinish phrase[25]
Soil our addition;[26] and indeed it takes
From our achievements, though perform'd at height,[27]
The pith and marrow of our attribute.[28]
So, oft it chances in particular men,[29]
That for some vicious mole of nature in them,
As, at their birth,—wherein they are not guilty,
Since nature cannot choose his origin,—

---

19. She troubled herself to counterfeit (to put on) a courtly cheer.

20. estatlich = stately.

21. digne = worthy.

22. That is, it is more honorable to break this custom than to observe it.

23. tax'd = charged, accused. The "of" also differs from Mod. Eng. practice. We would say "taxed *by*" or "charged *by*."

24. clepe = call. (Same as in "And she was cleped madame Eglentyne . . . ")

25. with swinish phrase = phrases which call us pigs.

26. soil our addition = soil (Mod. Eng. "sully"). For "addition," the Oxford English Dic-tionary gives this (obsolete) meaning: "Something annexed to a man's name, to show his rank, occupation, or place of residence, or otherwise to distinguish him." Thus to soil, or dirty, our addition would be to belittle our titles.

27. perform'd at height = our peak performance.

28. attribute = reputation.

29. in particular men = in individual men; i.e., as opposed to the habits of the nation at large which he has been talking about.

By the o'ergrowth of some complexion,
Oft breaking down the pales and forts of reason,
Or by some habit that too much o'er-leavens
The form of plausive[30] manners; that these men,—
Carrying, I say, the stamp of one defect,
Being nature's livery,[31] or fortune's star,—
Their virtues else—be they as pure as grace,
As infinite as man may undergo—
Shall in the general censure take corruption[32]
From all that particular fault; the dram of eale[33]
Doth all the noble substance of a doubt,[34]
To his own scandal.

Hor.   Look my lord, it comes!

Ham. Angels and ministers of grace defend us!

In reading this you probably have very little difficulty, and yet there are some constructions and some uses of words that are unfamiliar beyond what is attributable to the fact that this is poetry, as for instance, "clepe" in line 7 and "addition" in the next line. It is undoubtedly true, as one linguist notes, that the troubles experienced by many modern students in reading Shakespeare are as often caused by changes in the structure of the language as they are by running head-on into unfamiliar vocabulary.

Let us conclude this brief glance at the English of different periods of the language—which, you remember, is not a "history" of English but merely an illustration of how greatly it has changed—with a glance at a sample of contemporary English. To make the comparison more vivid I've selected the same New Testament verses which you looked at in Old English:

9. This is the way you should pray: "Our Father in heaven: May your name be kept holy,
10. May your Kingdom come, May your will be done on earth as it is in heaven.
11. Give us today the food we need;
12. Forgive us what we owe you as we forgive what others owe us;
13. Do not bring us to hard testing, but keep us safe from the Evil One."

---

30. plausive = pleasing.
31. nature's livery: that is, the "livery" (clothing or badge *or, by extension,* appearance) is natural, born in the man.
32. take corruption = be infected.
33. *eale.* This word, and the rest of its phrase, is responsible for seven (!) pages of small-type commentary in Furness's *Variorum Edition.* "Eale" is interpreted by some as "ale" and by others as "evil." It seems to me at least possible, since Shakespeare was a fast man with a pun, that both meanings are intended.
34. A variant reading: "Doth all the noble substance often dout," wherein the last word means "banish."

14. For if you forgive others the wrongs they have done you, your Father in heaven will forgive you.
15. But if you do not forgive others, then your Father in heaven will not forgive the wrongs you have done.
16. And when you fast, do not put on a sad face like the show-offs do. They go around with a hungry look so that everybody will be sure to see that they are fasting. Remember this! They have already been paid in full.[35]

You may prefer, as I do, an older translation, one with which you are more familiar, perhaps on the grounds that it is more poetic or more beautiful. At the same time, this one is undeniably modern English the way we know and use it.

So, as we said, it is very easy to demonstrate that English *has* changed. What is difficult for many people to accept is the idea that it *is changing* still. Nevertheless it is true, and we shall take a look in a later chapter at some of the implications of this for us.

It is a basic conclusion of modern language study that *all* languages in use—that is, "living languages"—are constantly changing. And what else could you expect when language is entrusted to the care of illogical, inconsistent, ever-changing beings like people? Perhaps if we always had the same needs, if our cultures remained constant, our speech would change less. But as we have seen, an alteration in the culture will inevitably produce a variation in the language. If it is true, as has often been observed, that the one unchanging fact in our history is "change," it is not the least surprising that language should change too.

An interesting question which might have been triggered in your mind as you looked at older samples of English is: What came before them? What did it look like? And before that? And back and back and back to the ultimate question: When was language invented? and where? and what was it like?

The answer to these final questions is very easy. Nobody knows. It is inconceivable in the nature of things that we shall ever know. Language is as old as man—indeed, some philosophers argue that man was not "man" until he had language. But writing is relatively recent. If man's entire history on this earth could be pictured as an hour, man has been writing for much less than a minute. Obviously as researchers attempt to discover the nature of very old languages all they have to go on is the written record. Where are the tape record-

---

35. From *Good News For Modern Man,* The New Testament in Today's English, American Bible Society, New York, 1966. Translation by Robert G. Bratcher. (Note that the "Good News" of the title is a translation of the Old English word "gospel.")

ings of pithecanthropus erectus chattering excitedly over a roast hunk of haunch? All we can do about language before writing (that is, literally, "prehistoric" language) is speculate. Of course, there has been plenty of speculation.

The nineteenth century philologists, as the students of language in that day liked to style themselves, were fascinated by the question of the origin of language and offered a number of theories. Since they were not handicapped by the necessity of offering supporting evidence, they were able to produce some pretty colorful ideas. One school of thought was that man learned language by imitating the sounds of animals. According to this idea, if you saw a lion menacing the neighborhood you tore back to the cave and made lion-like noises, thus alerting everybody. If you had seen a wild dog, you'd have come back barking, etc. This "explanation" has obvious limitations. For one, it would allow only a somewhat limited vocabulary. One irreverent German philologist expressed his evaluation of this hypothesis by labelling it "the bow-wow theory," and it died in the general laughter.

However, others were willing to take a flier at solving the riddle. A second theory was that language had its beginnings in the natural exclamations and utterances man produced in pain or fear, as when you burn your finger you might make a sharp hissing sound by drawing your breath in sharply between clenched teeth while you are shaking your hand and hopping around. The great Charles Darwin explained that when there is a feeling of contempt or disgust it is evidenced by a tendency to "blow out of the mouth or nostrils, and this produces sounds like *pooh* or *pish*." This suffers from the same sort of inadequacies as the "bow-wow" explanation and soon came to be generally known as "the pooh-pooh theory."

The same German who had laughed the "bow-wow" idea out of existence with his satiric lable tried his own hand at a hypothesis. According to his, there is a sort of harmony between man and nature, and as man tried to express his ideas the appropriate "natural" sounds magically sprang to his lips. The author, in a memorable but perhaps unfortunate phrase, said that in nature "everything which is struck rings with its own sound." He called his idea the "naturalistic" theory, but others, less impressed, called it the "ding-dong theory" and it became as much ridiculed as its predecessors.

One other idea we'll mention here, and that is the one known originally as the "work theory." The idea underlying this one was that as a man performs certain tasks, he is likely to make certain appropriate noises, and these noises somehow developed into language. If you lift a heavy load, you grunt, and perhaps you are thus expressing some prehistoric word. Naturally enough, this soon came to be known as the "yo-he-ho theory." It failed to attain a distinguished place in man's thoughts about language.

The modern linguist pays little attention to this sort of speculation, perhaps discouraged by the inglorious flops made by his forerunners. Further, he is reconciled to the idea that we can never know either how or where language originated, much less what it was like. Still the subject retains its fascination for us. I once heard the late Bernard Bloch, a distinguished linguist, offer a few observations on it. His idea was that the invention of language, however or whenever it happened, was certainly man's greatest accomplishment, alongside which the invention of the wheel was trifling, and that it was unlikely that this tremendous feat had occurred a number of times at scattered places around the earth. He felt it much more probable that language had been invented only once. If true, this would have important implications: For one thing, all the world's languages would have to be related somehow, and for a second, every language would be of exactly the same age as any other language. This would force some interesting conclusions as to how languages develop. But again, alas, we can never know.

Grammar, If You'll Pardon the Expression

So far we have considered in some detail a definition of language, which necesarily took us into some elementary observations about its nature, and we have noted that all language is constantly changing. Perhaps only for entertainment, we have also touched very lightly on some speculations about its origin. We have been carefully avoiding any talk about what is for most of us an ugly word with depressing connotations, and one which brings painful memories into the minds of many of us: "grammar." Not even the people who really work professionally with grammar seem to like the word, for as Paul Roberts has pointed out, they never, never call themselves "grammarians." Philologists, *si.* Linguists, *si.* Structuralists, transformationalists, stratificationalists, all *si.* But grammarians, *no!* However dodge and squirm as we will, procrastinate as we might, if we are going to consider language we are sooner or later going to have to confront grammar. The time has come.

Let's start with a question: What is grammar?

Like a lot of other simple questions, this one doesn't necessarily have a simple answer. Grammar means different things to different people, and it means different things to the same person at different times. It depends on how you're looking at it.

One way of answering the question would be to say that grammar is the system of signals which enables a language to work. This is the same "system" we talked about earlier in our effort to define language. Here are a couple of sentences:

> The whale swallowed Jonah.
> Jonah swallowed the whale.

That these two sentences have different meanings is a fact of English grammar. So is the difference in these two:

> I dance at all her weddings.
> I danced at all her weddings.

In the second sentence you hear a quick little "t" sound on the second word that you didn't hear on the second word of the first one and you derive a different meaning. That we often signal past tense in English with this little "t" is a *grammatical* fact.

English grammar, then, can be viewed as the total of all these signals. They add up to a fabric which I know and you know and all the English-speaking people we talk to know, and if they don't know it they don't speak English. You can't speak English without knowing it.

It is in this sense that the linguist is using the word "grammar" when he says that the average child trudging off to his first day at school already knows the grammar of his language. Little Johnny, and his sister Susan too, on their very first day in the classroom do already know the grammar of their language—*if* by "grammar" we mean this tremendously complex of signals which allows them to use the language. Of course they haven't mastered all the vocabulary of English. Neither has their teacher. Nor has anyone, ever. It's true too that Johnny and Susie wouldn't know a dangling participle if they tripped over one entering the school building. But they undeniably do know the grammar of their language in the sense that the linguist is using the word.

Picture Johnny's mother screaming at him on the evening *before* he goes off to school to learn all about life, including grammar: "Johnny!! I want you to take your red tricycle off the porch and put it in the garage with your sister's. Right now!" Does Johnny understand this? Sure. Does he maybe think his mother is asking him a question? Does he get the idea that the word "red" applies to the tricycle, or does he think it's the garage that is red? Does he believe that his mother thinks the tricycle is in the garage? Does he understand that his sister is in the garage or that her tricycle is? Does he think his mother would like all this done tomorrow? To all these questions the answer is "Of course not." Johnny understands full well what his mother wants and whether he actually bestirs himself immediately to do it is a matter of discipline, not language. Yet if you analyze grammatically what Johnny's mother shouted at him, you will find it fairly complicated. Though Johnny has no trouble comprehending it, it might give us trouble to diagram. Johnny has somehow managed to learn the system of English. He does indeed know its grammar.

In this sense every language has a grammar, even those never written, and even those never taught or studied in schools. There were stories in the papers not too long ago of a newly discovered language out in the boondocks of Australia. Of one thing we may be sure: it has a grammar. And all the little kids know it, too, though they perhaps aren't able to explain the structure of a sentence, if the language happens to have things like sentences.

Suppose you and I and a dozen or so of your friends were in some miraculous way to find a previously unknown island out in the South Pacific somewhere, and suppose further that we discover it is inhabited. After ascertaining that the natives don't have cannibalistic tendencies we make up our minds to stick around a while and learn something about them. We'll become famous and get our names in *Time.* The first problem we run into, naturally, is how to communicate with these people. Their language, which we decide to call Snangti, seems to consist of grunts, squeals, tongue clicks and assorted idiotic noises (for their sounds are different from ours and therefore ludicrous), and we are confronted with the problem of unravelling this mess. We need to discover its system, its grammar. Suppose we learn that a noise which sounds like "gnarf" means "she is singing," and that when it is repeated—like "gnarf-gnarf"—it means "she sang." Then we learn that "bronk" means "she is eating" and "bronk-bronk" means "she ate." Then we hear someone say "grunff" and learn, through gestures etc., that it means "she is dying." Ten minutes later we learn that a woman died. We'd feel pretty confident that we'd know how to express the concept, wouldn't we? And we probably would know how, too, unless "grunff" turned out to be one of those obnoxious "irregular" words which crop up so often as we struggle with languages. Anyhow, in some such manner as this, whether systematically or intuitively, we would go about learning the system of Snangti and, the system once learned, we would be able to speak it and understand it. The jumble of sounds which seemed so strange at first would no longer be so peculiar because we would have mastered its grammar.

Suppose further that one of us, prompted by a missionary spirit or a scientific spirit or something, decides to invent a way of writing this language and then to present in writing what he has learned about how Snangti works, perhaps for the benefit of latecomers to the island so they won't have quite so tough a time learning the language. What he would write would be a "grammar." The word now has a different sense from the way we were using it just a few minutes ago. Here it indicates a formal presentation of the study of the system of a language. So *grammar* can be the system itself or the completed (and usually written) study of that system.

Let us imagine one more thing. Suppose that each of us hardy pioneers took on the job of writing a grammar of Snangti, and suppose too that we agreed that we would each work completely independently. Unless we cheated, we would undoubtedly produce grammars quite unlike each other in a number of important ways. If there were fourteen of us, we would turn out fourteen different grammars. Is it likely that they would all be equally good? Of course not. Perhaps you might think yours far better than mine. So how could they be judged? How would anybody determine what he wants in a grammar of Snangti, assuming he wants one at all?

I think we could agree on certain standards, certain criteria with which to measure one grammar against another.

For a starter, we might consider accuracy. There isn't much virtue in a grammar that says things about the language that are not true. Say that one of the Snangti grammars our gang has written reports that "No speaker of this language ever ends a sentence with 'ugluk,' " but in reality 90 percent of Snangti speakers often do end sentences this way. It would seem to me that such a grammar would not be very useful, certainly not as to sentence endings. (If this example seems stupid to you, reflect on the grammars of English that say users of English do not end sentences with prepositions.) It is basic that a grammar should tell the truth about the language.

A second matter of importance is completeness. If your grammar of Snangti tells twice as much about the language as the rather slipshod job I did, even I would have to concede that yours is of more value. The ideal would be a grammar that would tell *every* fact about the language, but such a grammar would be extremely difficult to make, whether for Snangti or any other language. Natural languages are wonderfully complex, and to describe all the details that five-year-old Johnny (or Juanito or Jeannet) has learned is a very difficult proposition. For instance, no complete grammar of English has ever been written, though people have been trying for a long time. Completeness is obviously a goal, though, and would have to be a criterion as we judge one grammar against another.

Still a third basis on which to evaluate a grammar would be simplicity. At least it would be for me. If one grammar proposes 1,000 rules, each with seventeen exceptions, and some of the exceptions with exceptions, and another grammar offers only 100 rules which seem to work most of the time, would you hesitate very long between them? Simplicity, which essentially is universal applicability of "rules," is one of the things modern linguists constantly strive for as they attempt to describe "Language X," and as we shall see, some of the complicated-looking things they come up with work out to be simpler in the long run because they can make a few "rules" go a long way.

Many of the things observed about our imaginary Snangti, as you no doubt have recognized, are exactly true of English. An English grammar, for example, is an effort to describe the system of the English language. And there are many grammars of English: not just the one you learned in school, if you learned it. As with our hypothetical grammars there is variation in quality. Some are not too bad and others, let's be honest, are terrible. Some are more accurate than others, and some have so little accuracy that they seem to describe a language Johnny's teacher invented in her sleep, and which only she can understand. No grammar of English is complete, and none is as simple as we would desire. On this last point we must be reasonable. The English language, like other living languages, is an extremely complicated thing, so it would be unfair of us to expect an easy description in three short paragraphs. On the other hand, the secret of the system of the language can't be so overwhelmingly difficult, for you and I both know a number of really dull clods who speak the language fluently. We are compelled to figure that if some of *them* can learn it, it has to be easy. The trick is to discover and describe, simply, whatever simple thing it is that these boneheads learn. And that, so far, has stumped the best brains in the language business.

If you detect in the remarks made so far a certain disenchantment with the traditional grammar taught in the schools, there is nothing wrong with your powers of deduction. In the last thirty or forty years many scholars, dissatisfied with the older descriptions of English, have been trying their hands at creating something better. Perhaps in many ways many of the new grammars *are* better. However, there is still no grammar entirely accurate, there is still no grammar that can be called complete, and heaven knows many of the new efforts are not exactly simple. So if you, fresh from your triumphs at describing Snangti, want to take a whirl at describing English, come on in: there's plenty of room, and the criticisms of everyone presently working in the field will keep the water at least warm.

So far we have considered two meanings of the word *grammar:* (1) the system of a language, and (2) the description of that system. There is a third meaning which we haven't paid attention to, and oddly enough this is the one that almost everyone uses when he talks about grammar. This is the sense in which we might say of someone who says "He never told me nothing like that" that he uses "bad grammar." This is a meaning of "grammar" that the linguists never, never use. One needs a name for this sort of thing and the linguists have a number of them. One distinguished scholar refers to this problem as "linguistic etiquette," apparently dismissing it rather lightly. Others consider it a matter of "social dialects" of English. There are various terms, but never is it referred to as a matter of grammar.

The linguist is quick to appreciate that there are a number of different grammars of English, all in the sense in which we first used the word: the set of signals which enables the language to operate. To exemplify: your clergyman very likely employs different signals, at least some of them, than your auto mechanic. To a degree they are using different grammars, different sets of signals. Which is better? Let me re-punctuate: Which is "better"? The linguist refuses to answer that question, which he considers irrelevant. It all depends. If you are to live and work among day laborers, undoubtedly the grammar they employ will better serve your needs than the different grammar used by your physician or your lawyer. On the other hand, if you wish to work and live among professional people in your community, you had better learn to use the language as they use it.

This last observation might answer a question that may have occurred to you, and that is, why, if one "grammar" is as "good" as another, is there all the commotion you were exposed to in schools about teaching Johnny not to say "I ain't got none"? The answer is that presumably Johnny is attending school so that he can work among the professional types in the community rather than among the truckdrivers. If not, if Johnny wants to be a career truckdriver, then he is wasting his time learning to avoid certain signals of the grammar he already has. Thus no one—least of all the linguist—is saying that the difference between "I haven't any" and "I ain't got none" is unimportant. The linguist merely says that it's a *social* rather than a *linguistic* matter. He don't call the difference "grammar" and in this book we ain't going to neither. When we use that term we will mean either the set of signals inherent in the fabric of the language, or the formally presented study of that set of signals.

Who is "the linguist" that he dare challenge some of the most cherished superstitions about language? He's just a human being, really, like you and me, but undoubtedly unlike us he has devoted his professional life to the study of language and its problems. Further, it is a mistake to refer to "the linguist" as though he represents a single viewpoint, for in actuality there are many linguists and whenever you get three of them in a room, you find three schools of linguistics represented and a fight breaks out. Linguists have perhaps only two things in common: (1) they attempt to be scientific in their approach to language, and (2) perhaps because of this, they are often deprecated by those who are sure that they know how the language should work.

Linguistics might be, and has often been, defined as "the scientific study of language." With science as prestigious as it is in our society, everybody wants to be "scientific," even if he's a toothpaste huckster who puts on a surgical gown and peddles a dentifrice containing "Z-339," guaranteed to work wonders in your mouth. However, nobody considers such a salesman "scientific," in spite of his costume. Similarly, some academicians put on a "gown" of esoteric language and whip up a vast literature completely incomprehensible to the uninitiated in an effort to bestow a scientific aura on their discipline. Is the linguist guilty of this fraud? It is true that some linguists belabor us with an overdose of jargon, but it is also true that linguistics has a number of new and sometimes technical concepts for which names are necessary. But the existence of a technical vocabulary neither establishes nor disproves anything. More basic would be: "What do you consider the characteristics of a 'science'?" and "Does linguistics have these characteristics?"

Of the scientific approach to a problem we can make some observations that would certainly be generally agreed to. For one thing, there is a willingness to investigate, in search of truth, if you will, and there are no areas that are considered to be somehow beyond investigation. There are no "truths" which it is "unnecessary" or "in bad taste" to question. The scientific investigator does not start out with pre-conceived answers but works with his material, whatever its nature, and accepts the conclusions his investigations lead him to. Nor does he conceive that he arrives at "final" answers. He offers hypotheses which, hopefully, he is quite ready to change should subsequent research indicate the necessity. Further, his experiments are repeatable. Another scientist working with the same problem and materials and with the same method should get the same result. If not, back to the laboratory. Also, there is probably something in the nature of the materials with which the scientist works that allows the scientific method to be applicable. In this regard, for instance, the scholar we call a political scientist is doubtless handicapped, to the point where many of his colleagues on campus would dispute that he is a "scientist" at all.

The above characteristics do not delimit science very well, nor even describe it fully, but they are suggestive of the scientific approach to problem solving. It is notable that all of them apply to the linguist, so that perhaps his field really is what one language scholar called it: the most scientific of the social sciences. His material is something capable of being dealt with objectively. The modern linguist, for instance, can and does make extensive tape recordings, which he can then take into his study for various kinds of analysis, as the chemist retires to his lab to work with his materials. The linguist looks to his material for the answers to the problems he is investigating, nor does he assume he knows the answers before he makes the investigation. Of course his analyses lead him to hypotheses—and it is here that the fun starts, for the linguist takes great delight in knocking holes in the theories propounded by his fellows, meanwhile heatedly defending his own.

Indeed, these intra-disciplinary wars reverberate so through the halls of learning that they have been seized upon by those opposed to the linguist and all his works as a notable weakness of the "science." As one genuinely distinguished traditional grammarian has acidly observed, linguists often can't even agree with one another on the definition of some of their most basic terms. There is a great deal of truth in the charge, but that doesn't necessarily make it significant. Science makes progress through disagreement. If no long-held concepts were challenged, where would change come from? It should be considered also that linguistics, if a science, is a very young one. Modern linguistics, in this country at least, might well be said to date from the publication of Leonard Bloomfield's *Language* in 1933. If the older sciences still do not have all their problems worked out— What is the nature of life? What, really, is electricity? What is light?— it hardly seems reasonable to expect one in its fourth decade to have worked out final answers to everything.

As the linguist refuses to accept long-received "truths" about language, he finds himself in hot water with people who hold those "truths" sacred. As he refuses even to discuss the idea of "correctness" in language (see chapter on usage below), he is charged with "abandoning all standards,""destroying the purity of the language," etc. etc. Those who hurl such charges refuse to accept the linguist's explanation that he didn't "abandon" any standards because he didn't conceive of himself as guarding them in the first place. To the traditionalist schoolmarm the linguist is a sort of subversive devil who attacks mother, home and the flag. For instance, he asserts that a word that is "modifying" (whatever that is) a "noun" (whatever that is) is not necessarily an "adjective" (whatever that is) and he probably gets his ideas right out of Moscow. Even the linguist's interest in so-called primitive languages is held against him by defenders of English. Does he mean that he applies the same kind of analysis to a crude tongue like Snangti and to a refined, cultured, centuries-old, beautiful language like English? Horrors!

Whether or not you want to grant the linguist the accolade of "scientist" is not really important. What does matter is that you understand something of the way he approaches the study of language, the spirit in which he goes about his work. I remember a teacher of my own high-school days settling an argument over some grammatical point by slamming a book down on her desk and saying—not softly—that her contention was true "because I say it's true!" No linguist would ever do that. He wouldn't have to.

READING REFERENCES

Bloomfield, Leonard. *Language* ("The Use of Language," chapter 2). New York: Holt, Rinehart & Winston, 1961.

Bloomfield, Morton, and Newmark, Leonard. *A Linguistic Introduction to the History of English*. ("Language and the History of Language," chapter 2). New York: Alfred A. Knopf, Inc., 1963.

Brown, Dona Worral, Brown, Wallace C., and Bailey, Dudley. *Form in Modern English* ("Grammar in a New Key,"). New York: Oxford University Press, 1958.

Francis, W. Nelson. "Revolution in Grammar." *Quarterly Journal of Speech*, October, 1944. Reprinted in Allen, Harold B., *Applied English Linguistics*. 2nd. ed. New York: Appleton, Century, Crofts, 1958.

Fries, Charles C. *The Structure of English* ("Sentence Analysis: Meaning or Form," chapter 4). New York: Harcourt, Brace & World, 1952.

Gleason, H.A. Jr. *Linguistics and English Grammar* ("Grammar in the Schools," chapter 1). New York: Holt, Rinehart & Winston, 1956.

Hill, Archibald A. *Introduction to Linguistic Structures* ("What is Language?" chapter 1) New York: Harcourt, Brace & World, 1958.

Hook, J.N. and Mathews, E.G. *Modern American Grammar and Usage* (Changes in the English Language"). New York: Ronald Press, 1956.

Laird, Charlton. *The Miracle of Language* (chapters 1-3). Cleveland: World Publishing Co., 1953.

Langer, Suzanne. "The Lord of Creation." *Fortune,* January, 1944.

Sapir, Edward. *Language, an Introduction to the Study of Speech* ("Toward a Definition of Language"). New York: Harcourt, Brace & World, 1921.

Sturtevant, Edgar. *An Introduction to Linguistic Science* ("Lapses" pp. 37-39). New Haven: Yale University Press, 1960.

Warfel, Harry R. *Language: A Science of Human Behavior* ("The Nature of Language" chapter 1). Gainesville, Florida: Scholars' Facsimiles. 1962.

CHAPTER 2

THE NOISES WE MAKE

Since language is a system of noises, or vibrations, reaching through the air and not marks on paper, we need to investigate the nature of these noises. How are they produced? What are they like? How do they pattern together to form a system, which is to say "a language"? How are they received by a listener and how can they be interpreted?

The branch of linguistics that deals with questions like these and which attempts to provide answers is called "phonology," or the study of sounds. In popular speech phonology is often called "phonetics," but we are often going to want to reserve this latter term for something a bit more specialized, as you will see. We will say that "phonology" is made up of two areas: "phonetics" and "phonemics." Actually, "phonology" and "phonetics" are pretty nearly interchangeable terms, but there are times when we are going to want to contrast "phonetics" and "phonemics," which will then add up to "phonology." If this is somewhat confusing to you, don't worry about it. It's confusing because the words are not used with a great deal of precision even by those who use them professionally, and the reason they don't use them in a precise manner is that there apparently is no need to.

There are three branches of this study of sound. They are (1) "articulatory phonetics," or the study of how speech sounds are articulated or produced; (2) "acoustic phonetics," the study of how speech sounds are transmitted; and (3) "auditory phonetics," the study of how speech sounds are heard or received. Each of these areas is extremely important and is of vital professional concern to many people.

29

Auditory phonetics is of great interest to hearing aid manufacturers, many doctors of medicine, and psychologists, as well as to linguists. As the vibrations of air strike against the eardrum and are converted into signals that actually have meaning to that eardrum's owner—what is it exactly that happens? The little parts of the inner ear get to jingling around, they stir up vibrations in some liquid, which in turn excites energy (electric?) in cells, etc. etc. The study of all this is a matter of great importance, but we will not be able to deal with it here.

Similarly, acoustic phonetics is a significant area of study with which we are not going to concern ourselves. It is clearly of great importance to architects, as they design auditoriums, for instance, to telephone company engineers who are working with the transmission of sounds, and to people working with such things as radio and television.

We are going to be concerned with articulatory phonetics, how speech sounds are produced. This is for several reasons. For one thing, it is going to be of more practical use to us as we try to understand something of the nature of our language. And for another, you have almost all the equipment you need to study this area of phonetics, and the rest is easily obtainable. You already have vocal cords, a tongue, lips and teeth, unless something drastic has happened to you. In addition you should supply yourself with a small hand mirror, if you're male (girls will already have one) and a flashlight. For as technical as we're going to get, these items are all you'll need.

As people began to study the sounds of language, back in the nineteenth century, they had a number of ideal goals they were working toward. One was the recognition of all the different speech sounds made by humans as they use their many languages, and a second was to devise a set of symbols which would represent all these sounds. The written symbols, as far as they could be worked out, are known as the International Phonetic Alphabet, generally called the IPA. Theoretically a phonetician could study a sample of speech, transcribe it in IPA characters, and a third person could read it, reproducing *exactly* what the original speaker had said. Thus you, if you were thoroughly familiar with IPA characters and had practiced making the sounds they represent, could read a passage transcribed in some language totally unfamiliar to you and be able to sound just exactly like the native speaker of that language whose recorded speech you had just read.

This never worked out in practice. It worked to a degree, of course, and the IPA is still very valuable in language study today, but it never attained the ideals it sought. We have come to understand that the ideals are not attainable. We seem to be dealing with infinity. There is no discernible limit to the variety of speech sounds humans are capable of and actually produce. The most minute differences we can note turn out to have sub-differences. The numbers of sounds that can be heard, then, are limited only by the sharpness of the listener's hearing; and today with modern equipment such as the spectrograph, which gives us visual pictures of sounds, even those limits have been lifted. So far has this refinement of differentiating speech sounds gone that many phoneticians have concluded that even the same speaker never makes the same sound, identical in all respects, twice in his life. Thus if you were to say "cheese" twice, the two utterances of the word would be different, and if you were to say it fifty times, all fifty of them would be different. Nor is this theory. A spectrogram (the "sound picture" taken by a spectrograph) could offer visible proof. If the difficulties of noting and recording accurately all the differences in just your speech are so great, how in the world would we possibly sort out, list, and write down, *all* the sounds made by a couple of billion people speaking X number of languages? It can't be done, and that's all there is to it.

It was not until the concept of the "phoneme" was invented (by a Frenchman named de Saussure at the very end of last century) that really significant advances in phonology became possible, and it was a few decades later before the concept became widely understood in this country. We will get to know the phoneme a little later on, but first we need to consider something of how we make speech sounds and how the various sounds we make differ from each other.

Let's start with something simple, like blowing a trumpet. Have you ever stopped to think of what's involved when Al Hirt blows a rocking version of "Way Down Yonder in New Orleans"? Well, I'll tell you what he does. He spreads his lips tautly across his teeth, holding them lightly together, and then he blows through them. This produces a buzzing sound which he can raise or lower in pitch by stretching the lips tighter or relaxing them a bit. What's that? I forgot the trumpet? No, I just haven't come to it yet. The essential thing is the buzzing, vibrating lips, and after that the trumpet itself is just a refinement. Quite literally a refinement. When the mouthpiece of the horn is held against the lips their buzzing sets in motion the column of air trapped in the instrument's tubing and produces the sound with which we are familiar. Change the shape of the tubing and you change the sound—which is the technical difference between a cornet and a trumpet. Make the tubing bigger and longer and you might wind up with a trombone or even a tuba. But with all these instruments the principle is the same: the buzzing of the vibrating lips.

The production of speech sounds is very similar except that it is not the lips that you vibrate but the vocal cords or vocal bands. (The terms are interchangeable.) They are a couple of pieces of cartilage and muscle located in your larynx or voice box. This voice box (let's use that term) is located just inside of the Adam's apple. If you're a woman it's located inside of where the Adam's apple would be if you had one. These two vocal bands can be stretched or shortened, brought firmly together, held lightly together, or separated. Stretching or shortening them enables you to make your voice go up and down; the manner in which they are brought together, or kept apart, determines other things as we shall see in a moment.

Incidentally as we talk about the various "speech organs," as the physical parts you use to produce speech sounds are called, you might find it helpful to keep a finger stuck in the book at page 33, where there is a drawing intended to help you locate the parts we're talking about. We call this drawing Phonetic Man. You will notice he has no brain. We are not interested in what he thinks about, nor even at the moment in what he has to say, but merely in how he produces sounds.

The drawing doesn't show one of the most important elements in the production of speech: the lungs, which you can think of as the motor enabling everything else to function. If you didn't have breath to blow out through vocal bands, nothing would happen, just as if Al Hirt didn't have breath to blow and make his lips buzz he'd stand there looking silly with his lips spread against his teeth. As you expel air through, around and between the vocal organs—or as we say, through the "vocal tract"—you provide the power which makes your speech possible. As long as you have air coming out you can keep talking, but when you run out you have to quickly get a new supply in order to continue. One linguist writes of an unfortunate girl, a victim of polio, who was encased in an iron lung which did her breathing for her. She could talk only as the machine was compressing her lungs, and as it reversed direction she would sometimes get cut off in mid-sentence. This makes vivid the point that in English we talk only as we *exhale.* Some languages produce speech sounds on an indrawn breath, but I don't see how they do it. It seems like a good way to strangle.

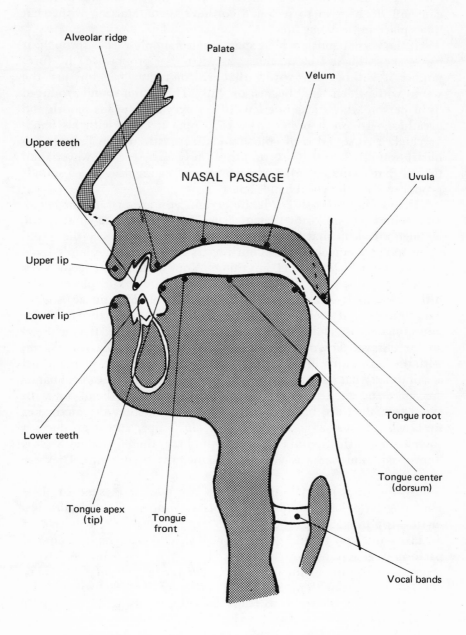

Alveolar ridge

Palate

Velum

Upper teeth

NASAL PASSAGE

Uvula

Upper lip

Lower lip

Lower teeth

Tongue root

Tongue center
(dorsum)

Tongue apex
(tip)

Tongue
front

Vocal bands

As you expel air out through the vocal tract a number of things can and do happen to it. Let's consider them, starting with what takes place in the voice box.

If the vocal bands are held apart, the air simply rushes through. It can make a slight friction noise, as when you pronounce "h" (pronounce it without any vowel—that is, don't say "ha" but just the sound with which "ha" begins, or "h.") This is the sound produced by a person who sticks one lens of his eyeglasses in his mouth and breathes hard on it preparatory to wiping it clean with his handkerchief. This sound is of course a characteristic one in English, the initial sound of *head, hot, hundred, holy cats,* etc. *H*owever (and there's that sound again), we have many other English speech sounds produced with the vocal bands apart.

Here's one: Sssssss! Try it. Be certain you are making the beginning sound of "sip," not that of "sure." Ssssssssss—like air escaping through a leak in that bald tire on your front wheel. Try the sound again and as you make it put your fingers firmly on the Adam's-apple area of your throat. Feel anything? You shouldn't, except your warm, tender, lovely throat. Keeping your fingers in place, try a different sound: Zzzzzzzz. The bumblebee or door buzzer sound. *Now* you should feel something: a vibrating in your throat, under your finger tips. Now place your hand firmly on top of your head and try Ssssss. Now, with your hand still there, try Zzzzzz. Again, with the Sssss you will feel nothing, but with the Zzzzz you will feel a vibrating. What has happened is that with the Ssssss the vocal bands are apart and air is merely passing through between them, but with the Zzzzz they are brought lightly together so that the air makes them vibrate, just as it does with Al Hirt's lips, and it produces a sound. We call this sound *voice.* We would say, therefore, that Sssss is "unvoiced" and Zzzzz is "voiced." Remember these terms. They are important.

By the way, just a moment ago when you were asked to place your finger tips on your throat, and later your hand flat and firmly on the top of your head, did you do it? If you didn't, you made a mistake—and you should go back through that paragraph again and perform the actions you were asked to. You are going to have a tough enough time in this chapter, understanding *sounds* from mere cold, silent type, without cavalierly cheating yourself of some of the opportunity provided you to really latch on firmly to what the text is trying to tell you.

So now we understand that the air can pass through the voice box either with the vocal bands apart and silent or lightly brought together and vibrating. Speech sounds are either voiced or unvoiced (often called "voiceless"), depending on this distinction.

Another major division of speech sounds is into "oral" and "nasal." If you'll look at our drawing of Phonetic Man you'll see at the back of the mouth, upper deck, a part labelled "velum." Hanging down from it is the "uvula," which you can see in your own mouth if you'll take a peek way in the back via your flashlight and mirror. The uvula is the little pink soft thing dangling there in the rear. It gets its name because some unidentified Roman, apparently suffering the after-effects of an orgy, thought it looked like a grape. However, at the moment it's the velum rather than the uvula which is demanding our attention. This thing can be raised and lowered, as the dotted lines on the drawing indicate. Looking at the drawing, you can easily see that if the velum is raised, it blocks off the passage of air through the nasal cavity. The sound produced with the velum in this position is called "oral," because the airstream is directed out through the mouth. However, if the velum is lowered, and especially if the oral cavity is blocked off, like when you have your lips tightly shut, the airstream will go out through the nasal passage, producing a sound we call a "nasal." If you happen to have a bad cold the air can't get through and your nasal sounds will be distorted, thus adding to your other miseries.

Another more-or-less useful differentiation between types of sounds is between those we call "stops" and those known as "continuants." You produce a stop when you block off the passage of the airstream entirely at some point and then release it. For example, when you say the word "upper" you produce the "p" by bringing your lips lightly together so that for a moment there is a cessation of the flow of air. For other sounds, as when you were going Ssssss a few minutes ago the airstream is *shaped* but not interrupted. Sounds like these, because they can be continued for at least as long as your air supply holds out, are called "continuants."

So we have three either/or propositions: a sound is either voiced or voiceless, oral or nasal, a stop or a continuant.

Let's look at some of the different sounds you make as you use English. We'll not even try to list them *all* (which would be impossible in any event) or even a very large number, but perhaps enough to demonstrate to you that you make more different kinds of sounds than you might think you do. We'll begin with stops.

We already talked about one stop, the middle sound in "upper." As we noted, this is made by bringing the lips together, building up a little air pressure behind them and then releasing it. Make the sound several times—but be sure you are just making the sound we are talking about. That is, do not follow your long habit of thinking of letters as sounds and pronouncing the name of the letter "p." If you do, you'll say something like the word "pea," whereas what we want is just the *beginning* sound of that word. So close your lips, build up a little air pressure, and release it. Do this a number of times with your fingertips placed on the Adam's apple region of your throat. If you are making the sound correctly you will not feel any vibration. You'll feel a little movement under your finger tips, of course, but not vibration.

Now, unless you had a good speech course which involved you in phonetics, you are probably unaware that in your speech you regularly make this sound in a number of different ways. You are likely to feel that as Gertrude Stein might have said, a "p" is a "p" is a "p." This isn't so. Say the word "pin" several times. Now try the word "spin." Can you hear the difference in the "p" sound in the two words? Perhaps not. In "pin" the "p" is followed by quite a sizable puff of air. This puff is missing in "spin." Maybe you can convince yourself of the difference in the "p's" of "pin" and "spin" just by holding the back of your hand close in front of your mouth and pronouncing the two words alternately. You will feel quite clearly the difference between "spin" and "pin."

We are going to need some way of referring to the various sounds of speech without going through the clumsy routine of saying, as we did above, "We mean the sound of the letter "p" but without the vowel that is present when you name the letter," or "Just the beginning sound of the word *pin.*" This will involve us in a bit of technical terminology which is really quite simple, though at first when the terms are still unfamiliar to you it might look formidable. It isn't. The key to our system of nomenclature is quite simple: we name the sounds according to how they are produced. If you look back at the sketch of Phonetic Man you'll observe that generally the lower parts of the mouth—the lower lip and the various parts of the tongue—are movable, while the upper parts are not. The movable parts are called *articulators,* and the upper, non-movable ones, are known as *points of articulation.* To describe a speech sound, or to be more accurate, to describe a consonant sound, we need to note at least four factors in its production:

1. whether it is voiced or voiceless
2. the articulator
3. the point of articulation
4. the manner of articulation.

Let's return now to our examination of what we're still awkwardly writing as "p." When a few moments ago you tried pronouncing it, by itself, with your fingertips on your throat, you felt no vibration. This means (remember the Sssss-Zzzzzz contrast?) that the vocal bands are not vibrating. Therefore, the sound is what we call "voiceless," or "unvoiced." So we have cited the first of the four factors in its production: "p" is voiceless.

In producing the "p" the articulator, the lower lip, is brought against the point of articulation, which is what? The upper lip. Where else would you place the lower lip to produce "p"? So we have stipulated items three and four in the list.

As for the manner of articulation, item four, we have already noted that "p" is a *stop*. There are, of course, other ways of making other sounds, which is to say there are other manners of articulation, but for the time being let's just note that "p" is a stop, which means—you remember—that the airstream is blocked off completely for a moment.

Thus we can satisfy the four points in the little list by saying that "p" is: a (1) voiceless, (2) lower lip, (3) upper lip (4) stop. This is simple enough, certainly. As a matter of fact, we want to make it just a bit simpler, phoneticians hating to spend extra effort just like the rest of us. Since you only have two lips, and one of them is clearly the lower and the other the upper, there isn't really any pressing need to name them. It might be different if you had four or five. So we'll just use the term "bilabial" (two lips) in this description of the "p." We'll call it a "voiceless bilabial stop." That's clear enough and easy enough.

If you've been reading carefully and attentively you might well at this point have a nagging little question in the back of your mind. "If this is an adequate description of the "p" how do we account for the differences we just noted between the "p" of "pin" and the "p" of "spin"? A good question. Let me remind you, though, that the statement was: "To describe a consonant sound we need to note *at least* four factors in its production." Now that we've seen how really simple those first four factors are, perhaps we can add an occasional extra refinement, as we're going to have to do with the case of the "p."

The phonetician calls the "p" of "pin" *aspirated,* which simply describes the puff of air we noted, and he writes it thus: [p'], Phonetic symbols are always enclosed in square brackets, and remember they are NOT letters; they are symbols to represent sounds. When we mean the letter we'll put it in quotes—"p"—and there's no way of telling what it might sound like. (Consider "pin," "phone," "psy-chology.") But when we write [p'] we always mean "the aspirated voiceless bilabial stop." Phonetic symbols and conventional spelling, then, have this difference: if you see the standard spelling of an English word that you've never seen before you *can't* be certain you know how to pronounce it, but if you should see it in phonetic transcription you would know with no doubt whatsoever. The same character always represents the same sound; the same sound is always represented by the same character; and the only limit to this is the precision of the set of symbols being used and the acuteness of the transcriber's hearing. A very precise, detailed representation of the sounds is said to be a "narrow" transcription. We are not going to get very "narrow" here, no narrower than we already have in describing the aspirated voiceless bilabial stop.

The "different" voiceless bilabial stop of "spin," the one we have discovered is relatively without the aspiration of [p'], is called, as you might expect, *unaspirated* and is written simply [p].

There is still a third very common way of making this voiceless bilabial stop. Ordinarily there are three steps involved in producing a stop: 1. the articulator is brought against the point of articulation (with the stop we've been discussing the lower lip is brought against the upper one), 2. a little air pressure is built up behind the block-age, and 3. the blockage is "released," resulting in a tiny explosion. (Many phoneticians often refer to stops as "plosives" for this reason, but to keep things simple we'll avoid that term.) Sometimes, when the stop in question is the final sound in a sentence, the articulator is never brought away from the point of articulation. Example: A tired mother hollers at her child, "Johnny, I want you to stop!" To pro-duce the final sound of that string of sounds she brings her lips together, naturally, but she might not then separate them. What happens to the air built up behind the lips? Maybe she swallows it. Maybe she exhales it through the nose. Anyhow the lips remain tightly together. Try it. That is, try the whole sentence: "I want you to stop!" and leave your lips closed at the end. It feels perfectly natural, doesn't it? It should. We all do it all the time. This version of the voiceless bilabial stop is called *unreleased,* and is written [p⁻].

What we originally thought of simply as "p," then, has become the aspirated, the unaspirated, and the unreleased voiceless bilabial stops, or: [p'], [p], and [p⁻]. More accurately, instead of saying that it "has become" those several varieties we should observe that they were there all the time, unnoticed by most of us. So: to say that a "p" is a "p" is a "p" is to be linguistically somewhat naive, isn't it?

Suppose now you again place your fingertips on your throat and say the sound [p] for [p']) several times. Having done that, see if you can produce the "same" sound with your voice box operating, that is with the vocal bands vibrating. Any luck? What did you discover? If you did it right you produced the sound we associate with the letter "b," the initial sound of "bin." Think a moment, now. In terms of our little list of four necessary points to be mentioned in describing a consonant sound, how are we going to describe this one? Here is the list again:

1. voiced or voiceless
2. the articulator
3. the point of articulation
4. the manner of articulation.

If you really thought about this, even only a little bit, you've concluded that it's about the same as [p] except for the first item, voicing. Thus we will call this sound a *"voiced bilabial stop"* and we will write it [b]. Does it, like the voiceless bilabial stop, have various kinds of refinement, is it actually produced in several ways? Unlike its voiceless opposite, it doesn't occur in English with aspiration. There is no [b']. Notice that we have to say that [b'] doesn't occur *in English.* As we have already seen, languages are quite unlike each other in many ways and certainly one of these ways is the system of sounds any language might use. [b'] is quite common in many languages and we often try to indicate this in English spelling by putting an "h" after the "b." Check your big Webster's and you will find words like "bhai," which we have borrowed from Hindi. It has the meaning of "brother" or "friend" and you'd probably never run across it except in a novel set in India in which it might be used to give flavor. If you were to pronounce "bhai" in the Hindi fashion, you would then have [b']. Anyhow, it's not a sound native to English so we won't worry about it any further.

The [b] does, however, have an unreleased version. In answer to the question, "Where's Johnny?" his mother might say, "He's in the tub," and she might very likely not separate her lips at all after that final stop. She would thus produce an unreleased voiced bilabial stop, or [b⁻].

There are other stops, too. Let's consider what happens if you bring the apex of your tongue (look at the diagram again) against the alveolar ridge (once more, the diagram!) and block off the passage of the airstream at that point. You can easily feel the alveolar ridge with your tongue tip—it's that bumpy area just in back of and above the front teeth, where the teeth are anchored. Place the tongue tip firmly against that alveolar ridge, let a little air pressure build up, and then let it release with a little pop. You have produced the sound we usually associate with the letter "t," the initial sound of "top."

How are you going to describe this one? For one final time here's the list of four things to be considered (if you need it later you'll have to look back):

1. voiced or voiceless
2. articulator
3. point of articulation
4. manner of articulation

Make this "t" sound several times with your fingertips on your throat. It's voiceless, isn't it? So we have the first of the needed statements.

The articulator, the movable part, is here clearly the tongue tip or apex. (There is actually a difference in these terms which we're going to ignore beyond noting that the "tip" is really the very tip, while the "apex" is back from the tip for half inch or so, and includes the tip. Ordinarily, and unless the distinction is clearly made, we'll be referring to the apex.) The point of articulation, that point against which the articulator is brought, is as we stipulated the alveolar ridge. And finally, we've already noted that it is a stop.

We have all we need to describe the "t": it's (1) voiceless, (2) apex, (3) alveolar ridge, (4) stop. We smooth this out a little by adopting the adjective form of "apex"—apico—and dropping the word "ridge." So we describe this sound as a "voiceless apico-alveolar stop."

We have a couple of refinements to note, which exactly parallel what we noted about the voiceless bilabial stop. In your pronunciation of "top" the initial sound will carry quite a puff of air with it, whereas in "stop" the "t" won't have this air puff. Give it the "back" of the hand" test by putting your hand close in front of your lips and pronouncing "top" and "stop" several times. It will make the contrast sharper, by the way, if you make the final stop [p⁻]. The sound in "top" we will call "aspirated" and will write [t']; that in "stop" we'll call "unaspirated" and will write [t]; and that in "not" unreleased [t⁻].

Now pronounce either [t'] or [t] a number of times with your fingertips on your throat, and as you keep making the sound get your vocal bands vibrating. Can you do it? If you did, you produced the sound we associate with "d." Now take your hand and cover up the next paragraph on this page and see if you can describe this sound in terms of our four items.

It's voiced. We just stipulated that. Also the tongue apex is locked firmly against the alveolar ridge. And the sound is still produced by interrupting the airstream, so it's a stop. Hence: "a voiced apico-alveolar stop."

This stop exactly parallels the voiced bilabial stop in its most common varieties. That is, it doesn't exist, in English, in aspirated form. There is no [d']. (However, in the big Webster's you'll find "dhak" and similar words. Can you explain that?) We are going to write this voiced apico-alveolar stop [d]. Would you be surprised to learn that [d], like [b], has an unreleased version? Well, it has, and of course we'll write it [d⁻]. If you were to say something like "How sad" the chances are pretty good that you'd leave the final sound unreleased.

We have now to consider still a third pair of stops. Since you probably already noticed that both the bilabial and the apico-alveolar stops come in pairs, one voiced and one voiceless, I'm probably not giving away any surprise ending in introducing this next set by observing that it's a pair. We move a bit further back in the mouth, along the tongue, to the area labelled the "dorsum" on the portrait of Phonetic Man. (You understand, I hope, that the dorsum is not a tiny dot on the tongue, as the drawing might indicate, but rather that area in general. Even if you look closely at your tongue in a mirror you won't find any lines marking off the apex from the front, or the front from the dorsum. Generally, the dorsum is the after half, until you get *way* to the back, where you gag if you stick your finger, and that's the root.) We're now dealing with the dorsum as an articulator and we want to bring it against the velum as the point of articulation. I'll not ask you to do this because perhaps I have not described the anatomical parts clearly enough. Instead, I'll ask you to make the sound we often spell with a "k," the initial sound in "kin." Do you feel that it's a stop? The part of the tongue involved is the dorsum; the part of the roof of the mouth is the velum. If you run your tongue back along the roof of your mouth from the alveolar ridge you come first to a hard, smooth area called the "palate" in the diagram, and as you go still further back you arrive at an area where the mouth-roof is much softer, though still smooth. This is the velum. It is often called the "soft palate," and people who call it that have to refer to the harder area further forward as the "hard palate." We're going to use the terms "palate" and "velum."

All right, so you've made a "k." Can you describe it? (1) it's voiceless. (2) The articulator is the dorsum, which has an adjective form "dorso." (3) The point of articulation is the velum, which also has an adjective form: "velar." (4) The manner of articulation is a stop. Ergo, the sound is "a voiceless dorso-velar stop."

Like the voiceless bilabial stop, and the voiceless apico-alveolar stop, this has a number of varieties, principally the aspirated, the unaspirated, and the unreleased. We write them, of course, [k'], [k], and [k⁻]. The aspirated version, as I think you might expect by this time, occurs initially: "kin." Add an "s" to the front of this word, as we did to "pin" to get "spin" and "top" to get "stop," and you will find that the stop has become unaspirated: "skin." Third, you might note that in final position—as in "What a hick!"—it's often unreleased.

This might be a good point to digress for a moment and point out that there are actually many other ways of making this "k," the unvoiced dorso-velar stop. For instance, try pronouncing, very carefully and being as observant as you possibly can, this series of words: *keel, kill, call, cool, cough.* Please be sharp enough to recognize that each of them begins with [k'] in spite of the fact that some have the letter "k" and others are letter "c." When we are discussing sounds spelling becomes irrelevant. However, there *is* a difference, or there *are* differences, in the initial sounds of these words. Just try again the first and the last of the series: *keel, cough.* If you can't hear a difference in the two beginning sounds, surely you can feel it. The [k'] of "keel" is made much further forward in the mouth than the first sound of "cough," which is made way, way in the back. True? In English this difference is unimportant so we ignore it, and it might well be that you never noticed it before. Why should you? But there are languages in which it makes a crucial difference whether you make a [k] toward the front of the mouth or toward the back, in which the difference between two words might be just this, and only this. And if you'd grown up speaking one of those languages you'd have no trouble hearing the difference. It's all in what you're used to, as they say. And we English speakers are used to ignoring that difference. So that now, having noticed that the difference is there and is real, let's go back to ignoring it.

Just as with the bilabial and apico-alveolar stops we had both voiced and unvoiced versions, so with the dorso-velar. What do you get if you voice [k]? You get what we used to call in school, as I remember, the "hard g," the initial sound of "get." Three of the elements of the description, of course, are going to be the same as for [k]. Which of the four is different? If you're on to the principle of describing these sounds, and I hope you are by this time, you have correctly called the sound under discussion 'a voiced dorso-velar stop."

Do you remember how the voiced stops we have considered differed from their voiceless opposite numbers—aside from the obvious fact that they're voiced, that is? Here, let me lay it out for you:

Stop	Voiceless			Voiced	
Bilabial	[p']	[p]	[p⁻]	[b]	[b⁻]
Apico-alveolar	[t']	[t]	[t⁻]	[d]	[d⁻]
Dorso-velar	[k']	[k]	[k⁻]		

Now, looking at that, the question is: what versions do we anticipate of the voiced dorso-velar stop? We expect that it will have an unaspirated version and an unreleased one, but that it will not exist (in English) in an aspirated variety. (Again peek at Webster's for words like "ghat." Notice how many of them are of Hindi origin? What do you conclude about the existence of aspirated voiced stops in Hindi? Incidentally, don't let the existence of English words with spellings like "ghost" mislead you, because we're still talking about *sounds,* remember? and the initial sound of "ghost" is simply [g].)

There is one other stop extremely common in English, but since it doesn't *mean* anything we go along quite blissfully unaware of its existence, though like the differences in the [k'] of "keep" and "cough" it is of vital importance in some languages. This sound is called the "glottal stop," it is written with a symbol [ʔ], like a question mark without the little dot under its tail, and it is going to demand just a wee bit of explanation, both to explain how it is made and to get you to hear it.

On our earlier tour of the vocal tract we left the voice box with the observation that the vocal bands can either be held apart with the air passing freely between them (Ssssss) or pressed lightly together, in which case the air passing through them makes them vibrate (Zzzzzz). There is a third possibility: they can be pressed firmly shut so that no air can get through them at all. When this is done and air pressure is built up behind the vocal bands, then abruptly released— what is produced is a stop. (We often get an exaggerated version of it, sort of a stifled grunt, when trying to lift a heavy load.) There's one other thing. Why is this stop called a glottal stop? Well, this voice box, as we've been calling it, and will continue to call it, is known more technically as the "glottis," and hence, using the adjective form of the word, the stop is a glottal stop.

Now to get you to hear it, which might be just a bit difficult since you're so used to ignoring it, quite properly for a speaker of English, let me hasten to add. Suppose you are listening to a friend who says:

At Bill's ranch last summer I saw threegles.

Your response would be something like, "Huh?" So he repeats, splitting up the vowel sound that seems to bother you:

At Bill's ranch last summer I saw three + eagles.

What he breaks it with is the glottal stop, right where I have put the plus sign. Try it yourself. Try "threegles" and then "three eagles." Can you feel the little catch in the voice box that we call the glottal stop? Probably you can. We use this [ʔ] commonly, though not always, to separate similar vowels that occur in sequence, especially when we want to stress that there is a separation between them. Try "oh, oh." Hear it? Feel it? This little stop is a very characteristic feature of English. You have one on almost every word you utter that begins with a stressed vowel. Say these words: "apple," "only," "each." They most likely begin with [ʔ], which is so normal a part of the word that it's hard to separate out. Of course the [ʔ] has a voiceless version, too: [ʔ̥] For instance, try *whispering* the test words above. The glottal stops might be even easier for you to notice than in their voiced versions.

Those are the principal stops of English. Don't they pattern neatly? In pairs, a perfect balance between voiced and voiceless, they underscore our earlier observation that a language is a system. Obviously the system extends even to the very sounds of the language. Right now, though, instead of stopping idly to admire what we've seen so far we need to press on and examine another category of English consonant sounds, the fricatives.

The word "fricative" rather reminds us of the word "friction." This class of sounds is characterized by the noise of the friction of the restricted airstream as it passes between an articulator held close to a point of articulation. The fricatives are all continuants, which is to say that unlike the stops they can be prolonged, and for just as long as your air supply holds out. You can't "hold" a [t], but the sound we associate with "s" you can hold and hold and hold: Sssss sssss sssss sssss sssss sssss sssss sssss ss - - - - gasp!

The first fricative we'll look at is the one we usually spell "f," though we spell it other ways too, like "*ph*one" and "lau*gh*." Let's describe this sound in terms of our list of four articulatory facts.

First, give it the fingertip test. Is it voiced or voiceless? Then determine which movable part (articulator) is brought against which non-
movable part (point of articulation). As for manner of articulation,
we've already stipulated that it's a fricative. You should arrive at
some list like this: (1) voiceless, (2) lower lip, (3) upper teeth, (4)
fricative. Actually we don't need all this information, for there isn't
any sound in English made by pressing the upper lip against the
lower teeth and blowing air through. So we don't have to state which
lip and which teeth and we can simplify our description. We describe
the sound, therefore, as "a voiceless labio-dental fricative," and we
write it [f].

You will recall that each voiceless stop has a voiced counterpart.
You probably expect now to find something like that with the fricatives. Try making a prolonged [f] and turning on your voice box.
What do you get? The sound we usually spell with a "v," the beginning sound of "very." Of course it has the same description as [f]
except for the voicing, so we call it "a voiced labio-dental fricative."

The next fricative we'll look at is a very common one in English,
though many languages get along okay without it, like French or
Latin-American Spanish, for instance. Actually, I should have called
this a "pair" of fricatives because like all the sounds we've considered
so far it has both voiced and voiceless versions. I might well caution
you at this point that for some reason students have a great deal of
trouble distinguishing the voiced and voiceless versions of this fricative. They have no trouble making these sounds properly in their
speech, for they do speak English. They just have trouble differentiating them on quizzes. The pair of fricatives being referred to are
the initial sounds in "thin" and "then." Stop right now and try
saying each of them, d-r-a-w-i-n-g out the initial sounds and giving
them the fingertip test. Can you tell which is voiced and which
voiceless? "Thin" is voiceless; "then" voiced.

We need a description of these two fricatives, which are the same
except that one is voiceless and the other voiced, of course. There is
some variance in how they are described. Some people feel that the
apex of the tongue is brought against the upper teeth and the air
blown through. Thus the voiceless version is called "a voiceless apico-
dental fricative," and the other "a voiced apico-dental fricative." I
prefer to think of the tongue as merely being stuck between the
upper and lower teeth. The sounds are then *interdental* fricatives. In
any event, the voiceless version is written with the Greek theta, [θ],
and the voiced with what is called an "eth" (with the "th" voiced,

naturally) and is written like a "d" with the shaft curving and a slash through it: [ð].

The next pair of fricatives are the familiar ones we started this whole business with: Sssssssssss and Zzzzzzzzzz. Often phoneticians separate these (and the following pair too) from the fricatives and call them "sibilants" because of the hissing noise they have, but they are still produced by friction so I propose to go the simpler route with you and not have an extra class of sounds. We'll just call them fricatives. Note that for the "s," the initial sound of "sin," the apex of the tongue is brought near the alveolar ridge and a stream of air is forced through. It's voiceless, of course. We call it, then, "a voiceless apico-alveolar fricative," and we write it [s]. If you will get out your hand mirror and flashlight, look inside your mouth as you produce [s]. Notice the deep channel or groove in your tongue through which you are directing the air against the alveolar ridge. Because of this the [s] is often referred to as a "groove" fricative.

Naturally, if you turn on your voice box while pronouncing [s] you'll get the voiced equivalent, which we'll write as [z]. It's a "voiced apico-alveolar fricative." Neither [s] nor [z] has any significant variations.

Now we need to consider another common pair of fricatives. Let's start with the voiceless version and then take up its voiced opposite number. This fricative is the one we usually spell 'sh," the initial sound in "shirt." (We can, let me remind you, spell it in a variety of ways: "ti" in "nation," "ss" in "fissure," and with simple "s" as in "sugar." You may remember the old joke about the teacher who was declaiming emphatically to her class that "sugar" is the only word in English in which this sound has the "s" spelling, when one of her bright boys interrupted to ask, "Teacher, are you *sure*?" There are also a number of other ways to spell this sound, but enough of that for now.) This fricative is made somewhat like the [s] but further back on the tongue. The part of the tongue we call the "front" (see diagram" is the articulator and is brought near to the palate. So we'll describe it as "a voiceless frontopalatal fricative." The International Phonetic Alphabet (IPA) symbol for this sound is [ʃ], but we'll use the symbol much more common among American phoneticians, an "s" with a little check over it: [š]. If you have occasion to refer to [š] in speech, it is most simply called the "esh." If you didn't put away your mirror and flashlight after studying your tongue while making the [s], take a look at it while it shapes the [š]. You'll discover that the deep groove you used in making the [s] has now been widened considerably and is much shallower. The air is

being forced out through a slit, sort of, and for this reason the [š] is
often called a "slit fricative." But to describe it adequately (and to
differentiate it from other fricatives which are also called "slit fricatives") we need to call it "a voiceless fronto-palatal fricative."

Now let's consider briefly the voiced equivalent of [š]. First, try
making it. Make a sustained [š] and turn on your voice. You produce
a sound like the middle one in "pleasure," "measure," and "azure."
Many people (but by no means all, so be careful) also make this
sound at the ends of words like "garage" and "rouge." We'll have an
additional remark to make on this in a moment. We call this sound,
of course "a voiced fronto-palatal fricative" and we write it thus: [ž].
The IPA symbol for this sound is [ʒ].

Up until this point all the sounds we've discussed, with the exception of the glottal stop, which isn't a "significant" sound in English anyway, can occur at all points in words. That is, they can occur
at the beginning of a word, or in the middle, or at the end. Or as the
linguist says, more economically, they can be "initial," "medial," or
"final." To be precisely correct, this statement must be taken rather
broadly. That is, [p'] is nearly always initial, and [p⁻] has to be final,
for obvious reasons. But speaking more broadly, the *voiceless bilabial
stop,* in one or another of its sub-varieties, can occur initially, medially or finally. With [ž] we come to the first break in the regularity
of our pattern: it is not used initially in English and it appears finally
in only a few words, mostly borrowed from French (like "rouge"
above). To say it is *never* used initially in English is not quite exact,
for some people, being nattily imitative of French, use it in a few
words borrowed from French, like "genre" or the French proper
name "Jean." But it is certainly correct to say that it is not *natively*
used in the initial position and only very rarely in final position.

This leaves us with only one more fricative to talk about. It's the
"voiceless glottal fricative" which we associate with the written letter
"h." It's the initial sound (only) of words like "hot," "head,"
"how." It is produced by leaving the vocal bands separated and
pouring air through them. We write it [h]. It is occasionally voiced in
English, kind of by accident. You can hear it, if you listen carefully,
in a word like "ahead." What apparently happens is that we have the
voice box turned on for the initial vowel, "a," and we want it on for
the second vowel also, here spelled "ea," and being lazy we just leave
it on through the fricative too. When this occurs we write it [ɦ],
with a bent stem, if we are making a "narrow" transcription.

We now have to look at a class of sounds called "affricates," a
very small class consisting of only two sounds, one voiced and the

other unvoiced, as you might well expect. The affricate is halfway
between a stop and a fricative, or perhaps it is better described as
both a stop and a fricative. Let's take on the voiceless variety first.
Suppose you start to make a [t] but instead release it quickly into a
[š]. Try [t] and [š] quickly one after the other. Don't let any sort
of vowel sound intervene but go directly from [t] into [š]. If I'm
describing it well enough for you to follow, you're getting the familiar English sound initial in "chop," medial in "itchy," and final in
"ouch." This is the voiceless affricate which, since it's the only one,
might be adequately described with just that label, and we'll write it
[č]. (The IPA writes it [tʃ], which has the virtue of describing how
it's made.)

   The [č] has a voiced partner, the initial and final sound in
"judge" and the medial sound in "edgy." Just as we called [č] the
"voiceless affricate" we'll call this sound the "voiced affricate," and
we'll write it [ǰ]. Many Americans use this sound rather than [ž] at
the end of "rouge," "garage," etc.

   Remember a few pages back where we noted that sounds are
either oral or nasal? So far all the sounds we've been considering have
been oral, and it's about time we looked at the nasals. English has
three of them.

   First we need to consider what happens if you close your lips
tightly, vibrate the vocal cords, and let the sound go out through
your nose. It can't exit orally since you have your lips tightly shut. If
you try this you're going to produce "mmmmm mmmmm," the
initial sound of "mother," the medial sound in "Amy," and the final
sound in "some." Since all nasals in English are voiced (though in
many languages this isn't true) we can ignore voicing-voicelessness in
our description, and we call this sound simply "the bilabial nasal"
and write it [m]. There are no important sub-varieties of it.

   Another important nasal is made this way: put your tongue apex
firmly against the alveolar ridge, as though you were going to make a
[t], but turn on the voice and send the sound out through the nasal
passage. Can you do it from that sketchy description? If so, what
you get is the beginning sound of "no." It occurs medially ("any")
and finally ("tan"). It, too, is always voiced in English. It's called the
"apico-alveolar nasal."

   There is one other nasal: the final sound in "sing" and the medial
sound in "hanger." This sound never, ever, under any circumstances
occurs initially in our language. Say the word "sing" and hang onto
the final sound. Can you tell how it's made? You're blocking off the
airstream with the dorsum and the velum, that's how, and sending it
on out through the nasal passage. So of course we call it "the dorso-

velar nasal." In English it's always voiced. We write it like an "n" with a tail: [ŋ], and call it "eng."

It is interesting to note, speaking of the symmetry of our sound system as we were a while back, that the three nasals are made with the same articulators and points of articulation as the three pairs of stops: bilabial, apico-alveolar, and dorso-velar.

We've now covered all the consonants of English except four, and I'd like to put those off briefly until after we've sneaked a look at the vowels. I think they'll be easier that way.

The vowels differ from the consonants in a couple of important ways. In the first place they are all voiced. In the second, they are all continuants and the airstream flows smoothly through the vocal tract while they are being made. So, third, and as a result, we don't describe them in terms of articulators and points of articulation. Just how we do describe them needs a bit of explanation, though it's easy enough.

Consider a moment. The vocal bands are vibrating, the airstream is unimpeded—and yet there's clearly a difference between the vowels of "see" and "saw." What is it that makes this difference? In effect, we change the shape of the mouth. As the sound of the vibrating vocal bands issues through the oral cavity, it is made to "resonate" in this space. The amount and the shape of the space provided is going to change the distinctive sound that issues forth. But, you say, "I don't think I go around making my mouth bigger or smaller, or one shape as opposed to another." In reality this is true, of course, but *in effect* you can and do make these changes. You do it with your tongue. You do this in two principal ways: you move it up or down in your mouth, and you move it forward and back. Actually the "frontness" or "backness" of the tongue (these are linguists' terms which you'll get used to) is not quite precise: during the act of speech the tongue often has a hump in it, like an angry cat's back, and it is this hump which is moved front or back as you make different vowel sounds. So we describe vowel sounds in terms of two items: whether the top of that hump is high or low, and whether it is relatively front or back. We make a rough representation of the mouth thus:

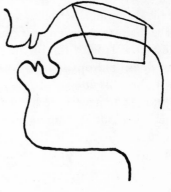

The box (as drawn in the mouth, above) is divided up into squares, as you will see, and the vowels are put into the squares according to the tongue's position as they are made. Thus a vowel made with the tongue's hump high to the front or upper left corner of "the vowel quadrangle," as this box is called, is called "a high front vowel," one low to the back, or right, would be "a low back vowel," and so on. It is for this reason, rather than any political implications, that Phonetic Man is always drawn facing left.

One other general observation before we go on to a more-or-less detailed look at the vowels: the tongue as it moves around the mouth is not put into fixed positions. That is, it's not like the keys on a piano, where you have to hit one note or the other, but rather like the finger moving on a violin string, or like the slide on a trombone, in that it might not be exactly in position for one note or another but might quite well be in between two of them. This is a caution that as we deal with these tongue positions we are not dealing in absolutely precise matters but in approximations. In terms of the piano keyboard, we are quite easily able to play in the cracks as well as on the keys.

Now: get out your mirror and flashlight. If you are going to follow (and especially if you are going to believe) this discussion of vowels it is important for you to see for yourself what happens. Pronounce this series of words: *beet, bit, bait, bet, bat.* Now pronounce the series again, watching what happens in your mouth, but *without* the initial consonant on each word. What you see happening is that the tongue is humped forward in the mouth and that it stays that way. These are all *front* vowels, then. But you also notice that as you go from one to another of these sounds in sequence, the tongue keeps dropping. Actually, your whole jaw drops, but that isn't necessary, it's just convenient. Consider the pipe smoker who can produce these vowels with the bit of his pipe clamped between his teeth. *His* jaw doesn't drop or he'd lose his pipe and probably set fire to his shirt, but his *tongue* drops or he wouldn't be able to make these sounds. Admittedly he has a bit of trouble, and that's why it's sometimes difficult to understand a guy talking around a pipestem, but essentially he does it. The tongue, then, is front in the mouth, but it goes from high front to low front. We would represent it diagrammatically this way:

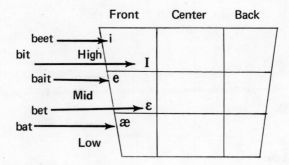

Now, again with the mirror and flashlight, try: *beet, Bert,* boot,*
again omitting the view-obscuring stops. What do you see? The hump
in the tongue moves steadily back, doesn't it? Thus on the diagram:

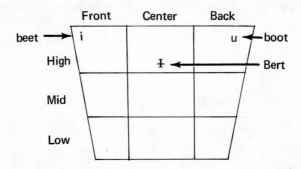

These, obviously, are all high vowels.

Now, as it were, let's try running down the scale at the back of
the quadrangle, which means also of course the back of the mouth.
Try these words: *boot, foot, obey, taught.* Actually, all we need here
is the vowels, and of course in "obey" it's the first one we want.
(There is one more vowel in this series, the bottom-most one, but not
many Americans have it in their speech: it's the sound in British
"not," if you're familiar with that. Probably we needn't worry about
this one.) As you pronounce this series you can again feel the tongue
going down, but this time it is clearly way in the back of the mouth.
Observing it in the mirror will be helpful again. The vowels just
considered are these:

---

*See page 52 for more precise description of this sound.

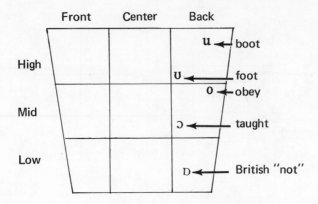

Now we need to consider the central vowels. In the most common analyses there are about seven of them, and you will have trouble distinguishing some of them from one another. For this reason it is impractical to give you a list of words to pronounce as samples. I'll try to describe them as best I can. Starting from the top and going down, then:

	Front	Center	Back
High		ɨ	
Mid		3 3˞	
		ə ʌ ɚ	
Low		a	

At the top is a sound usually called "the barred i" because of the way it is written, a letter "i" with a hyphen or bar struck through it: [ɨ]. It is the sound we often use in pronouncing the word "just" in a statement like "He's just a boy." Novelists often spell the word "jist" in trying to suggest the sound, but we actually don't quite say this "jist" the same way we do "gist." The tongue is not quite so far front in the mouth. Another place where this sound commonly occurs is in syllables like the second one of "hated."

The next symbol is [3] and is the vowel sound, without the "r," of "bird." It is, in fact, the sound most New Englanders and Southerners use in "bird."

The symbol to the right of [3] is the sound of "bird" *with* the "r." Phoneticians argue whether this is a vowel in its own right or whether it's simply [3] followed by "r." As you can see, the essential dispute here is over how to analyse "r," and we'll have to consider that (but not try to settle it) a little later. The symbol is [ɝ].

The next sound, moving down, is written as an inverted "e," is called the *schwa,* and is undoubtedly the most common vowel in English because of our tendency to "de-color" unaccented vowels. That is, they tend to become schwa. Here are some examples, with the underlined letters representing this sound: around, telephone, continental, conjugate, ricochet. (It doesn't make much difference what way it is spelled, does it?) It is written [ə].

A very similar sound is indicated by the schwa symbol with a little tail on it: [ɚ]. This is the second syllable of "father," assuming you speak a dialect that actually puts the "r" coloration on that syllable. Otherwise you use the schwa there too.

The next symbol is an inverted "v" ---- [ʌ] ---- and is the vowel sound of *cup, some, mud, tough, fudge.* Many people argue that this is the same as the schwa and that the only difference is one of stress. Whatever the truth of this argument, I include both "sounds" in this sketch of the vowel system because it's so often done that way.

The bottom-most symbol, [a], is the first vowel of "father" as most Americans pronounce it.

This completes in rough outline, at least, our listing of the most common vowels of American English. Here they are all together:

	Front	Center	Back
High	i ɪ	ɨ	u ʌ
Mid	e ɛ	3 ɝ ə ɚ ʌ	o ɔ
Low	ae	a	ɒ

There are a few observations that must be made about them:

First, there is the matter of "rounding" and "unrounding," which refers to the shape of the lips as vowels are produced. If you pronounce the word "peel" and watch your lips in your mirror you'll observe a slight spreading of them. Now pronounce "pool." You see the lips push out a bit and form a sort of O. They are "rounded." In describing the vowels of many languages it is necessary to describe whether the lips are rounded or unrounded as each vowel is uttered. French, for instance, has a high front rounded vowel. Shape your lips to say [u], as in "pool," but instead say [i], as in "see." That's that French vowel so difficult for so many American students. However, in English we have a fortunate situation, at least for purposes of vowel description: all the back vowels are rounded and none of the others are. Thus in English it is not necessary, in talking about any given vowel, to mention whether or not it is rounded. It's automatic.

Another thing: in English the tongue is very seldom still even as it pronounces a vowel—a stressed vowel, at least—and tends to glide from one vowel position into another. This produces, what we call "diphthongs," which we'll discuss at some length when we talk about phonemes. Right now, though, for purposes of illustration, let me remind you of the [o] from our vowel chart. To clue you in on its pronunciation I said it's the first vowel in "obey," and I could have said it's the last vowel in "Chicago." But I couldn't have said it's the vowel sound of English "no." Why not? Say this word in front of your mirror, and use the flashlight, and watch the tongue as well as the lips. You will see that you start out with [o], all right, but that then your lips round further and your tongue goes higher and backer (as the linguist says), and you have slid from [o] into [u]. This is a diphthong. (This is the difference, too, between Spanish "no" and English "no." Spanish uses a pure [o] and we "diphthongize" it.) Some speakers of other languages have told me that this constant slipping around of the tongue is to them one of the most striking characteristics of English.

One other thing and we'll have the vowels wrapped up for the moment. Just because these vowels we have been talking about are "the vowels of American English" (at least the most common ones) does certainly *not* mean that every American speaker has them in his own speech. In fact it is very unlikely that you have them all. (At the bottom of the *front* vowels, for instance, should be [ɑ], which is the way a New Englander says "bath," or at least some of them do, and it isn't the same vowel as the [a] in "father," which most of the rest of us make when trying to imitate Bostonians.) So if you don't have them all, don't fret about it. You're normal.

Now, a few pages back we left some unfinished business with the consonants. Let's get that cleaned up.

We'll consider first the sound we associate with the letter "l," the initial sound of "leap" and the final sound of "full." Actually, the sound in "leap" and the sound in "full" are quite different. Can you hear the difference? Try saying "full" and leaving your tongue in exactly the position in which you make the final sound. Then try beginning the word "leap" with that position. It's a bit clumsy, isn't it? As a matter of fact, there are several varieties of the sound we associate with "l," but we refer to all of them as "laterals" because they have in common that the sound, the airstream, issues around the *sides* of the tongue. There is a common version that is voiceless. It occurs very often after voiceless stops. Try, for instance, pronouncing the word "clip" with your fingertips on your throat. You'll probably find that you have pronounced clean through the "l" by the time the voice is turned on for the vowel. Still another version, made with the articulator and point of articulation further back in the mouth so that it's a voiced *dorsovelar* lateral, is fairly common in American speech. In making this one, the tongue apex is placed behind the *lower* teeth. You'll find it occurring, if it occurs at all in your speech, in words like "film."

Another consonant, if it is a consonant, which we've so far not dealt with is the one we think of as "r." There are those who argue that this sound is really a sort of coloration put on a vowel. Great uncertainty prevails, but we'll go with what seems to be the most usual analysis, and also the easiest, and call this sound a *consonant*. It is, like the various varieties of the lateral, a continuant. We describe it as "the voiced apico-alveolar retroflex." Very learned! Well, it's not really so rough. Let's look at it a minute. "Voiced" we understand, and also "apico-alveolar," though with this latter term we must understand that the apex is merely brought near the alveolar ridge and not smack up against it. "Retroflex" means that the tongue tip is curled back on itself. Take a look in the mirror and you'll see that this is true, at least approximately—the tip doesn't lie flat but sticks up, and almost, at least, curls back.[1]

We have to stop here and stipulate that the "r" we are talking about is the good, hard, ringing "r" that you would find in the

---

1. What is being given here is the "classical" description of the production of [r]. As a matter of fact, many Americans who do indeed have the [r] don't make it this way. For them, the tongue tip is depressed, in back of the lower teeth, and the back of the tongue is humped up. So if your mirror doesn't show the tongue tip curling back, but instead reveals this formation, you have a lot of speakers of good American English for company. However, for the sake of convenience we will still refer to it as the "retroflex"—meaning to include by the term both ways of producing this sound, which are, by the way, indistinguishable to the ear.

speech of a Middlewesterner. When he says "bird" there is sure an "r" sound in it. Now, the New Englander and the Southerner have a different kind of sound, at least in this position in a word. We might most easily say they have no "r" at all in "bird." What we call the "retroflex r" as made by the Ohioan—and by the New Englander and the Southerner too in words like "red"—we will write [r].

However, are you familiar with the British pronunciation of a word like "very"? In this one the apex, or tip, of the tongue is bounced off the alveolar ridge, making what is called a "flap r." To some people it sounds like a [t] or a [d]. When old-time columnist Walter Winchell used to want to make fun of something as being just too, too preciously British he would write it "veddy, veddy," trying to suggest this pronunciation. We write this [ř]. Sometimes, but very rarely in American English, the tongue tip is actually trilled against the alveolar ridge. You'll hear this in Scots dialect, and it is a normal feature of Spanish (as in "perro"). We would write this [ȓ], if you care. The "guttural" kind of "r," characteristic of French and German isn't made in American English. If it crops up we're ready for it: [Ȓ].

There is a voiceless version of the retroflex in our American speech, however, and it occurs, like the voiceless lateral, after voiceless stops. Try it on the word "cripple." It works just like voiceless [l]—you're all through with the "r" before you turn on your voice for the vowel.

We have two other "consonants" to consider and we'll have done with the common sounds of English. I put "consonants" in quotes because these are equally often called "semivowels." The problem is that they have the usual qualities of vowels, but they occur in words where consonants ordinarily do. The term "semivowels" turns out to be kind of a compromise. These are the sounds we usually associate with the letters "w" and "y."

The "w" is called "a voiced labiovelar semivowel," probably for lack of anything better to call it. The "labio" element gets in because the sound is accompanied by lip rounding. Try it and take a look. The "velar" part of the label is perhaps appropriate because the dorsum is raised a bit toward the velum. What happens after the lips are rounded and the velum is poised is that the tongue quickly slides into position for the vowel that is to follow, and if that vowel is a front or central one the tongue movement is accompanied by a simultaneous unrounding of the lips. Again, try it. We'll write the sound [w].

Incidentally, if you are one of those who carefully differentiate words like "wen" and "when" (as I am not), the "wh" variety is most easily considered a voiceless version of [w] and is written [w̥].

The sound usually spelled "y" we will write [y] (though the IPA writes it [j] and reserves the [y] for that French high front rounded vowel). The [y] has the same appearance as the letter we usually spell it with and will be easy to remember. Like [w] it is a quick gliding movement of the tongue, the front part of which is brought close to the palate and then quickly shifted into position for the following vowel. Therefore we'll call it "the voiced fronto-palatal semivowel."

Finally, then, we have listed the common sounds of our language. It has seemed like a long list, with many, many details to try to remember, and yet this treatment of it has not been at all thorough. If one wants any understanding of English, it is simply an unavoidable necessity to look at least a little bit at how the sounds of it are made, for language *is* sounds, as we have seen. If you are going to try to remember any of the mass of details in this treatment of English sounds, and of course you should, I suggest that as you look back over this chapter you pay less attention to detail than you do to how these sounds fall into patterns, and note too the close resemblances in the ways quite different sounds are produced. As you contemplate the patterns, the details will fall into place.

Something for you to remember: all of the intricacies of producing these sounds, and all of the complexities of fitting them together into speech patterns, is something of which you've been a master ever since you left the playpen. All we've done here is isolate, look at, and list something you've "known" all your life.

SUGGESTED READING

Buchanan, Cynthia. *A Programed Introduction to Linguistics* (to p. 82). Boston: D.C. Heath & Co., 1963.

Francis, W. Nelson. *The Structure of American English* ("The Sounds of Speech: Phonetics," chapter 2). New York: Ronald Press, 1958.

Thomas, Charles Kenneth. *An Introduction to the Phonetics of American English.* New York: Ronald Press, 1958.

CHAPTER 3

SOUNDS INTO BUNDLES

Suppose that for every sound listed in the preceding section we managed to discover 100 sub-sounds, and to devise a symbol to represent every one of them. What would we have then? We'd have a mess of finely-discriminated speech sounds, that's for sure. But what good would it all be? What could we do with it? What would it tell us about speech beyond the fact that speech sounds really may be infinite in variety?—which we already have theorized. What we need, if language analysis is to be possible, is not ever-spreading chaos but some way of bringing order to the endless variety of observable details.

With the advent of the phoneme, the language analyst had the tool he needed. You will need to understand the concept of the phoneme. Fortunately it's very simple. Unfortunately some simple things aren't always easy to grasp at first. We can do it, however, if you'll just patiently and carefully follow the explanation step by step, keeping in mind all the time my assurance that really this is pretty easy. And suddenly a great light will burst upon you and you'll have learned it once and for all.

Put yourself back, in your imagination, to the condition you were in before you learned that the [p'] in "pin," and the [p] in "spin," and the unreleased [p⁻] you might find on "stop" were all actually and demonstrably different. You might well have said to anyone asking you to comment on the differences among them: "Differences? What differences? They're all the same as far as I can see." And now along comes phonemics to say that *as far as English goes* you were right all the time. A "p" is a "p" is a "p." Essentially, that's what phonemics is all about.

But, you object, I've just gone to a lot of trouble and I find that there really *are* different kinds of voiceless bilabial stops. How about aspiration, lack of aspiration, failure to release—how about all that? How can we on the one hand go to a great deal of effort to point out differences and then turn around and say they don't exist? A good question. We can't. But we can say, and phonemics does say, that some differences don't *matter*. (Remember, please, as we say this we can be talking about *one* language only. Unless otherwise stated, we'll be talking about English.)

Suppose you were to say of some female you didn't like very much, "What a cat!" Would it make very much difference if your final apico-alveolar stop was aspirated, unaspirated or even unreleased? If the woman happened to overhear you would she understand what you meant, regardless of how you made that final stop? You'd better believe it. Suppose, however, you *voiced* that last stop, and said "What a cad." Would she still understand the same thing? Of course not. Whether the stop is voiced or voiceless makes a difference in meaning. That is, it is a *significant* difference. Thus the "t" ending and the "d" ending are different phonemes. But the [t], [t'] and [t˺] endings are not significant, compared one to another, so the differences are not phonemic.

I want to digress a few minutes and build a rather elaborate analogy, if you'll bear with me. Let's forget about speech sounds for a short spell and talk about dogs.

How many dachshunds do you reckon there are in the world? Two or three million? Four or five million? Anyhow there are a lot. Would you agree to the proposition that probably no two of them are exactly alike, if we get down to such refinements as the exact number of body cells, number and variety of corpuscles, etc? It would be at least unlikely that there would be two absolutely identical in all respects, wouldn't it?

At the same time they all have certain characteristics in common: short legs, long back, floppy ears, deep chest. You wouldn't mistake one for a Great Dane, nor for a French poodle, nor for a wire-haired terrier.

Now, as we contemplate this vast number of dachshunds we note that there are several varieties of them. There is a kind of grouping. There are the red ones, the black and tans, and the longhaireds. Also, there are the standards and the miniatures. A black and tan one is clearly different from a red one. Yet they're certainly both dachshunds.

Surely this is all very simple. You might even be thinking it's somewhat simple-minded. Let's see what relevance it has to the concept of the phoneme.

The linguist thinks of an individual speech sound as a "phone." (We'll have a few technical terms in this discussion, but not very many—and I'll try to make them clear.) A phone occurs once and is gone forever. Thinking of the voiceless bilabial stop, the sound we associate with the letter "p," in all the various varieties of it we have noted: suppose you say a word that has that sound in it, and so does someone in Chicago, someone in London, someone in San Francisco, someone in Birmingham, and so do I. That's six times that voiceless bilabial stop has been uttered, and no two of them exactly alike. How many times would you think that sound, the voiceless bilabial stop, gets made each day in the English-speaking world? Truly an astronomical total. And yet it can be argued that no two of them are perfectly identical in every respect. Though we are dealing with a vastly greater number than with the dachshunds, the principle is the same.

And just as with the dachshunds, we notice that there are different varieties of this unvoiced bilabial stop. That is, of course: [p'], [p] and [p⁻]. Yet they are all noticeably dachshunds/voiceless bilabial stops. And they are not to be confused with, say, a voiceless bilabial nasal or a German shepherd.

With the dachshunds we called the various groupings—reds, black-and-tans, etc.—varieties. Varieties of the dachshund. With the various versions of the voiceless bilabial stop we use a technical term: they are allophones. Allophones of what?

They are allophones of the phoneme /p/. And now, perhaps, we have arrived at some idea of the phoneme, which we always write between slant lines—/p/—to distinguish it from phonetic symbols [p'] and from mere letters, "p."

Remember, now: we have the billions and billions of individual occurrences of the voiceless bilabial stop, in all its varieties, each one a phone. As we observe these phones we find they tend to fall into types (aspirated, unaspirated, unreleased, and others which we haven't described), which clearly differ from one another. We call these types allophones. But though they are different from each other (like the various varieties of dachshunds) they all clearly belong to the same breed (dachshund, or voiceless bilabial stop) which we call the phoneme /p/.

I need to emphasize that *the phoneme is an abstraction.* We don't talk in phonemes but in *phones,* which we know how to sort into phonemes. The phoneme is a device that lets us create some order out of the chaos of zillions of phones. For instance, if I ask you how to pronounce /p/ *you can't do it.* You can't do it because you don't know which allophone is called for. Now, if you saw it in context, even in a made-up word, one of two things would happen: either you would automatically know, as a speaker of English, which allophone to select, or it wouldn't make any difference. If I give you the word "ponk" to pronounce, you will undoubtedly begin it with [p']; if I give you the word "sponk," the allophone you choose will be [p]; but if I give you "kanop," you might choose [p'], [p], *or* [p⁻] and it won't make any difference. (Actually, you *could* use an unaspirated stop on "ponk"—it's just that you wouldn't, and if you did you'd sound a little foreign, like a person with a Spanish accent.)

So far we haven't offered a definition of the phoneme. It will be adequate for our purposes to think of it as "the smallest significant unit of language." (It is important here to be thinking of language as speech, for clearly the concept of the phoneme is based on sound.) A "significant unit" is a unit that makes a difference in meaning. Thus whether we pronounce "cat" with [k'], which is normal, or [k], which would sound a little foreign to our ears, makes no difference in meaning, and we would have to conclude that [k'] and [k] are simply allophones of the same phoneme. But if we *voice* that initial dorso-velar stop [g] it makes a big difference. "He was arrested for carrying a cat" and "He was arrested for carrying a gat" are quite different things. Therefore, [k'] and [g] are allophones of *different* phonemes, and we have to deduce that /k/ and /g/ (as we'll write them) are two phonemes. It is an axiom, then, that a difference that makes a difference is a phonemic difference. (It is important to note that we are not saying that /k/ and /g/ have meaning in themselves but only that the choice of one or the other can effect changes of meaning in larger units, like words.)

Any time we can find two words or constructions which are identical in all respects *but one,* and which have different meanings, we are confronted with two different phonemes. Words or constructions like this are said to be "minimal pairs" and the sounds that differ are said to be "in contrast." Example: "Yale" and "jail" are identical except for the initial sound, and they are obviously different in meaning. "My boyfriend's in Yale" and "My boyfriend's in jail" are not the same. So we have a minimal pair. And, the initial sounds are in contrast. Anytime we can establish a minimal pair, then, we can be sure that we are dealing with two different phonemes.

We need to consider, and set forth in a list, these significant sounds of our language. Naturally this listing is going to be considerably shorter than our earlier look at the "sounds" of English, for not all of those sounds are "significant," as we have seen. We will compile them into bundles. First we need to note that these phonemes, these significant sounds, are of two main kinds. One set is called the "segmental" phonemes. Actually, these multi-syllable labels are easy enough because, as we shall see, they are descriptive. But they will take just a minute of explaining. Let's look at the segmentals first, just keeping in the back of our minds the awareness that the "supra-segmentals" will be dealt with later. This is simpler than trying to do two things at once.

Spoken language is really, as the linguists say, a continuum. That is, from the time you begin to say something until you finish saying it, the sounds tumble forth in a stream. You've noticed this as you've listened to a language you don't understand. You can't begin to tell where one word ends and another begins: it's all just a steady pouring forth of sounds. It's perhaps a bit more difficult to see this with English because we know where the word boundaries are, but if you listen closely to any random sample of speech you'll convince yourself of the truth of this: sounds blend and blur into one continuous stream.

We can't very well analyze the whole stream. We need some way of breaking it up into manageable bits: into segments. We segment the stream, and hence the name *segmental* phonemes. When we do this we are in fact perpetrating a friction because the phonemes that go to make up a word do not really neatly succeed one another in beautiful separateness like so many boxcars in a string. Rather they tend to fuse together so that sometimes they seem practically inseparable. Consider the crying child wailing to his mother that he doesn't want to do something. Does he say, "I don't want to, mama," with each sound distinct and carefully separated from its neighbor? No, he doesn't. "I don' wanna, mama"—and even the [d] might drop out and you get something like "Iowanna." But as long as we keep in mind that our neatly segmented phonemes are something of a fiction, we're not kidding ourselves at least, and we do have a useful tool.

There are thirty-three of these segmental phonemes in English: twenty-four consonants and nine vowels. This is quite a reduction from the lengthy list of sounds we examined earlier (which, at that, was quite superficial). Thirty-three is something manageable. This we can work with, and for English speakers who know which allophone of a phoneme to use where, or know when the choice doesn't matter, this comparatively short list is enough. Let's look at these phonemes. We'll break them up into categories (stops, fricatives, etc.) with which you are already familiar.

The Stops

We have already seen that the voiceless bilabial stop /p/ is a phoneme in English and we know its principal allophones: [p'], [p], and [p⁻]. It occurs in all positions in words: that is, initially, medially, and finally.

Its voiced opposite, which we'll write /b/, is a phoneme too. We have noticed that it doesn't have, in English, an allophone with aspiration. It has "general distribution" too, which is to say it also occurs initially, medially, and finally.

The apico-alveolar stops, voiced and voiceless, are phonemes too. So we have /t/ and /d/. (For allophonic variations you can turn back to the previous chapter, remembering that by no means all the allophones are listed. For instance, with both /t/ and /d/ we have the frequent occurrence of "nasal release." If you try the word "button," or "sudden," you will discover that the stop is not really released, but that with the tongue apex still against the alveolar ridge, the airstream is directed out through the nasal passage. This would be written [tᴺ] or [dᴺ]. A somewhat similar thing happens when these sounds are followed by a lateral.) These stops have general distribution.

The remaining two of the stop phonemes are /k/ and /g/, the dorso-velar stops. They too have general distribution.

The glottal stop is not phonemic in English. There is no word differentiated from any other word by the presence or absence of this stop. In some dialects of American English the glottal stop does serve as an allophone of /t/, as in the often-heard New York pronunciation of "bottle," in which the stop is made in the voice box and the tongue tip never touches the alveolar ridge.

The Fricatives

There are nine fricatives, and like the stops they come in voiced-voiceless pairs, until we come to the ninth one.

First, we have the labio-dentals /f/ and /v/, which occur in all positions.

Then we have the pair of interdentals /θ/ and /ð/. You will remember that /θ/ is the voiceless fricative, the initial sound of "thigh," and that /ð/ is voiced, the beginning sound of "thy." Both of these fricatives have general distribution.

Next we have the apico-alveolar fricatives (sometimes called sibilants), /s/ and /z/. They have no allophonic variations, so here is one time, at least, that you could, contrary to what I said some pages ago in discussing /p/, give the pronunciation from the phoneme symbol /s/ or /z/. Both of these have general distribution.

The last pair of fricatives are the fronto-palatal /š/ and /ž/, the sounds, you will recall, of "*sh*oe" and of "plea*s*ure." /š/ has general distribution (*shoot, issue, mush*), but /ž/ is limited. It doesn't occur initially at all (not natively) and occurs finally only in a few words where it is interchangeable with the voiced affricate (see below).

This leaves us only one more fricative: /h/, the initial sound of "heaven," and the other place too. The /h/ occurs initially and medially, but not finally, except as an element of a diphthong—which we'll discuss later.

The Affricates

Here again we find a pair, one voiced and the other voiceless, the apico-alveolar affricates. They have general distribution. We will write them /č/ and /ǰ/, though this pair of symbols is by no means universal. Many prefer to write /č/ as /tš/, which is certainly a logical transcription and which indicates something of how the sound is made. Often students practicing writing in phonemic symbols will come to a word like "much" and insist that they hear a /t/ in it. They do hear it, of course. But as we're going to use the symbol, /č/ *equals* /tš/. You might say it has the /t/ built in. Exactly a parallel situation occurs with /ǰ/, which is often written /dž/. As for which is preferable, it seems six of one and half a dozen of the other. However, using /č/ we do have to write only one symbol instead of two, /tš/. Economy in effort is a great thing. There's no telling how many man hours we might save in this way. These affricates, by the way, can be used in all positions in words.

The Nasals

We have three nasals: the bilabial /m/, the apico-alveolar /n/, and the dorso-velar /ŋ/. All are voiced. While /m/ and /n/ have general distribution, /ŋ/ is used only medially and finally, never initially. (Students have objected to me that "England" begins with this sound, but it doesn't. It begins with a vowel, which is followed by /ŋ/.)

The Rest

We have only four consonant phonemes left to consider. These are the retroflex, the lateral, and two semivowels. Let's list them quickly and move on to a consideration of the vowels.

The retroflex, which we are going to write /r/, has, as we noted earlier, approximately seventeen thousand different ways of being made. It has allophones until they won't quit. Speakers of different dialects make this sound in varying ways. Even whether it's properly a consonant or a vowel is disputed by phoneticians. But you and I know what we're talking about. The initial sound in "red." The medial sound in "Harold," and the final sound in "bore" (if you have the /r/ there). Since we really do know what we're talking about, and since the sound is so difficult to pin down precisely, let's let it go at that for the time being.

As for the lateral, which we'll write /l/, it will offer us no difficulty, though as noted earlier it really has quite an assortment of allophones. However, a name like "Lil" begins with /l/ and ends with /l/. All the allophones simply add up to /l/, and we'll have no trouble with that.

As for the labiovelar semivowel, which we will write /w/, we have no problem either. We might note that what we earlier called the voiceless version of this, if you differentiate "we" and "whee" is spelled out in phonemics. That is, the voiced version will be /w/ but the voiceless will be /hw/. If you stop to think about it, that's the sequence in which the sounds actually occur, isn't it? /hwen/ is much closer to what we actually say than is "when"—if we say it. Many of us simply say /wen/.

The other semivowel, and the last of our list of consonants, is the voiced fronto-palatal semivowel, which we'll write /y/. We need no description of it beyond what we've already had.

That completes our list of consonant phonemes. Six stops, nine fricatives, two affricates, three nasals, one lateral, one retroflex, and two semivowels. Can you name them all? If not, stop right here and try again. Get a real familiarity with them. You'll notice how their very neat patterning serves as a memory aid. Here they are, laid out for you: (See the consonant phonemes on page 66.)

Pursuing our description, or listing rather, of the segmental phonemes of English, we need to turn our attention to the vowels. We said there are nine of them. Here they are in a streamlined, cut-down version of the "vowel quadrangle" we were using earlier. (Phonetic

Stops	Voiceless	Voiced
Bilabial	/p/ (*p*in, u*pp*er, cu*p*)	/b/ (*b*ib, ru*bb*er)
Apico-alveolar	/t/ (*t*ip, pi*t*, pa*tt*y)	/d/ (*d*id*d*led)
Dorso-velar	/k/ (*k*ick, hi*cc*up)	/g/ (*g*ag, ea*g*er)
Fricatives		
Labio-dental	/f/ (*f*ife, o*f*ten)	/v/ (*v*i*v*id, ali*v*e)
Interdental	/θ/ (*th*igh, e*th*er, wi*th*)	/ð/ (*th*y, ei*th*er, la*th*e)
Apico-alveolar	/s/ (*s*i*s*ter, hi*ss*)	/z/ (*z*ip, sci*ss*or, hi*s*)
Fronto-palatal	/š/ (*sh*u*sh*, i*ss*ue)	/ž/ (a*z*ure, rou*g*e)
Glottal	/h/ (*h*ymn, a*h*ead)	
Affricates		
Apico-alveolar	/č/ (*ch*ur*ch*, i*tch*y)	/ǰ/ (*j*ud*g*e, e*dg*y)
Nasals		
Bilabial		/m/ (*m*a*m*a, ha*m*)
Apico-alveolar		/n/ (*N*a*n*a, si*n*)
Dorso-velar		/ŋ/ (si*ng*er, ha*ng*)
Semivowels		
Retroflex		/r/ (*r*oare*r*)
Lateral		/l/ (*l*ull, oi*l*y)
Labiovelar		/w/ (*w*art, a*w*ay)
Fronto-palatal		/y/ (*y*ou

Man is still facing left. That is, high front is to the top left, low back to the bottom right, etc.)

	Front	Central	Back
High	i	ɨ	u
Mid	e	ə	o
Low	æ	a	ɔ

What these symbols represent, with some little additional comment to help avoid confusion, is as follows:

The front vowel phonemes, from top to bottom, are /i/ as in "sit," /e/ as in "set," and /æ/ as in "sat." (Note that these symbols are *different from* the phonetic symbols in the last chapter.)

The back vowel phonemes, again from top to bottom, are /u/ as in "put," /o/ as in "*o*bey," and /ɔ/ as in "awe." This last symbol is usually referred to in speech as "open o."

The low central vowel, /a/, is the sound of the first vowel in "father."

The mid-central vowel, /ə/, is the vowel in "mud." This is the "schwa" sound, and you will notice that now that we're dealing with phonemes, we have forgotten such finicky refinements as whether the first vowel in "about" is the same as or different from the vowel of "come." If there is a difference it's so slight it won't bother us here, and it certainly isn't a *phonemic* difference anyhow.

This leaves only the high central vowel to be considered, the so-called "barred-i," and it still offers the same difficulties it did earlier, no more and no less. It's the vowel sound of "just" in "he's just a kid." (Note that the vowel of "just" in "he's a just man" is clearly the schwa, /ə/.) It's also the second syllable vowel, commonly, in words like "rancid." If you think your second vowel in "rancid" is a schwa, /ə/, and I suggest that it's more likely /ɨ/, don't worry about it. It might be /ə/ and again it might be /ɨ/—and again it might be something exactly in between. These efforts to describe phonemes are only approximations. We are the piano player with the ability to play the cracks, remember? So if you can't really decide to call a given sound, jump one way or the other. It doubtless won't matter much. But do remember that basic principle of minimal pairs. (See p. 61) If one vowel sound seems to you different from another, and *if it differentiates two words,* then it is different. It's a different phoneme. (Example: a good friend of mine differentiates "fir" and "fur," and can always tell which is which. There is, therefore, a phonemic difference involved. In this case, she seems to use barred i /ɨ/ for "fir" and schwa /ə/ for "fur." Anyhow in her speech they are different phonemes. In mine there is no difference, and I could buy a "fir coat" and "chop down a fur" with equal ease.)

If you really looked over and thought about the vowel quadrangle as presented above you are likely to have a complaint: Okay, /i/ is as in "sit." So what happened to the vowel sound in "seat"? You could go on to point out quite a few other familiar English vowel sounds that are not represented in that vowel quadrangle. What about them?

The explanation—which will need further explanation—is that these apparently-omitted vowels are all diphthongs, and we are going to need a slight modification of our symbols to accommodate them. Let's see how this works.

If you pronounce /a/ as in "father," and then quickly glide high front, without a glottal stop, to /i/, only higher and farther forward,—well, let's try it. A-a-a-eeeee. Aaaa—eee. (Trying to represent it in conventional spelling.) Now make the glide quickly. You get "I," the first person singular pronoun, the vowel of "mine," "side," "height." (Note: as always in discussions of speech sounds, dialects get in the way. If you come from the Deep South, where language is represented in print as "ah'm eatin' mah lunch," you might not have this diphthong in quite the same way as other dialects have it.) In other words, the "vowel" of "hide" is not "a" vowel but two of them blended and fused. We can define a diphthong as one vowel quickly sliding into another.

This is a very good time to get out the flashlight and mirror again. While watching your tongue closely, pronounce "I." You will see that it starts in low central position, /a/, then makes quite a spectacular leap high to the front (even higher and further forward than the /i/ of "sit,"). We are going to use a /y/ to represent the conclusion of this diphthong. Thus "hod" (the thing laborers carry bricks in) is /had/, and "hide" is /hayd/. So we have "time" /taym/, "style" /stayl/, "height" /hayt/, etc.

This diphthong, and others like it, is called a "fronting diphthong" because the tongue is moving forward, and also higher.

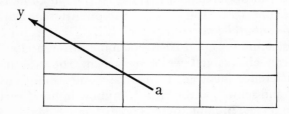

Suppose we make a similar glide with the tongue, but start further back with /ɔ/. This is what we do as we pronounce words like "boil" /bɔyl/, "coin" /kɔyn/, etc. (It should be remarked that many American speakers do not start these diphthongs quite so low, beginning instead with /o/. Thus: /boyl/, /koyn/, etc. This is, generally speaking, characteristic of Southern speech.) Try this one too with the mirror and flashlight routine. Did you ever realize your tongue was quite so active?

If a similar glide is started from the mid-front vowel /e/ we produce the familiar "vowel" sound of "slate," "freight," "wait," etc. Try "bet" /bet/ a few times. Then during the vowel let the tongue ride high and front and you will produce "bait" /beyt/.

Something very much like that will happen if you pronounce "sit" /sit/ and during the production of the vowel force the tongue higher and further forward. You'll get "seat" /siyt/. Here especially the flashlight and mirror are useful, for otherwise you might think you're being kidded. With the /a/ to /y/ glide the tongue moves so far, physically, that you don't really have to look to convince yourself—you can feel it. But the difference between /sit/—/siyt/ is not much of a tongue movement and you may have to witness it to believe it. But if you look you will see it.

I hasten to point out that if you do think you're being kidded by this description of the vowel in "seat" as a diphthong, /siyt/, a lot of distinguished phonologists would agree with you. They insist that this is not a diphthong but a pure, simple vowel and would assign it a symbol of its own, /i/. The vowel of "sit" then becomes /ɪ/. The most telling point of their argument, it seems to me, is that you can't prolong a "true" diphthong, like that of "might" /mayt/, but that you can prolong the vowel of "seat" as long as your breath holds out. They make precisely the same objection to the description we will consider, in the next page or two, of the vowel sound of "pool" as a diphthong. Describing the vowels of "seat" and "pool" as diphthongs is a widespread practice, however, so we will go along with it, with the full awareness that this matter, like so many others in language study, is far from universally agreed upon and that somewhere a distinguished linguist reading these lines will be clucking his tongue and shaking his head sadly.

We have a second major kind of diphthong, the "retracting" or "backing" diphthong. The principle is exactly the same as with the fronting diphthongs we were just considering, but the tongue instead of moving high and front moves high and back. You will notice that in our phonemic vowel quadrangle we have /u/, which is the vowel of "should." We don't have the higher and further back sound of "shoed," as in "He shoed the pony," because, again, this is a diphthong. We are going to write this very high, back sound as /w/.

Let's start again with the /a/ of "father." Suppose while making it we suddenly make the tongue glide high to the back. We'll get "aaa—oooo"—only do it real fast. What you're supposed to be coming up with is the "vowel" sound of "house," which we'll write /haws/. Thus: "round" /rawnd/, "lout" /lawt/, "scrounge" /skrawnǰ/, etc.

We ought to observe right here, in case you're having insuperable trouble with this, that many—and maybe most—of the pronunciation differences among various American dialects occur in the diphthongs. Thus the Virginian, who is libeled in print as saying "aboot the hoose" really starts this diphthong from the mid-central position. He says /hǝws/. Try it. Start with the schwa, the vowel of "but," and then glide higher and backer. In like manner, some Americans start this glide with /æ/. Thus they pronounce "cow" as /kæw/. These dialectal differences are merely dialectal differences: there is no "right" or "wrong" except that each of us is likely to think his English is normal and everyone else's is a bit funny. But as you can see, these differences complicate the discussion of our vowel sounds.

This glide high and back to /w/ starts from other positions than /a/, of course. One of the most common is the beginning from /o/, giving us the diphthong of "road" /rowd/, "no" /now/, "stone" /stown/, etc. If you watch your lips as you pronounce one of these words you will notice how they protrude further and round as the glide from /o/ to /w/ gets under way.

Another very common backing glide is /uw/, the diphthong of "pool" /puwl/ (contrast "pull" /pul/). Again, if you are skeptical that this really is a glide, the best evidence I can offer is your own mirror. Try it on "rude" /ruwd/, "lewd" /luwd/, and "booed" /buwd/. Try contrasting "stood" /stud/ with "stewed" /stuwd/.

Backing Diphthongs

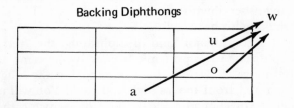

There is also in English a "centering diphthong," which we are going to represent with /h/. This diphthong occurs when the tongue shifts from another vowel position, say /i/, into mid-central area en route to some succeeding sound, and something of the mid-central vowel gets into the act. Since the tongue position for /r/ is close to that for /ǝ/, the centering diphthong is heard commonly after a vowel preceding /r/. Thus "beer" is much more likely to be /bihr/ than /bir/. Similarly: "chair" /čehr/, "poor" /puhr/, "four" /fohr/ or /fɔhr/, and so on.

Centering Diphthongs

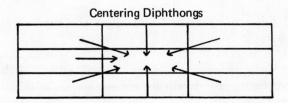

Theoretically at least, since there are nine vowels and any of them can glide front, back or center, it should be possible to produce twenty-seven diphthongs. These plus the original nine would give us a total of thirty-six *vowel sounds* in English, which is a far cry from the "a,e,i,o,u, and sometimes y" that we learned in school. (Of course, there our books and teachers were not thinking of vowels, but of *letters,* which are something else again.) Perhaps in one dialect or another of English all of these combinations exist. I don't know. But certainly none of us has all of them, and it's a good bet for any one speaker that he doesn't even have all nine of the vowel phonemes in the quadrangle.

There might be nagging in your mind one very good question that needs answering. It would go like this: "I thought we were going to use /y/ and /w/ as semivowels, as in "yes" /yes/ and "watt" /wat/, and /h/ was to be the glottal fricative as in "hot" /hat/. So what's all this jazz about using them to indicate glides in diphthongs?"

Phonemicists seem to have agreed to use these three symbols in *both* ways. The chance of confusion is nil, however. When you see /y,w,h/ *before* a vowel, in what is called "pre-vocalic" position, it's the semivowel or the fricative. When you see one of them *after* a vowel ("post-vocalic") it's the glide. And you couldn't possibly pronounce them the other way around if you tried.

Oddly enough, and perhaps lending some validity to this double use of these symbols, if you had a tape recorder which would play sounds backwards and you recorded a word like "wow" /waw/ you would find that it would sound the same either frontwards or backwards. This is also true of "yea" /yey/ and of "ha" /hah/, which is perhaps why some phonemicists like to call the pre-vocalic /h/ a semivowel rather than a fricative.

So we have run through our list of thirty-three segmental phonemes, twenty-four consonants and nine vowels, for we are viewing the diphthongs as combinations of other phonemes rather than as phonemes in their own right.

We need now to turn our attention to the suprasegmental phonemes, which topic is going to be a challenge to your ability to read imaginatively as well as to my ability to make clear explanations, for we are going to be required to listen to the "music" of the language and instead of being able to do it face to face we're obviously going to have to operate through the medium of marks on paper. Writing is a great invention but it has its limitations. We're going to have to extend them just as far as we can.

First let me hasten to tell you that the analysis of the suprasegmental phonemes which follows is only *one* analysis, though a fairly common one. There are others, and they differ. There is much less agreement among phonemicists on the suprasegmentals than there is on the phonemes we've already looked at. They seem not to have attracted as much serious attention, certainly not for so long a time. Perhaps, too, they're trickier.

Here are two sentences for you to read out loud:

1. She is my sister.
2. She is my sister?

The first thing we notice as we compare the two readings is that the segmental phonemes of the two sentences are identical. Dividing it into "words," which certainly isn't the way we'd read it, either sentence would perhaps look like this: /šiy ɨz may sistər/. (We'd really read it more like /sɨyzmə sistər/.) However, though the segmental phonemes are identical, the two utterances are different, are they not? The first is a simple statement, while the second is not only a question but one with a faint note of surprise, as though she's the last person in the world you thought would be taken for your sister. What is different in the two sentences is the "tune." In the first, your voice rises on the first syllable of "sister" and then drops off sharply. In the second sentence, instead of dropping off, your voice continues rising through the final syllable.

Now, remember back when we were taking our first look at the phoneme and trying to pin it down? We said then that when two words or constructions are identical in all respects but one, and have a different meaning, the difference is a phonemic difference.

So in our two sentences we have a phonemic difference, *by definition.* The phonemes involved are called suprasegmental, which would seem to indicate their being laid on over or above the segmental ones, and many of the symbols for them actually are literally written "above" the symbols for the segmental phonemes.

The suprasegmentals are of three kinds: *stress, pitch,* and *juncture.* There are (in the analysis we are considering) four levels of stress, four of pitch, and four of juncture, for a total of twelve.

Stress has to do with the degree of loudness given to some sounds, usually syllables, and withheld from others. This refers specifically to *relative* loudness within a construction. The fact that your friend consistently speaks in a louder voice than you do has nothing to do with it. We are considering degrees of loudness within one of his constructions (or one of yours, maybe) and the comparison between his and yours is irrelevant. In fact, at times you talk more loudly than at other times, and that's irrelevant too. What we're hitting at, then, is the degree of emphasis you choose to put on certain elements within a given construction. We can and do shift stress around in sentences to change meanings. Consider: *She* is my sister. (Not that one, stupid, this one.) She *is* my sister. (Why do you deny it?) She is *my* sister. (No, not his. Mine.) She is my *sister.* (You don't think I'd have my girlfriend here in my dorm room, do you?) Emphatic shifts in stress like these are obvious enough. They're real enough, too. But we need to look at subtler ones which are just as important and much more common.

How do you pronounce /insens/ and what does it mean? Careful! That's a trick question. You can't tell how to pronounce it until you know where to put the stress, and you don't know what it means until then either. If you stress the first syllable it's a perfumed kind of smoke (and is a noun). If you stress the second syllable it means "to make angry" (and is a verb). Clearly the segmental phonemes are identical. The difference is one of stress. We have quite a few pairs of words like this: *permit, imprint, inlay, insert, insult, transfer, reject,* and others. So—stress is phonemic.

Suppose you have occasion to say the following construction: "a new windshield wiper." Now, of course, you *can* put the stresses wherever you want them in this phrase, just as we did with the "She is my sister" routine a minute ago. But what I want you to do is say it simply and normally, as though it just popped up in conversation somehow. Say it several times and listen carefully to it. Does one syllable sound noticeably louder to you than the others? If so, and if this is working the way I hope it is, it's the "wind-" syllable. Now, are there syllables which while not quite as loud as "wind-" are still just a bit louder than the others? Try it several times again. For me, they are the word "new" and the syllable "wip-." They are noticeably louder than "-shield." However, "-shield," while not quite so loud as "new" or "wip-," is still louder than the "a" or the final "-er" of "wiper."

This little exercise has been an attempt to demonstrate the four stress levels of English. Here are their names and the symbols used to designate them as phonemes:

′ = primary (loudest)
^ = secondary (next loud)
` = tertiary (third level)
˘ = weak

Our phrase, assuming you agreed with me on where the stresses are, would look like this:

ă nêw wíndshièld ŵipĕr

It isn't too hard to demonstrate that English speakers have four stresses in their speech. But there are problems, nevertheless. It's very difficult to prove that these four stresses represent four different phonemes, for there are no minimal pairs. (The /insens/ example simply proves that stress is phonemic; it's a far cry from demonstrating four phonemes.) One thing compounding the problem, especially here, where you and I can't communicate face to face, is that people have different stress systems, and often as not when you give someone an example he says it differently. One theory is that when you listen to a person whose stress system differs from your own you are constantly and subconsciously translating it into your system, somewhat as you do when you listen to someone with a dialect greatly different from yours. If he doesn't put /r/ where you expect it, you mentally supply it.

We can't resolve the problem here, and fortunately we don't have to. But we can take the time to note some of the results of subtle shifts in stress. We'll proceed with constructions in minimal pairs and I'll mark the stresses to indicate the intended readings. Instead of writing these examples in phonemics I'll use standard spelling and punctuation, which are sometimes a clue to stress patterns, as in our very first example:

It's the mâin stréet càr. (the principal one)
It's the Máin Strèet câr. (the one running on Main Street)

I saw him bỳ the bánk. (near the bank)
I saw him bŭy the bánk.

. . . some nîce tŷpe wríters who use nîce týpewritĕrs.

She's an Énglǐsh teàchěr. (She teaches English.)

She's an Ênglǐsh téachěr. (She's from England.)

She's going to be a grèat-grándmòthěr. (Her grand-daughter is expecting.)

She's going to be a grêat grándmòthěr. (As a grandmother she'll be a wow.)

He's an odd féllǒw. (peculiar chap)

He's an Ódd Fèllǒw. (member of a lodge.)

. . . a robbery by twô aȓmed mén.

. . . a robbery by two-arȉmed mén.

. . . the country of our fórefàthěrs.

. . . the country of our fôur fáthěrs.

I heard a stress pattern once on the radio news that rather startled me, to say the least. Do you remember a few years ago when a huge dam in Italy broke and wiped out a whole village? It was a spectacular tragedy and occupied the newspapers and news magazines and news broadcasts. Of course one does not crack wise about such a topic, so I was considerably shaken to turn on the radio news and hear: "Here's some more news about that dȁmn disáster in Italy." It took a minute or so to realize that the announcer had meant to refer to "that dám disaȉstěr." When you consider how subtle are some of these stress shifts and what complete (and sometimes ludicrous) changes in meaning they effect, it is surprising that we don't pull bloopers with them more often. And yet all of us who speak English have mastered the whole repertoire, and more. Further, we do it all unaware of the wonderful complexity of what we're doing, just like our friend little Johnny and his sister going off to their first day of school. Johnny knows a lot about this stress system, too, and delights in playing with it. "The country of our four fathers" would break him up.

Next on the agenda is pitch. Like stress, pitch has four levels. We designate them with numbers—1, 2, 3, and 4—from lowest (1) to highest (4), for pitch represents voice "level," the "high-ness" or "low-ness" of the tone. Again, this is a matter of higher or lower pitch within an individual's voice range in a construction. The fact that a man's voice is pitched lower than a woman's is irrelevant, as is the fact that some women are sopranos and some altos. What counts is the way an individual's voice rises and falls within a given stretch of speech.

Consider again "She's my sister," made as a simple statement of fact. The voice begins at a pitch level we arbitrarily designate "2" and continues more or less at that level until it comes to the first syllable of "sister" where it rises abruptly. On the weak syllable of "sister" ("-er") it falls abruptly to the lowest level in the sentence. This pitch pattern, often called the "normal statement pattern," is frequently represented with a diagram:

$$^2\text{She is my}^3\ \big|\ \text{sist\r{e}r.}^1$$

But because of the sequence of pitches, the statement pattern in English is often called simply "the 2-3-1" pattern.

On the other hand, let's consider what happens if we make it a question.

$$^2\ \ \ \ \ \ \ ^3\underline{\ \ \ \ \ }/^3$$
$$\underline{\text{She is my}\ /\text{sister?}}$$

Here the voice begins on level 2 and continues again to "sis-" where it rises abruptly. But this time it does not fall but stays approximately at level 3, even continuing to rise as the voice ends. This is called the "2-3-3 intonation pattern" and is most often associated with questions, though not all kinds of questions employ this pattern.

We say that the voice begins at level 2 and holds that level until it arrives at "sis-." Actually, of course, it does *not* stay at exactly the same pitch, but we ignore the minor changes as sub-phonemic. What counts is when the voice jumps to level 3, as in:

$$^2\text{She is}^3\ \big|\ \text{my sister.}^1 \qquad \text{(i.e., not his, mine.)}$$

Because so very often the rise in pitch occurs on the word or syllable with the heaviest stress, many students get the mistaken idea that pitch and stress are tied together. This is not so. Any pitch can occur on any stress. We can easily say:

Y e s , s h e i s m y s i s t e r — and we can put the stress wherever we choose to in this series of descending tones.

As for pitch level four, it would most likely indicate a considerable degree of excitement, or emphasis:

2   4   1
She's my ⌐sister!   (You dope!)

The whole business of questions and their signaling, by intonation or otherwise, is very complex in English, as is the subtle shading of differences among them. For instance, we noted above that "She is my sister?" with a rising intonation indicates an element of surprise. Ordinarily the question would be "Is she my sister?" with the same 2-3-3 intonation but with subject and verb reversed. This is the simple question without any suggestion of the speaker's being surprised by someone's prior remark.

"Is she my sister?" is one of the most frequent kinds of questions. It is called a "yes/no" question because ordinarily the answer expected is a *yes* or a *no.* "Do you like it here?" "Have you been waiting long?" "Is your teacher hard?" These are all yes/no questions and would ordinarily have the 2-3-3 intonation pattern. Note the difference in meaning when such a "question" has the 2-3-1 pattern:

2   3   1
" Is his teacher ⌐hard !"

is an exclamation because of intonation pattern, not a question because of subject-verb reversal.

The other most frequently occurring kind of question, besides the yes/no question is the "information question," to which the expected answer is not a simple yes/no but some item of information. Examples: "What color is your dog?" "What's your sister's name?" "Who is that difficult teacher?" If the answer to any of these came back, "Yes," you would think the person you were talking to had misunderstood you, was acting smart, or had flipped. Note that the information question *ordinarily* has the 2-3-1 intonation of a statement.

2   3⌐1
How long have you lived in Chicago?

In fact, if you give it the 2-3-3 intonation the meaning of your question is quite different:

2   3   3
How long have you lived in Chicago?

would mean "Aw, come on, I don't believe you!" or "I didn't quite catch that. Would you repeat it?" Here's a little four-line playlet which makes perfectly good sense if you give the lines the proper intonation. You should be able to figure it out:

Mr. Smith:	I apologized to him.
Miss Jones:	What did you say?
Mr. Smith:	I apologized to him.
Miss Jones:	What did you say?

If you have trouble with this, try giving the first question a 2-3-3 intonation and the second a 2-3-1. Notice that the questions ask two very difference things. Could we have any clearer demonstration that pitch is indeed phonemic?

Now let's turn our attention to the third set of intonation phonemes, those dealing with juncture. Juncture is a bit harder to explain than either stress or pitch, but it is easy to exemplify. Briefly, juncture is the way two segmental phonemes are held apart, or in its absence fused together. In a word like /lemǝnéyd/, in which the sounds all fuse together one into another, we say there is "close" or "zero" juncture. This seems foolish, this going out of our way to note the *absence* of what we're going to call juncture, but we do want the ability to contrast a construction with juncture with one without it.

Omitting the *absence* of juncture from our consideration, we have four degrees of juncture. From the least to the greatest they are plus juncture, /+/, single bar juncture, /|/, double bar juncture, /||/, and double cross or double plus juncture, /#/. We need to illustrate each of these.

Consider this pair:

1. That's tough
2. That stuff

As for segmental phonemes, these are identical: /ðætstǝf/. Yet there certainly is a difference. You could say one or the other of these time after time, mixing them up in all sorts of random sequences, and a friend of yours could spot which one you had said every time. The difference between them, what it is your friend is hearing, is plus juncture: /+/. We would write them phonemically:

1. /ðæts + tǝf/
2. /ðæt + stǝf/

In *phonetic* terms we can note some significant differences in the two utterances. For instance, in the first version the "t" of "tough" is aspirated, [t'], whereas in the second it has got itself incorporated into "stuff," where it follows /s/, and is not aspirated, [t]. We could also comment on the way the [t] of /ðæt/ is released or fails to be released. But in phonemic terms we don't need to give that sort of description: we just note where the separation occurs and we call it plus juncture: /+/. This particular juncture occurs constantly in our speech, but of course it isn't always crucial in distinguishing minimal pairs. Here are a few pairs, though, that I've gathered to help illustrate the point:

> It was a great rain. /greyt+reyn/
> It was a grey train. /grey+treyn/
>
> I wonder where Elsie's been. (In "Elsie's" there is "close" juncture.)
> I wonder where else he's been. /éls+iyz+bı̂n/
>
> They're all so nice. /ɔhl+sow/
> They're also nice. (Close or zero juncture.)
>
> He was a nice man.
> He was an ice man.
>
> He wanted the night rate.
> He wanted the nitrate.
>
> You make all the arrangements.
> You may call the arrangements.
>
> I'd rank it up. (i.e., give it a higher grade)
> I drank it up.

Note that sometimes the contrast is between /+/ and the absence of /+/, whereas at other times the contrast depends on the placement of /+/. Perhaps before leaving plus juncture for the time being it would be well to point out that it is not reflected, in writing, in our system of punctuation.

Single bar juncture, /|/, is a little more pronounced. In fact it's noticeable enough that sometimes we do actually indicate it with a comma—and often we "make a mistake" when we do. Students who have been told, or who have perhaps discovered on their own, that they should put a comma where they "hear a pause" often punctuate where they really shouldn't, because after all they do hear a pause. What they hear is this single bar juncture.

It is characterized by a slight slowing of tempo just before the juncture occurs, with perhaps an accompanying drawing out of the last phonemes before the juncture, and a resumption of tempo after the juncture has been bridged. Like the /+/ this is perhaps more easily illustrated than described. Consider this sentence:

It left the students involved in a state of confusion.

As with so many, many sentences, what this one means depends on "how you read it," or more specifically in this case where you put the single bar juncture. We can read it like this:

It left the students | involved in a state of confusion.

This means clearly that the students we're talking about, all of them, were left in a confused sort of condition. Now let's read it with the single bar at a different point:

It left the students involved | in a state of confusion.

Now we're not talking about all the students, but just the ones who were involved. We don't know what they were involved in, but the ones who were involved in whatever it was are now confused. There were other students who were not involved and they are not mixed-up at all. Try reading it each way, and notice how just before you come to the crucial point, the juncture, your tempo slows and you l-e-n-g-t-h-e-n out the sounds, and then the juncture once over you zip right along again.

In the example we just considered, the contrast depended upon the location of the single bar, but as with the /+/ the contrast is sometimes between the presence and the absence of the juncture. Here is a pair to illustrate that:

I saw a mán | eâting shárk.
I saw a mân-eàting shárk.

Here are some more examples for you to practice on:

It might clear up | a little later.
It might clear up a little | later.

He's outstanding in the rain.
He's out | standing in the rain.

I drank two | much too fast.
I drank too much | too fast.

I heard you both loud and clear.
I heard you both | loud and clear.

She was brought up here.
She was brought | up here.

It may be her singing.
It may be her | singing.

They are both | small and comfortable.
They are both small | and comfortable.

These are clothes I wore | out on the beach.
These are clothes I wore out | on the beach.

Unlike single bar juncture, double bar is most often reflected in writing with a comma, though with modern loose punctuation practices it's difficult to make such an assertion and make it stick. The double bar is characterized by a falling of the voice followed by a slight rise. I think I can get you to hear it if you will count, slowly, to seven: One, two, three, four, five, six, seven. We can represent what's happening to the voice diagrammatically:

one two three four five six seven.

I suggested you do it slowly only so that you could hear it better. Actually, the same phenomenon occurs no matter how fast you count.

Of course if we used the double bar only in counting it would be of limited interest, but it occurs all the time in our speech. Listen carefully to this one: "Maltilda, my old maid cousin, is coming to dinner." Thus what we were taught to call an appositive and to set off in commas is more basically set off in speech with double bar junctures. If commas give you a lot of trouble, as they do many of us, you might try training yourself to hear the double bar juncture, and when you hear it, put a comma. It's not foolproof—what is?—but it's not the worst approach to the problem either.

Notice that above, when we were counting from one to seven, the double bar juncture had the effect of advising the listener that there was more coming. It seems to say: "Message to be continued."

However, when you arrived at the end and said "seven," the voice fell off completely and signalled the end of the string. That is the double cross juncture /#/. Thus if I say: /wən ‖ tuw ‖ θ riy ‖ fɔhr ‖ / you keep waiting for the list to continue, but as soon as I say /fayv#/ you understand that that's the end.

This /#/ is often called something like "the sentence final (or phrase final) intonation contour pattern," which simply means that it is a pattern, an intonation pattern, we use to end sentences, or phrases. We must note, though, that there is more than one intonation contour that makes up /#/—we can say it has allophones. Thus the sentence "She is my sister" ends with /#/, but the yes/no question "Is she my sister?" ends with /#/ also.

We have now at least looked at and considered the twelve suprasegmental phonemes: four of pitch, four of stress, and four of juncture. This gives us a total of forty-five phonemes in English. (Let me caution you again that this is only one analysis. Some other person might well insist that there are fewer, or more. The *language* is a reality; analyses are imposed upon it.) Our phonemes, as we have looked at them, are:

24 consonants
9 vowels   } 33 segmentals

4 stress
4 pitch   } 12 suprasegmentals
4 juncture

Which, let us say, pretty well lays out the sound system of English.

CHAPTER 4

ANOTHER -EME AND
SOME MORE ALLO-'S

It is possible to consider language on many different levels. For instance, in my school days, "grammar" consisted very largely of examining sentences and determining their parts and how they fit together. On another level we have just been examining the individual speech sounds of language and how they bundle together into phonemes. It would be possible, and indeed it has been done, to take sub-sentence elements like noun phrases and study and describe their typical constructions in English. But there is a level of complexity a step or two down from phrase construction, but a step above the phoneme. The level I have in mind is that of the *morpheme* and the study of it is called *morphology* or *morphemics.* Heaven help us, you say, more technical jargon! I concede, but it won't amount to very much and the terms we are going to use are very widely used (so that you should understand them in any event). And the terms *are* necessary; we still need labels to discuss things conveniently.

For one thing, we aren't going to probe very deeply into *morphology,* just enough so that you will understand the nature of the beast; something of the function it has in language, and specifically the English language. I think you'll find it an interesting concept. Certainly the role of the morpheme is a vital one. One linguist, in a happy phrase, entitled his study of morphemes "The Building Blocks of Language," and that's a pretty fair description of the part they play.

Oddly enough, for such an important concept, linguists are by no means in agreement as to what a morpheme is or how to identify one. It was specifically morphemes that were in the mind of the distinguished traditional grammarian I referred to earlier when he bitingly observed that linguists cannot even agree on some of their most basic terms. He is right, too. I once spent an idle summer afternoon looking up and copying down the definitions of "morpheme" in various linguistics books. I quit when I had copied out about fifteen—all different. Yet the differences were in detail, and especially of how morphemes are to be identified. All the authors of the books I looked into would agree, I am sure, to the "building blocks" concept. For language *is* built out of morphemes, and that is the aspect of them with which we are going to concern ourselves.

A large part of the difficulty with the morpheme, and especially with its identification, springs from the fact that the morpheme has *meaning,* and meaning is a very slippery thing in language analysis. One of the great American linguists, Charles Fries, pointed this out vividly, strikingly and memorably in his denunciation of the traditionalists's approach to the analysis of a sentence. The traditionalist will show how the parts of the sentence relate to each other according to how they fit into the total meaning, but he never says *how he knows* what the sentence means. And this is the basic question, at least if we are doing more than playing language games. How does language work? How do humans manage to make a string of sounds convey meaning? In other words, Fries' point was that if you start your analysis by basing it on meaning, you're cheating. Therefore many linguists, whom I think of as purists, try not to employ meaning at all as a tool of language analysis. They are as much aware as you and I that the purpose of language is to carry meaning. But they don't want to use meaning in trying to discover how meaning is conveyed. It's not quite cricket, that is, to use the answer as one of the devices in solving the problem.

One way of attempting an analysis without recourse to meaning *per se,* is through the use of "native informants." Remember our experience with Snangti in Chapter 1? The speakers of Snangti would be our informants. We do not pick out one and ask him what a sentence means, if only because he doesn't speak English and so couldn't tell us anyhow. No, we scratch around until we get a toehold in the language and then we begin asking questions, largely questions of comparison. Is this the same as that? How does this differ from that? (You'd better believe this is a grotesquely simplified sketch of a highly complicated operation.) With English, the approach is the same, but one significant, and convenient, compromise is reached. One always has a good, interested and trained native-speaking informant at hand: himself. Of course the researcher is not limited to himself as informant, but there would seem to be no reason why he should not ask himself some of the questions which he would have to ask someone else if he was researching Snangti.

Part of the difficulty in identifying the morpheme, then, springs from the basic approach of the analyzer. Does he candidly recognize that the morpheme has meaning and use his knowledge of that meaning to spot morphemes? Or does he take the more rigorous course, and the perhaps more scientifically honorable course, and try to identify them without availing himself of meaning? It makes a difference.

Some language students, particularly those inclined to the traditional anyhow, are prone to view the existence of an unresolved problem like this as invalidating linguistics entirely. The logic of this attitude is a bit difficult to appreciate. Must everything be settled, cut and dried, before a discipline can be of any value? Must the physicist and the biologist, for example, suspend work until they can agree on the nature of light or of life? Must the physician suspend practice until he knows all the answers about cancer? To ask these questions is to demonstrate their asininity. So the student satisfying his curiosity about linguistics will quickly find that not all the work is done, not all questions answered. He can, in fact, view himself as a participant in the search for better solutions to language problems. He is no longer merely bolting down gospel supplied by some unknown divinity but questioning, probing, offering tentative answers himself. It is one of the refreshing aspects of modern language study.

What *is* a morpheme? Well, here's a definition that might make a linguist break down and cry, but which will do for our purposes: A morpheme is the smallest *meaningful* element of a language. It is important that you notice how this differs from the definition of the phoneme as the smallest *significant* element of language. Phonemes signal differences in meaning but they don't have meaning themselves. It does make a lot of difference whether you say "I admired her /niys/" or "I admired her /niyz/," but the /s/ and the /z/ mean nothing in themselves. You can't just go around saying /s/, /s/, /s/, /s/ and expect to communicate much of anything to anybody.

The morpheme, though, does have meaning inherent in itself and just as the phoneme is made of allophones which in turn are made of literally billions of phones, so the morpheme has its "allomorphs" which are comprised of countless numbers of "morphs." The arrangement is exactly parallel, so if you really got the concept of the phoneme, the way the morpheme is developed won't bother you at all.

Without further introduction, let's meet a few morphemes.

Suppose we are interrogating an informant, a native speaker of English, and we ask him, "Is /buk/ the same as /buks/?" He tells us that it isn't. So we ask him, please, to tell us the difference, if he can. And he says, " 'Book' refers to one book, whereas 'books' always refers to more than one." Then we ask him about *rock* and *rocks,* and we get the same answer. (Except where phonemic transcription is needed here we'll stick to standard spelling on the theory that you can read it easier.) So we keep on asking this same kind of question. We ask about *hat—hats, cop—cops, tariff—tariffs, Baby Ruth—Baby Ruths, cigarette—cigarettes, clock—clocks,* and always we get the same answer, the difference is between one and more than one. "Aha!" we say, "We have discovered the principle of making plurals in English. You just add /s/."

So we decide that we will call /s/ a morpheme because it has meaning. It means "more than one." And to distinguish it in writing from the phoneme, /s/, we will write it between braces, like these: { }.

Alas for our lack of sophistication! Pretty soon, eavesdropping on a conversation between a couple of English speakers, we hear one of them refer to one /biyn/ and then to two /biynz/. And another soon refers to one /ruwm/ and to two /ruwmz/. So again we start asking questions and we discover plurals like "buds," "boobs," "oars," "bulls," "bows," "bees," "pies," and so on. So we back off from our original conclusion and revise our statement: "To form the plural in English you add either /s/ or /z/."

But once again we have gone too fast. Sooner or later we are going to stumble across /kawč/—/káwčɨz/, /kis/—/kisɨz/ and others: *judge—judges, wish—wishes, rose—roses* /rówz—rówzɨz/. Now, at last, we figure we've got it. The plural in English is formed by adding /s/, /z/, or /ɨz/. One of those three. Now all we've got to do is find out when you use which and we can make a full description of the plural in this language.

After a great deal of listening we might come up with a set of "rules" like this:

The English Plural

1. Add /s/ to all words ending in unvoiced consonants except /s,š,č/.
2. Add /ɨz/ after /s,z,š,ž,č,ǰ/.
3. Add /z/ everywhere else.

And we would be almost right—something like 99+ percent. In a minute we'll take a look at the few times we wouldn't be right. (Incidentally, "rules" is in quotes above because these are not some kind of regulations you have to follow but rather simply a description of the way the speaker of English forms plurals. This is all language "rules" ever really are anyhow.)

Notice the results this painstaking questioning of informants has produced. (I know all this was imaginary, but it would have been painstaking if it had been for real, wouldn't it?) The thing you do *not* do is ask the informant to solve your problem for you, because most speakers are really rather naive about their language. For example, suppose you ask the average English speaker how the English plural is formed. "Say, Joe, how do you form the plural on English words?" If Joe went to the same school I did, (or, I'll bet, to the same school you did), he'll answer, "Oh, you just add 's' or "es.' " This is worse than an over-simplification. It's misleading. It's wrong.

Now we need a name and a symbol for this thing we've discovered, this little set of sounds that pluralizes nouns when added to them. Since it certainly has meaning—it means "plural"—and since it can't be divided into smaller meaningful units, it's a morpheme. Let's call it "the plural morpheme." Now we need a symbol, some way of writing it quickly, easily and recognizably. We've already noted that we'll put the symbol between braces, { }, to distinguish it from standard spelling ("p"), from phonetic symbols ([p']) and from phonemes (/p/). What symbol we use doesn't really matter, so long as we understand the same thing by it. And as a matter of fact you'll find in various books different symbols for this. I remember one uses {P}, apparently to indicate "plural," and another uses {-es}, perhaps suggested by the ordinary spelling of the plural. The most common symbol, though, seems to be {Z}, and that's the one we'll use.

What does {Z} mean? It means "plural." What do we call it? We call it the "plural morpheme." How do we pronounce it? We don't. Ever. How could we? We've just seen it has three quite different sounds. How do you know which sound to select? If you speak English you just *know*, automatically. Here are three nonsense words for you to demonstrate this with:

1. If we have one *praak,* we would have two _____.
2. If we have one *rheen,* we would have two _____.
3. If we have one *bletch,* we would have two _____ .

(You might look back at the "rules" which "govern" the distribution of these plural sounds and see if you got them right—that is, if there could possibly be any smidgin of doubt in your mind.)

How many times a day do you suppose /s/ is used to form a plural in your home state? Not to mention the United States, or the entire English-speaking world. Let's not guess; it's too much like working with light years, or the national debt. Anyhow, every single individual occurrence of that /s/ *used with that meaning* is a "morph." Now, we are going to need some way of referring to all those occurrences of /s/ as a totality.

We are going to call it the /s/ allomorph of the plural morpheme {Z}. Now what do you think we'll call all the occurrences of /z/ *as they mean plural*? And how about all the occurrences of /ɨz/? Of course. Allomorphs of {Z}.

The parallel with the phoneme is quite exact, then. Just as phones *make up* allophones which *make up* phonemes, so do we have morphs which *make up* allomorphs which in turn comprise morphemes.

Before pursuing further this matter of the plural in English, to attempt to plug up a few little chinks which you might have noticed, we need to stop a moment to notice that there are two huge classes of morphemes: "free" and "bound." After considering them we'll come back to the problem of {Z}.

As the names "bound" and "free" would seem to imply, bound morphemes can occur only when they are fastened onto something else. We use a hyphen to indicate in which direction it fastens them on, thus {-Z}. Free morphemes can occur in isolation. It is usually, though not always, a free morpheme to which a bound morpheme is attached. Thus in the word "dogs" we have *two* morphemes: one is the free morpheme {dog} and the other is our new-found friend {-Z}. You might wonder whether the idea of morphs and allomorphs is extended to free morphemes, and the answer is that it is. Every time "dog" is uttered (with the same meaning) it is a morph contributing to the structure of the morpheme {dog}. It may well turn out that the morpheme {dog} has only one allomorph, just as the phoneme /s/ has only one allophone. There's nothing wrong with that. But there will be times when free morphemes will have more than one allomorph, and when we need the concept it's useful to have it around.

Let's consider what happens when we have, as we say, one "word" with different meanings. Take "rat" /ræt/. This can mean the repulsive rodent. It can also be a verb: "Don't trust Joe. He'll rat on you every time." It is also at times a device women wear in their hair, described by Webster's as: "A pad with tapering ends over which a woman's hair is arranged for an illusion of greater quantity." Thus we have the same sounds, /ræt/, but with quite different meanings. We are dealing with three *different* free morphemes. In order for allomorphs, or morphs, to belong to the same morpheme *they must mean the same*. The allomorphs of a morpheme needn't sound alike (example, /-s/, /-ɨz/ and /-z/) but they do have to share the same meaning (as /-s/, /-ɨz/ and /-z/ all indicate plurality in the examples above.)

This is an important point, which we need to pursue a bit further. We won't listen to our native-speaking informants long before we hear some such thing as "the horse's mouth." "Horse's?" Yes, "Horse's." But we had that /-ɨz/ set aside for an allomorph of our plural, and as we inquire we learn that in "the horse's mouth" there is no idea of more than one horse. The /-ɨz/ seems to be fulfilling quite another function. Further, as we continue our observations we're surely going to run across things like "the dog's bark" and "the cat's meow," and we find that all the sounds we were considering allomorphs of {-Z} are living double lives. On top of that, we find they are distributed just exactly as they were in our set of "rules" for forming the English plural.

So what do we do? Easy. We adjust the symbols to accommodate both these sets of sounds, and what we were calling the plural morpheme is now {-Z$_1$}. This new morpheme, the possessive morpheme we might as well call it, will be {-Z$_2$}. Clear enough? Then here's a little problem: "The /kæts/ fur was grey." "There were three /kæts/." In each case /kæt/ has an /s/ added to it. What is the relationship of the first /s/ to the second? Perhaps the most obvious answer is the one you'll give: there's really no relationship. But you might want to go on to explain. The first /-s/ is an allomorph of {-Z$_2$} and the second is an allomorph of {-Z$_1$}. They cannot be allomorphs of the same morpheme because they differ in meaning.

So we have established the principle that the allomorphs of a morpheme will have the same meaning, though they may and often do differ in sound. And we have also established that we have two kinds of morphemes, bound and free. Let's go back now to that unfinished business with the formation of the English plural, {-Z$_1$}.

We observed that /-s/, /-z/, and /-ɨz/ will make up something like 99+% of the plurals in English. (Incidentally, we can write them more economically as /-s ~ -z ~ -ɨz/ which means they alternate with each other.) You probably find exceptions springing to your lips. How about that remnant, for instance, of Old English that we noted in Chapter 1: "oxen" /áksɨn/? We observe that /aks/ adds /ɨn/ to form its plural. This means simply that {-Z$_1$} has another allomorph, one that happens to be hauled out and used very rarely: /-ɨn/.

But, you ask, what about words like "deer"? If our rule is going to stand up, we are going to have to add $\{-Z_1\}$ to "deer" singular in order to arrive at "deer" plural. The limitless ingenuity of the linguist has solved this crisis by inventing ("positing" might be a better word) a *zero* allomorph, which is written $\emptyset$. Thus to "deer" singular we add zero, $\emptyset$, and get "deer." (Note how the little child, is likely to tell us he saw "three deers." He's smart, he is. He's learned where to put the /-z/ allomorph and sees no reason to make an exception for three crummy deer and the rest of us would be smart to let a little child lead us and do away with some of these nonsensical irregularities.)

At this point perhaps you are thinking that this is a pretty silly process, this inventing of such a fiction as the zero allomorph in order to explain plurals like "deer," "sheep," and "fish" (sometimes). Not so. We want a rule which will describe how the plural is formed, and we have one that describes the overwhelming majority of plurals. You'll probably concede that in most matters, especially where people are concerned, a rule with 99 percent applicability is a pretty useful rule. So we want to keep the rule if we can and s-t-r-e-t-c-h it a bit where necessary to make it apply all the time, if possible. If it should turn out that we can't, we can list the handful of exceptions *as* exceptions and treat them specially. In the meantime, we want to keep the list of exceptions as small as possible, and let the rule have as great an applicability as we can.

We need to note another phenomenon before we get on to looking at some other plurals you're no doubt burning to ask about (like *man-men, foot-feet*). We need to note that some free morphemes ($\{$house$\}$ and $\{$knife$\}$ are good examples) have allomorphs which are used *only* when a bound morpheme is to be attached to them. Consider: we talk about one /nayf/ and the way the distribution of the allomorphs of $\{-Z_1\}$ goes (see our "rules" above) we would expect to talk about two /nayfs/. But we don't. We talk instead about two /nayvz/. The way we're going to make this fit our set of rules is to say that $\{$knife$\}$ has two allomorphs, /nayf/ which we use ordinarily, and /nayv-/ which we use only when we want to add $\{-Z_1\}$. Now then if we look at our distribution rules we find that when the free morpheme ends in /v/ we add the /-z/ allomorph, which gives us /nayvz/.

Something like this happens with $\{$house$\}$ /haws/. We would expect the plural to be /háwsɨz/, but it isn't. It's /háwzɨz/. So we stipulate that house has two allomorphs, /haws/ which we use ordinarily and /hawz-/ which we use only when we're going to add a bound morpheme, such as $\{-Z_1 .\}$

Now we're ready to go with *foot-feet*. It turns out that {foot} has two allomorphs: /fut ~ fiyt/, both singular, and we use the second of them only when we wish to add an allomorph of {-Z_1}. Now, which allomorph of {-Z_1} will we select? Correct. We choose ∅ . Thus /fiyt/ + ∅ equals /fiyt/.

You should now be able to explain without help how we go from the singular "man" to the plural "men." (A hint if you need it: it exactly parallels "foot-feet.")

We use the same gimmick to derive "children" from "child." We say that child has two allomorphs: /čayld~čildr-/, and that we use the second only when we want to add an allomorph of {-Z_1}, in this instance /-ɨn/. And so with "brother-brethren."

The allomorphs of {-Z_1} now look like this: /-s ~ -z ~ - z ~ɨn ~ -∅ /. Certainly not too formidable a list, considering all that we can do with it. As a sort of review let's see how some of these work.

{cat}	+	{-Z_1}	=	/kæts/ (/-s/ allomorph selected)
{dog}	+	{-Z_1}	=	/dɔgz/ (/-z/ allomorph)
{kiss}	+	{-Z_1}	=	/kisɨz/ (/ ɨz/ allomorph)
{sheep}	+	{-Z_1}	=	/šiyp/ (∅ allomorph)
{knife} /nayf/ /nayv-/	+	{-Z_1}	=	/nayvz/ (/nayv-/ allomorph of knife and /-z/ allomorph of {-Z_1} selected.
{man} /mæn/ /men/	+	{-Z_1}	=	/men/ (/men/ allomorph man selected and then ∅ allomorph of { -Z_1} added.[1]

The rule that we add {-Z_1} to form the plural is, with a few adjustments and modifications, applicable to nearly all English words. There is still a small group of words which we have borrowed from other languages and which still retain their native plurals. (I don't know why we always refer to "borrowing" these words, and even call them "loan words," when we never seem to give any of them back. What we really do is appropriate them.) These are words,

---

1. Some speakers would use /min/ instead of /men/.

of course, like *alumnus-alumni, alumna-alumnae, appendix-appendices, cherub-cherubim,* etc.

Probably the only practical thing to do with these words in any comprehensive discussion of the plural in English is simply to list them as exceptions. Since they are not originally English, even though naturalized, they don't conform to English patterns. We perhaps should note, though, that the ones that get used a lot often get themselves wrenched into the English pattern. Thus with "cherub" above, you might much more likely pluralize it with the /-z/ allomorph. In fact, did you even know the "cherubim" plural? The plural of "cactus" is still "cacti" to Easterners, but Southwesterners, for whom it is a common bit of the environment instead of something exotic, are more likely to say "cactuses." And when is the last time you heard "stadia" as the plural of "stadium"? As loan words become very widely used they are quite likely to become forced into the English pattern. Except among the very elegant. *The New Yorker* once printed a little squib about a Harvard freshman who wrote home to his mother expressing his delight in the apartment he had found, which even had Bendix washing machines in the basement. Or, as he put it, "Bendices."

It is probably well to stop here and remind you of something we observed earlier: all of this we've been doing, with allophones and phonemes and allomorphs and morphemes is, in a sense, unreal. It is an attempt to *create a description* of the system of English, and is not to be confused with the system itself. The language is a reality. The description is an invention. It might do a very good job of describing or a very poor one, but either way it won't affect the language itself. Whether it is a good or a bad description must be judged. Who's to do it? Well, for a starter, why not you? Actually, you can't help it, and you've doubtless been doing it right along. Is there any reason why you shouldn't? No. We're not in the business of dispensing gospel here. For example, reflect on the way we've just described the formation of the noun plural in English. As theory, how does it square with the facts of the language as you know them? Is it a neat, systematic, clear hypothesis? How complete is it? Perhaps more important, do you see any easier way of doing it that will fit the facts of the language? Improvements are always welcome. In this very real and very important sense, perhaps we'll never be done writing a grammar of English, for there is always someone who sees a better way of doing something.

So far, other than free morphemes, all we've discussed is $\{-Z_1\}$. There are, of course, many, many, other bound morphemes, and we

are not going to discuss them all, nor even try to list them. All you
need have, really, is an awareness of the morpheme as a concept, and
an idea of the role it plays in the analysis of English. We do need to
glance at some groupings of morphemes, and then as a kind of review
we'll look at one you haven't yet met: {-D$_1$}.

Generally, bound morphemes are "affixes," which means naturally that they are "affixed" either to free morphemes or to combinations of them and bound morphemes. Affixes are known as "prefixes" if they fit on the front end of the free morpheme (often called
the *root* or the *base*) and "suffixes" if they are attached to the back
end. For example: let's take "ready" as the free morpheme. We can
add as a prefix the bound morpheme {un-} to give us "unready." Or
we can add the suffix {-ness} to give us "readiness." Or we can add
them both: "unreadiness." To this we can still add {-Z$_1$}, if it doesn't
offend your sense of proper English, and get "unreadinesses." "His
unreadinesses were a pain in the neck." It isn't very elegant, but it
seems "English" enough, don't you think?

(Many languages, but not English, have affixes occurring in the
middle of roots, where they are called "infixes." An example would
be Spanish *Carlos,* Charles, which can become *Carlitos,* Charley.)

One problem which irritates linguists occurs when two bound
morphemes apparently hook up to each other. Such a thing seems to
happen with these for instance:

$$\{\text{con-}\}\ \{\text{-ceive}\}$$
$$\{\text{de-}\}\ \{\text{-fer}\}$$

Note that we can have "confer" as well as "conceive," "deceive" as
well as "defer." The irritating thing is that we have defined the
morpheme as the smallest element of language with meaning, and it
is extremely difficult to pin a meaning on such a thing as {-ceive}.
Well, that's a problem we don't have to work out. I bring it up only
to show you that there are unresolved problems—and believe me
there are many of them.

Suffixes fall into two broad classes: "derivational" suffixes and
"inflectional" suffixes. (All *prefixes* in English are derivational.) How
useful this distinction will be to you I can't say, but it might be an
interesting thing to know. {-Z$_1$} is an example of an inflectional
suffix (so is {-Z$_2$}), and the {-ness} we used a moment ago is a derivational suffix. There are these differences between the two kinds:

1. Generally speaking, when a derivational suffix has been
    added to a word it is still possible to add other suffixes, but

when an inflectional suffix has been added it is nearly always the end of the road. Consider the famous "antidisestablishmentarianism," which we've all been told is "the longest word in English." As you can see, it's made up of a root and a lot of affixes. Ignoring the prefixes, which don't matter at the moment, let's consider "establish" as the root. We add {-ment}, {-arian}, and {-ism}, and we can still add {-Z_1} if we wish and make the whole thing plural. But suppose to "establish" we add (in spelling) "es." We can't add anything to "establishes"—not {-ment} nor {-arian} nor {-ism} nor anything. (Incidentally, remember the distribution of the allomorphs of {-Z_1} and {-Z_2}? Well, you might like to know that the inflection on the third person singular of the verb has exactly the same distribution and we refer to it as {-Z_3}.) If to "establish" we add {-Z_3} we get "establishes" and that's all we can get—we can't add any more suffixes.

2. Very often, but by no means always, a derivational suffix changes the "part of speech" of the root to which it is added. Thus *agree-agreement, defer-deferment, establish-establishment, argue-argument,* and so on. Verbs into nouns, nouns into adjectives, adjectives into adverbs, etc. The inflectional suffix does not do this. If you add {-Z_1} to a noun it's still a noun.

3. Another difference between these two kinds of suffixes is what the linguist calls their "distribution." He would say that inflectional suffixes have a very "wide distribution," which means that they are incessantly popping up, whereas derivational suffixes have a "limited distribution," which is to say that they occur *comparatively* seldom. Consider a moment: to how many adjectives can you add {ness} to convert them into nouns? Like *ugly-ugliness, happy-happiness, sweet-sweetness.* Fifty? A hundred? Five hundred? Maybe a thousand? But compare: to how many nouns can we add {-Z_1} to form a plural? Practically the whole durn dictionary full, that's how many. And how many verbs will accept {-Z_3}? Nearly all of them, of course. So it *is* correct to observe that the inflectional suffixes have much wider distribution than the derivational ones.

Incidentally, some of these derivational suffixes are more "live" than others, which is to say that like other things they ebb and flow in popularity. Right now {-ize} is quite popular, to the dismay of those who would guard our language against corruption. It makes verbs out of nouns and adjectives, like *organize, synthesize, idolize.* The bane of the purists is "finalize." Currently, {-ness} is also a very live suffix. It crops up in the oddest places. My students would never think of writing of "sorrow." It's always "sadness." A word like "sociability" is a dead duck, being replaced by "sociableness." Not long ago I read a student paper which referred to a young girl's "beautifulness." But it isn't only students who like {-ness}. In a recent smash hit book on psychology the word "candidness" appears three times in as many pages. Whatever happened to "candor"? Is there in language an equivalent to the economist's point of diminishing returns? Sometimes I hope so with ferventness. Otherwise I'll never finalize my ableness to have an understandability of my own language. (And I don't think I have much conservativeness!)

Let's look in detail at one more morpheme—{-D₁}. It's the bound morpheme, an inflectional suffix, with which we signal that something has already happened—in other words, past tense. Let's observe something of how past tense is formed on English verbs.

We have a large group of verbs like *belch-belched, cough-coughed, kiss-kissed,* and *scoff-scoffed.* To all these verbs, and to others in this category, we form the past tense by adding /t/. But we're too sophisticated now to assume that we can call /-t/ the past tense morpheme. We assume it's an allomorph only, and we look around a bit more.

And sure enough, we come across verbs like: *bug-bugged, fizz-fizzed, adorn-adorned,* and *bomb-bombed.* So we note down that the past tense morpheme also has an allomorph /-d/.

As we look further we quickly find verbs like hate-hated and skid-skidded, so we discover a third allomorph /-ɨd/. As we continue our examination of our body of material, which is a sample, however large or small it may be, of spoken English, we learn that the allomorphs we've listed, /-t~-d~-ɨd/, describe correctly the process of adding {-D₁} to the overwhelming preponderance of English verbs. Again the applicability might be something like 99+%, so we think we've got a pretty good rule. As for the distribution of these allomorphs, it's easily described:

/-t/ after /p k č f θ s š/, voiceless consonants except /t/

/-ɨd/ after both apico-alveolar stops, /t d/

/-d/ everywhere else

However, as with {-Z₁}, we find we have a number of irregularities to account for. The past of /riyč/ is /riyčt/, as the above distribution schedule would lead us to believe, but the past of /tiyč/ is /tɔht/.

What are we going to do about this kind of thing? Well, if you were wide awake as we accounted for the irregular noun plurals you know full well how we're going to iron out the wrinkles in $\{-D_1\}$. We will use the razzle-dazzle of the zero allomorph ($\emptyset$) again, and we will theorize that many of the free morphemes which are verbs have allomorphs which are called into play only when we are going to add $\{-D_1\}$. And the justification for this outrageous procedure is the same as it was before: out of all the zillions of verbs in English, only a relative handful are "irregular" and need to be given special handling. With a rule as widely applicable as ours for the past tense morpheme it is worth a little extra work not to have to junk it.

There is, incidentally, a $\{-D_2\}$. It is the bound morpheme which signals the past participle, and with all our regular verbs, and quite a few of the irregulars, it is the same as $\{-D_1\}$. However, there are exceptions: "I ate," but "I have eaten," "I threw," but "I have thrown," etc. So we have to have $\{-D_2\}$.

You might be interested in noting, as a sort of aside, that very often our irregularly-inflected words in English become regular when they acquire new and different meanings. Thus of a very awkward couple on the dance floor you would not say "Look at those clumsy oxen," but "Look at those clumsy oxes." Consider the verb "fly," past tense "flew." It's not "flew" in baseball. You wouldn't say "Mickey Mantle flew out to center field," or if you did you'd plant a strange picture in your listener's mind. "Mickey Mantle flied out to center field." It's as though we were tired of the bother of these irregularities and when a word gets a new meaning we want to give it a fresh start.

Write off that bit of information as a digression. Let's get back to business. How many morphemes in this sentence?

The farmer killed the ugly ducklings.

Obviously we start with the first "the." It's not divisible into smaller meaningful parts and, though its meaning is perhaps a bit difficult to state (see next chapter), it certainly does have meaning. Therefore, it's a morpheme.

"Farmer" is made up of two morphemes, the free morpheme $\{farm\}$ and the bound morpheme $\{-er\}$, which indicates one who does something. Compare *dance-dancer, swim-swimmer, kill-killer, sing-singer.*

"Killed" is the free morpheme $\{kill\}$ plus our new acquaintance $\{-D_1\}$.

The second "the" is a free morpheme as the first one was.

"Ugly" has to be considered a free morpheme. You might object that we certainly have a bound morpheme -ly , as in *sweet-sweetly, slow-slowly, beautiful-beautifully.* However, the /lɨ/ syllable of "ugly" doesn't seem to be the same morpheme, nor in fact a morpheme at all. The "-ly" on "sweetly" *et al* is a derivational suffix with a grammatical "meaning" of something like "adverb signal," but the /lɨ/ of "ugly" doesn't have this meaning at all. Further, we have stipulated that the morpheme is not divisible into smaller meaningful parts. That's "parts," plural. Thus we note that while "hat" /hæt/ has within it the sound /æt/, which is certainly a free morpheme under other circumstances, if we take /æt/ out of /hæt/ that leaves an isolated /h/, which certainly has no meaning—and we conclude that "hat" is not divisible into smaller meaningful elements. So with "ugly." If we subtract /lɨ/ we are stuck with /əg/, which while it can have meaning in certain circumstances (Ugh!) certainly doesn't have that meaning here. There is no adjective /əg/ which we are converting into an adverb with the addition of /lɨ/. All that happens, then, with the second syllable of "ugly" is that it is made up of the same sounds that coincidentally, under other circumstances, make up a bound morpheme. But we are not dealing with that morpheme here and we conclude that "ugly" is not divisible into smaller meaningful parts.

This leaves for our consideration the last word, "ducklings." We note that it is plural (We can certainly have one duckling as opposed to what we have here), so we observe that it ends with {-Z₁}. Then we scrutinize the "ling" element, and also the "duck" syllable. We know that {duck} occurs frequently as a free morpheme, and we want to consider it a morpheme now. When we find that {"ling"} occurs elsewhere with the meaning of "diminutive" (as gosling, princeling), we observe that that meaning fits here (we can go ask a native speaker if we wish, to keep our scientific procedures pure), and we conclude that {-ling} is a bound morpheme, a derivational suffix.

So we see that our six word sentence is made up of ten morphemes, and we also see something of the way morphemes, both free and bound, function together to make up the fabric of our language.

Interestingly enough, morphemes don't always combine to form "words" but sometimes combine directly into phrases, which when divided into their logical parts do not divide at word boundaries. Here is an example: In the sentence "He was a criminal lawyer," the phrase "criminal lawyer" ordinarily would mean "a man who practices criminal law." It would not usually be interpreted as a lawyer who is criminal. What we have is an allomorph /-yər/ of the mor-

pheme {-er} (as in *farmer, singer, dancer*) attaching not to the word
"law" but to the phrase "criminal law." Thus logically the phrase
would have to be divided into parts: criminal-law / yer. Similarly, in
the phrase "a fire fighter," the bound morpheme {-er} clearly applies
to the whole phrase, meaning one who fights fires—"fire-fight / er."

It is easy to produce many, many examples of this kind of thing.
Here is one involving {-ist}, a morpheme quite similar in meaning to
{-er} (as in *jurist, pianist,* etc.): "He's an artifical florist." Clearly this
doesn't refer to a florist who is somehow artifical but to a man who
works with artificial flowers. Cutting the phrase into its logical parts
would produce: artificial-flor / ist. A "total stranger" is not a
stranger who is total but a person who is totally strange. Just so "an
American Indian linguist" is probably not a linguist who is an American Indian but rather one who studies American Indian languages.
Having seen the principle involved here, you could go on and make
up scads of examples of your own.

Here are a couple of superficially-similar sentences with a real
difference in patterning caused by the way {-Z$_2$} attaches:

> George is the king of England's people.
> Elizabeth is the king of England's daughter.

Note that in the first sentence {-Z$_2$} attaches to the word "England,"
but in the second it obviously applies to the whole phrase, "king of
England." Our analysis of the two phrases would have to be:

1. the king / of England's people
2. the king of England / 's (daughter)

All of this interesting kind of observation has led to some real
headaches for the linguist, the net result of which is a great deal of
uncertainty as to how to define the concept of the "word" in English. The ordinary man on the street, or student on the campus, is
likely to feel that any fool knows what a word is, and in the rest of
this book we're going to proceed on the assumption that we do
indeed know a "word" when we hear one, but we might just keep in
the back of our minds the awareness that the linguist is uncertain.
(Any fool knows what light is, but the physicist doesn't.) The problem, of course, springs from the fact that to make things neat we
would like to say that words combine to form larger constructions,
such as phrases, and conversely that phrases are made up of words.
But as we have just seen, this isn't entirely true, unless in our definition of "word" we want to include certain occurrences of {-er}, {-ist},
{-Z$_2$}, and so on, and that would seem to violate our common-sense

knowledge of our own language. Well, this is not a problem we have to resolve, fortunately, but it is well to be reminded that some very simple and obvious things turn out to be tougher than leather spaghetti when we really try to get our teeth into them.

If we define the morpheme as a meaningful unit of language it follows that any unit that has meaning must, necessarily, be a morpheme. Right? Now consider this pair:

> He saw a black bird.
> He saw a blackbird.

The difference is the stress phonemes, of course, and we have in the first "black bird" and in the second "bláckbird." In the first utterance we are obviously talking about any old bird that happens to be black, but in the second a particular kind of bird. The point is that since there is a difference in meaning we must have two different morphemes. If we could find other pairs like this—and we can find many (remember English teácher—Ehglish teácher?)—we would have to conclude that there are two morphemes: {ˆ´} and {´ˋ}.

This whole huge, and important, area of what we might as well call "intonation morphemes" is even less well worked out, and accordingly less well agreed upon, than the rest of morphemics, which we noted as we first took up the subject is a field wherein linguists dispute one another even more vehemently than usual. And all of the uncertainty appears to be due to the entry into the analysis of that slippery concept, meaning. Just to reemphasize for ourselves that the business of morphemics is not all wrapped up, consider these:

> kitchenette
> cigarette
> luncheonette
> majorette

In each we have added /-et/. Is it one morpheme? It wouldn't seem to be. Certainly not only *one* morpheme. A kitchenette is a little kitchen—or is it? A cigarette (or cigaret) wouldn't seem to me to be a little cigar. Certainly a luncheonette is not a little luncheon, and most emphatically a majorette is not a little major. And how about a "marionette"? Would that be a little "marion"? If so, what in blazes is a "marion"? Certainly the /et/ adds something to all these words and to the many others where we add it (*dinette, launderette, suffragette*) But what? If it has meaning, what is it? It's difficult to say.

One linguist also points out the difficulty of assigning "meaning" to what might be called "grammatical signals"—if they are even that. He contrasts "I want to go" with "I can go" and asks the meaning of "to." These two sentences are certainly different, but the difference is clearly assignable to "want" and "can." We *could* set up a morpheme {want to} /wántə/, or one {to go} / təgów/, but this is undesirable for a number of reasons, not the least of which is the usual independent existence as free morphemes of both {want} and {go}. So it looks as though we're stuck with a morpheme {to}, to which we can't easily assign a meaning. (If the "to" is essential, why don't we say "I can to go"?)

In closing, we can still note that there really does seem to be an element in the language which we might as well call "the morpheme," and its reality is not negated by the difficulty of defining it, isolating it, and agreeing in all instances on the meaning of individual occurrences of it. The morpheme is not only a useful concept but one which must be taken into account in any realistic analysis of language at a higher and more complicated level: i.e., grammar. As one scholar put it in a lecture: "You can't write a grammar without listing morphemes any more than you could write a phonology without listing phonemes." You can't, that is, analyze a whole without noting its constituent parts and how they function.

SUGGESTED READING

Gleason, H.A. Jr. *Workbook in Descriptive Linguistics*. New York: Holt, Rinehart & Winston, 1965. The exercises on morphemes are fun and not too difficult. Try especially pp. 26-7 where one exercise is in Swahili, the other in Tepehua.

Nida, Eugene A. *Morphology*. Ann Arbor: U. of Michigan Press, 1949. Though this gets quite technical, you may enjoy working out some of the earlier exercises, say the first ten.

Stageberg, Norman C. *An Introductory English Grammar* ("Morphemes," chapter 8). New York: Holt, Rinehart & Winston, 1965.

CHAPTER 5

SOME WORDS HAVE FAMILIES

Let's begin this chapter with a scandalous question: "Is there in English such a thing as a noun?" Your answer, if you've been paying attention thus far, will be: "No, there isn't." What's actually in the language is a series of sounds which are combined in various ways, and—if we want to include writing—which are represented by variously shaped symbols which we combine in regular ways on paper, or incise into marble or paint on highway signs. This is the reality. Now, if we want to isolate certain of those sounds and call them "nouns" there is nothing to stop us. We can also extract other sounds and call them "quangs." It's a bit difficult to see what we would gain thereby, but certainly we could do it if we wanted to.

What we have to keep clearly in mind, then, is that the realities of the language are one thing, and the things we dream up to help us analyze those realities are something else again, and something entirely different.

It follows that if we are trying to create an analysis—a description, if you please—of English (or any language, for that matter) we are free to go about it in any way we wish. Is there any reason why not? Where are the laws which tell us we can't? The only thing we need consult is our own convenience. What will be *useful* to do? What devices, gimmicks, can we come up with which will help us make an accurate, concise, coherent and as-simple-as-possible description of the language and the way it works? That is all that counts. We are not dealing here with "Truth," though we do want of course to describe the real language as it actually is. We understand that the so-called "rules of grammar" are not of divine origin. Moses did not discover a footnote to the Ten Commandments which laid out the "laws" of language. The only thing that governs us in our search for a description of our language is *expedience.*

We can, if we want, select a group of words and call them "nouns." We could say: "In English any word both beginning and ending with a vowel, like /íni/, we will call a noun." And we could go on and say further: "Any word beginning and ending with a stop, like /pæd/, is an adjective." "All words beginning with nasals, /m,n/, are to be known as adverbs." Sure we could. But we probably wouldn't, simply because it wouldn't prove very useful. Suppose we did laboriously sort out all the words beginning and ending with stops. What could we do with them? How could such a list possibly help us in an effort to describe English? It wouldn't, that I can see, and it would therefore be wasted effort. But observe: it wouldn't be immoral. It would only be impractical.

We do notice, as we watch the language in action, that certain words seem to act like certain other words. They seem, in a way, to come in families. For example: "Her _____ was on the table." How many words can be put in that blank? Quite a few, no? *Hat, notebook, purse, foot, beer, pencil, elbow, blouse, cocker-spaniel, baby, lipstick.* . . and on and on and on. At the same time we observe that there are a lot of words that won't fit there: *wonderful, if, when, excruciatingly, bookish, because, nasty, sad, quickly, traditional* . . . and thousands and thousands more.

Similarly, in "He _____ there yesterday" there are many words that will fill the blank and not offend your sense of proper English, but they are not the same ones that went in the blank above.

It turns out that in our discussions of English it will be useful to have some kind of labels so that we can conveniently refer to these "words of a feather." What the labels are doesn't matter much, if at all. We could call the words that go in the first blank "alpha words" and those that fit the second "beta words." We could follow the practice of Charles Fries and designate them with numbers. We could make up names. Or we could use the old labels, "nouns" and "verbs." However, please notice carefully that there is a danger in using the old words, because we won't be meaning the same thing by them as the old grammarians have meant. All we mean, at this moment, is that a "noun" (or alpha word" or "type 1 word" or whatever) is any word that will fill the blank in "Her _____ was on the table." And that is *all* we mean. Regardless of what anyone else has meant. We have the right to define our own terms in our own way, and we mean to do it.

As we observed, the labels don't matter. But how we group things does. We want to be sure that when we put words in the same family—let's say "class"—they really belong there. Also, we want the classes to be useful to us. There's no point in going to a lot of work that isn't going to have a significant payoff somehow. Consider this test frame (as we call these sentences with blanks in them): "He ate _____ ." Here we can fill the blank with *hors d'oeuvres, meat, snails, parsnips,* etc., but we can also fill it with *greedily, well, yesterday, outdoors,* etc. This is all right, of course, but it turns out not to be too useful. The trouble is that the words in the first list don't act like the words in the second list in other environments. Thus the two lists are alike in that the words in them fill *that* blank, but they won't work alike in other places. The trouble seems to be with the test frame we've used. It isn't demanding enough, perhaps. We can sharpen it a bit: "He ate very _____ ." Now none of the words in the first list will fill the blank. We can't say *"He ate very snails." (An asterisk preceding a construction indicates that it is impossible or "un-English.") Two of the words from the second list, *well* and *greedily,* will fit, but the other two won't. There is no *"He ate very yesterday." So we will have to conclude that in some respects "well" and "yesterday" are not alike. The point is that as we construct the various sets of criteria, whether test frames or other types, we need to be constantly observing what they do and testing the results by asking ourselves, "How useful is this? What of value does it show us? Does it help us in making a description of the language?"

Notice that we do *not* ask "Is the result true?" In the first place asking such a question would presume that there is somewhere "A Truth." In the second place, we would be presuming that we already know this Truth, and if we do, then what's the point of all the struggling we're doing? In other words, we're not playing tricks in an attempt to make the analysis arrive at a foreordained answer.

This means that in all honesty we are either going to have to accept the results of the criteria we set up for sorting words into groups, or else change the criteria. If we say, for instance, that any word that will fill a given blank is "an adjective," and some word comes along and fills it that for some reason we feel shouldn't be included with the other words we're calling adjectives, we're stuck with it nevertheless, unless we want to revise our criteria. We are not going to weasel on this, the way traditional grammar so often seems to do.

Let's pause a brief moment for a quick glance at what we're calling "traditional grammar," which is more accurately called "school grammar" if we mean by it the superficial, dogmatic, prescriptive stuff which was taught for many years in our schools. Actually there have been, and are, "traditionalists" whose work is not superficial, not dogmatic, and not prescriptive—men like Otto Jespersen, George O. Curme, and Ralph Long. If the linguist takes issue with their work it is not on the grounds that it lacks seriousness, profundity, and intellectual honesty, but simply that the linguist urges another analysis which he thinks somehow better. However, in school many of us were not exposed to the likes of Jespersen, Curme, or Long, but instead to an authoritarian, shallow, inaccurate, self-contradictory, intellectually-disreputable assortment of "rules" presented as revealed truth and as something that would be "good for us" and make us educated citizens and polished writers. The question is, where does this stuff come from?

Very briefly, and to be more than a little superficial ourselves, it goes back to the so-called "Age of Reason," the eighteenth century. Perhaps influenced by Newtonian explanations of the orderliness and the system of the universe, people of that day sought order and system in everything. This was the period of geometrically patterned gardens, a la Versailles, of geometrically patterned dances like the minuet, of geometrically patterned music like Mozart's. Order, beautiful order everywhere. Until, that is, the Englishman looked at his language, where he saw, or thought he saw, chaos. Untrammeled, unfettered by "rules," it was changing and shifting, and people lacked an authority to appeal to for standards of right and wrong, which there obviously had to be. Samuel Johnson's great Dictionary was published in 1755 and immediately proved tremendously influential. It met a need. It served as an authority. Interestingly, Johnson confessed that one of his purposes in compiling the dictionary had been to "fix" (i.e., stablize) the language, but he was later forced to recognize the impossibility of attaining this objective. Finally, he even hoped, in his Preface, that "the spirit of English liberty" would prevent the founding of a Royal Academy, such as was being proposed in various quarters, to "cultivate our stile."

We must not suppose, of course, that the masses were concerned about the disorderliness of English. It was rather the educated, the cultured, who were disturbed. And they, practically by definition, knew Latin. Hadn't they been to "grammar school"? And what did one study in grammar school? Grammar, that's what. But *Latin* grammar. It was considered unnecessary to teach kids English, which they spoke perfectly well without special instruction, but Latin, that useful tool and hallmark of the educated—of course they had to be taught Latin.

So they knew Latin grammar. Furthermore, they had a tremendous admiration for the classics, and often, in fact, referred to their own great era as the new "Augustan Age." So what could have been more natural when they became concerned about the absence of a grammar for English than that they should turn to Latin and borrow the rules of *its* grammar? This solution was obvious, but it was unfortunate, and generations of schoolchildren in the English-speaking world have suffered because of it. For, as we have seen, Latin and English are quite different in many important ways, and while Latin grammar might be just dandy as a description of what happens in Latin, it is something of a bust when applied to English. This Latin origin of our traditional school grammar accounts for many of the puzzling things (at least they were puzzling to me) that I had to learn in school. For instance, "case." Nominative, dative, accusative, etc. Did you have to learn that too? "John has a book." "I gave John the book." "I gave John to the cops." Do you detect any difference in the three occurrences of "John"? Do they look somewhat similar to you? They do to me, too, and they did when I was a schoolboy, and I never could see much reason for the different labels we had to learn for them. But look at them in Latin:

> *Johannis* habet librum. (John has a book.)
> Dēdī *Johanni* librum. (I gave John the book.)
> Dēdī aedilibus *Johannem*. (I gave John to the cops.)

Thus the distinction has validity in Latin. Endings actually differ as the word is used in one case or the other, and you will remember from the example in Chapter 1 the extreme flexibility of Latin word order which renders these endings necessary, and which these endings, at the same time, made possible. But in English, excepting the pronouns, case is almost irrelevant, and as a matter of fact it's not too vital with the pronouns, except as a matter of prestige. Consider this example:

> They gave the loot to she and I.

Immediately you spot this as one of those old chestnuts which you used to correct by the pageful in some English drillbook. But right now the question is not whether it's "right" or "wrong" but whether you understand it. Do you know who did the giving and who got the loot? Certainly. But how can you if the "case" is wrong on the pronouns? Simply because the case of pronouns isn't a very strong signal in English. Word order is, however, and you know the direction the loot moved by the sequence of the words. In Latin if you get the case endings wrong you've really scrambled the meaning.

Case is only one example of the difficulty of using Latin grammar to describe English. It's like trying to cram a size ten foot into a size eight shoe. You might make it, but it isn't going to be really satisfactory. No wonder so many people say, as my son said to me a few years ago after he had studied Latin some. "I never really understood English grammar until I had studied Latin." The reason is plain enough: it had been Latin grammar the poor kid had been struggling with all the time, and he was only able really to understand it when he saw it applied to the language where it belonged. Applied to English it takes a lively imagination as well as what Coleridge called, in another context, "a willing suspension of disbelief."

Back to the eighteenth century for a minute or two. The "English grammars" that began to be produced were resounding successes because they met a demand. One of the first, and one of tremendous influence, was Bishop Robert Lowth's *A Short Introduction to English Grammar,* published in 1762. Not a great deal later Lindley Murray published *English Grammar Adapted to the Different Classes of Learners,* soon followed by an exercise book. His work too was wonderfully influential, passing through more than fifty different reprintings.

What accounts for the great appeal of these books? As we said, they filled a need, but what was the need? It sprang not only from the desire for order but, especially among the "masses," from the ever growing possibilities of social mobility. The child of a chimney sweep or a shoemaker was no longer condemned to a career as a chimney sweep or shoemaker: he could achieve a great deal better station in life than his father had before him. Parents then, as now, were deeply concerned to see that their offspring had the best opportunities. And they recognized the truth we have touched on before: if a person wants to live and work among the prestigious echelons of his society, he had better conform to the ways they do things, and especially he has to learn to use the language the way they use it. The urgent cry, then, was "What is correct English?" and, more importantly, "Where do we send our children to learn it?" That Lowth's and Murray's books appeared like answers to prayers is deducible from the practically instantaneous and overwhelming reception they were given.

One more thing should be noted in this regard. What was desperately wanted was authority. It was assumed that there was "a" correct way of saying (or writing) things and the demand was for a no-nonsense book that would state flat out what that correct way was. From this derives the prescriptivism of these school grammars. They taught, for instance, the *who-whom* distinction in all its refinements, and the fact that not all the books always agreed on every point, and that some educated persons differed in their usage was irrelevant. The books stated *rules* which were meant to be followed, and anybody whose usage differed, be he king or commoner, was *wrong*, that's all. As we shall see later, much of this attitude still persists, and at least partly for the same reason. The PTA is not interested in Webster III's assertion that "ain't" is "used orally in most parts of the U.S. by many cultivated speakers," even though all you have to do to be convinced of the truth of this is go around with your ears open. No, it is better to have the kids told firmly what to say and what not to say. So prescriptivism is still a feature of many school grammars.

That these grammars are filled with wrong assertions, inadequate definitions, and superficial analyses is very easy to demonstrate. It's almost too easy to be much fun, but let's look at a few cases in point just by way of illustration.

As for their prescriptiveness on points of usage, we need only note that this kind of "grammar" doesn't have too good a grip on reality. It warns us never to split infinitives, it advises against "It's me," and it stipulates that a preposition is a bad word to end a sentence with. It informs us that "only" in "He only had five bucks" means that he *alone* had five bucks, whereas you and I and all other Americans would understand that five bucks was all the money the guy had. In short, in these and practically countless similar matters it preaches a language that never was on land or sea, which is why numberless Johnnies and Susies tend to feel that what goes on in the English classroom has little relation to the outside world. It also causes the general public to regard the English teacher as more than a little bit peculiar, something I personally am inclined to resent.

But this kind of stricture aside, let's look briefly at school grammar coming to grips with a description of the language. First and foremost (and some think *only*) it attaches importance to labeling the "parts of speech." In most grammars there are eight, but not in all of them. Some have fewer and some more. There is less agreement among these grammars than one might think without deliberately comparing them.

"A noun is the name of a person, place or thing." Is it? I always had trouble with this. A woman might say of a dress material, "That yellow is very pretty." My teacher wanted to call "yellow" a noun, and when I asked what kind of person, place or thing it was I was told that it was a "quality" and that a quality is a thing. (Perhaps part of the difficulty with this definition is the vagueness of "thing.") So then I saw a sentence like "Her dress is yellow" and I knew that "yellow" was a noun. Wrong, I was told. It's an adjective. But I didn't see why. Isn't it still a quality? And isn't a quality a thing? Not here it isn't, they told me. Well, is "yellow" a quality which is in turn a thing, or isn't it? Consider these:

> Her dress was yellow.
> Her dress was a pretty yellow.

You can argue if you wish that "yellow" in the first sentence "modifies" *dress*. And I can argue that it "modifies" it in the second sentence too. Yet the grammar wants to call it a noun one time and not the other. When is a quality not a thing?

Then there's the verb, defined usually as a "word that indicates action or state of being." Good. So in "He arrived on time" the verb, the word carrying the action, is clearly "arrived." That's easy. Now how about "His arrival was on time"? "Arrival" is certainly an action. No, I'm told. You're wrong again. "Arrival" is a noun. So I say, "Oh yes, of course. It's a 'thing'—or is it a 'place'?" And I get accused of being a smart-aleck. So I say the heck with the verb. Let's turn to something easier.

Like the pronoun. That one should be clear enough. It's a word used in the place of a noun, or nouns. If instead of saying "Myrtle and Gertrude had a terrific fight" I say "They had a terrific fight," then "they" is a pronoun. Right? Right. So now I say it this way: "The girls had a terrific fight." "The girls" is used in place of "Myrtle and Gertrude" so it's a pronoun. Right? Wrong. But I don't see *how* it's wrong—I followed the instructions of the rule and substituted "the girls" for "Myrtle and Gertrude." And the word I substituted turns out to be a noun. You know what? I'm beginning to have a suspicion that maybe the weakness is in the definition.

When we turn to the adjective and the adverb we find ourselves in a morass. They depend on the concept of "modification" and the whole thing is pretty difficult. I suppose we could say that when a word is modified by another the original concept in your mind is altered or "modified" somehow. Thus if I say "a house" the picture conjured up in your mind might be of almost any kind of house, but "a brick house" is clearly more specific, and it might be a modification of your original picture, unless you were visualizing a brick house in the first place. Let's pursue this matter a bit further. Suppose I say "the grandmother." You get a certain mental picture. Now I say "the red-haired grandmother" and perhaps the picture is refined a bit. Let me put the phrase into a sentence:

> The red-haired grandmother sitting at the bar was getting smashed on martinis.

You and I might agree that the martinis had modified grandma somehow, but the grammarian wouldn't. But I'll bet the ending of that sentence "modified" the mental image you had of the old lady. The point is that in a very real sense all of the words in a sentence modify each other, and it is very difficult to pin down exactly what modified which, and how. This concept of "modification" is much thornier than you would expect if you just gulp down the definition that "a word that modifies a noun is an adjective." Perhaps it is not a good thing to look critically at these hoary definitions. However, I am comforted by an observation once made by that grand rascal Wilson Mizner: "Faith is a beautiful thing, but it's skepticism that gets you an education."

Let's turn to the prepositions, little-enough words so that they shouldn't cause much trouble. One standard grammar within easy reach on my shelf defines it thus: "A preposition is a connective *placed before* a substantive (called its object) in order to subordinate the substantive to some other word in the sentence." In effect, a preposition is the word which introduces the noun in a prepositional phrase, which is splendid if you happen to be able to spot prepositional phrases, and if you don't really care about the definition of a preposition.

One basic trouble with these definitions is that they don't sort words into categories according to consistent standards. It's as though we were to set about sorting all the cars in the world into categories and we came up with groupings like these:

1. Four cylinder cars
2. Blue cars
3. Convertibles
4. Diesel-powered cars
5. Rear engine cars

The obvious trouble is that there is no consistency of perspective. Clearly some cars wouldn't fit into any of the groups, and we might have some that would fit all of them.

School grammar has a similar inconsistency. Some words are classified according to their meanings, such as nouns and verbs. Some are defined according to function, such as the preposition or the conjunction ("A conjunction is a word used to *join together* words, phrases, clauses, or sentences"). And two large classes, adjectives and adverbs, are defined in terms of *both* meaning and function. It is perhaps no wonder that the results are not entirely satisfactory.

As a matter of fact, the school traditionalist doesn't really *use* the definitions he insists upon. Remember the familiar opening stanza of Lewis Carroll's "Jabberwocky"?

> 'Twas brillig, and the slithy toves
> Did gyre and gimble in the wabe;
> All mimsy were the borogroves,
> And the mome raths outgrabe . . . .

Ask any teacher the part of speech of "toves" and she will promptly inform you it's a noun, and a plural noun at that. She might go on to volunteer the information that this noun is modified by "slithy." But it would be mean of you to pursue the thing further and ask her what kind of person, place or thing a tove is or in just what way it is modified by "slithy." If she *can't* look at the meaning and determine the person, place or thing business, and if she *can't* tell in what way the toves are modified by their slithiness, then she *must* be basing her decision on factors which are not included in the definitions.

An even more extreme case would be the following "skeleton sentence."

The _____ _____-ed the _____ some _____-s.
      (1)   (2)   (3)   (4)

Here she wouldn't hesitate a minute to pronounce (1) a noun and (2) a verb, though what kind of person, place or thing, or what kind of action or state of being, these blanks indicate is perhaps somewhat difficult to say. Similarly, she would confidently assert that (3) and (4) are also nouns, and she might go on to point out that (1) is the subject, (2) is the verb in the past tense (3) is the indirect object, and (4), which is plural, is the direct object.

I wouldn't argue with any of those conclusions. Would you? But I would insist that it is impossible to reach them on the basis of the traditional definitions. Therefore, our school teacher friend is using something else. It will be interesting, and certainly part of our purpose, to see what some of those other things might be.

While reading these nasty remarks about school grammar you might have been asking yourself, especially if you were one of those rare students who was good in grammar, whether the linguist has anything better to offer in its place. The answer is certainly "yes," but with a timid, little, following qualifying "no." That is, it is easy to offer something *better* but it isn't at all easy to come up with something airtight and foolproof. At least nobody's done it yet.

Perhaps the solution is impossible. This, at least, is the suggestion thrown out by H.A. Gleason, one of the country's top linguists, who says: "Definitions are probably not possible, at least for unlimited classes like Fries' four major form classes."[1] He says further that "many" linguists today doubt the "feasibility" of defining parts of speech.

Recognizing, then, that the job of defining the so-called parts of speech perhaps can't be done, at least not for the major classes, let's nevertheless take the time to learn something of what modern attempts to do it look like. Maybe in the course of this effort we can learn something of what it is that makes the task so difficult.

As the Gleason quote above indicates, Charles Fries identified four main parts of speech, which he called "form classes." The label is itself significant, for the effort was to identify the members of these classes on the basis of form, including the way they fit into certain "slots" (or filled certain blanks, that is) in sentences. Meaning was not a criterion. Also, the classes were identified by numbers, so that he speaks of a given word as a "Class 1" word or a "Class 2" word. Since the classes were being newly defined, it seemed appropriate to give them new labels. However, later linguists have not followed Fries in this, preferring to keep the old familiar names— noun, verb, adverb, adjective—but defining them differently. (In my opinion, we would have done much better to follow Fries' lead, for many students have it so deeply ingrained that anything that modifies a noun is an adjective that they are permanently branded. They drink the new wine from the old bottles subconsciously assuming all the time that it's the old wine still.)

In this book we will follow general practice and use the old names, but it cannot be stressed too much that they don't mean the same as in school grammar, and if you go along assuming that they

---

1. *Linguistics and English Grammar,* p. 119.

do you're going to be badly confused.[2] A noun is going to be *what we say it is*. Likewise a verb, an adjective, and an adverb. And what it might have meant in some other grammar is completely irrelevant.

We should stress once more, too, that when we finish looking at the "parts of speech" we will *not* have them all neatly wrapped up, settled once and for all. There will be loose ends all over the place and unresolved problems by the bushel. We are not trying in the little time available to us to finalize anything. Rather we are merely going to note the kinds of approaches linguists are taking today and some of the tentative answers they are giving. Unlike the traditionalist, the linguist is capable of saying quite honestly and earnestly: "I don't know."

As we watch the vast array of English words in action we find that many of them have similarities of form, of bound morphemes they will accept and of places in larger patterns they will fill. These *formal characteristics* generally are the basis on which they are sorted into categories. For instance, we noted that in the frame sentence "Her _____ was on the table" only certain words, certain *kinds* of words we might as well say, would fit. We can approximately double the list if we create an option with "was," so that we make the frame: "Her _____ (was) (were) on the table." Now we can have not only "foot" but "feet," not only "lipstick" but "lipsticks." We noted similarly that in "He _____ there yesterday" quite a different group of words would fit, and we see readily that we would change their *form* if we substituted "tomorrow" or "right now" for "yesterday." That is, in "He ate there yesterday," "He will eat there tomorrow," and "He is eating there right now" we don't feel any *class* difference in "ate," "will eat," and "is eating."

Let's start looking at how words are assigned to classes by considering the kinds of formal characteristics the linguist is looking for.

First we have to recognize two major subdivisions of words into groups: these are the "content words" and the "function words." Content words, often called "lexical words," are the ones we think of as "having meaning." They are the ones you would look up in a dictionary (or "lexicon," hence "lexical words") for their "mean-

---

2. One thing that will tend to lessen the differences that will be apparent to you is that, as we have noted, the school-traditionalist didn't really *use* the definitions he gave. Since he used, instead, something like the things we are going to note, it is not too surprising that the results are often similar. The difference is, then, that we are making the criteria explicit, not leaving them unstated while insisting that we use something else. It could well be that those who were "good at grammar" in their schooldays had somehow discovered a number of these criteria for themselves.

ing," and they have a meaning that can more or less easily be explained. They would be words like: *lexicon, regurgitate, bellicose, spontaneously, book, depart, sad, ill.* Function words, on the other hand, you would probably never have to look up anywhere—if you speak English, that is—and their "meaning" is hard to state anyhow. They are words like: *up, and, about, if, to, why, the, a, with.*

Let's illustrate this point with a sentence:

> *The* pretty girl stood *on the* curb *in the* rain, waving frantically *at* passing taxis.

The function words are italicized. Note how they give a framework to the sentence, serving the *function,* that is, of relating the content or lexical words to each other. Note how easily we can substitute other content words and retain the same structure:

> *The* belligerent sailor sat *on the* pier *in the* fog, cursing furiously *at* floating bottles.

Even if we substitute nonsense items for the content words we retain the appearance of English. We might say it's *English* nonsense:

> *The* gludgeous krankle drilted *on the* whopple *in the* drangst, stangling flardously *at* slanding bloogers.

We can pretty well identify the parts of speech of that, too, and again we might wonder how. Perhaps the following is a tip. If we keep the original content words but substitute nonsense for the function words we don't have even "English nonsense," but sheer gibberish:

> Scrab pretty girl stood pringle groff curb krang blunk rain waving frantically slark passing taxis.

Reading these last two versions out loud shows us something. Try it. The first one sounds like what used to be called "double talk," and it at least has normal English intonation patterns. The second one sounds like reading items in a list.

We see, then, that these homely little function words have a vital role to play. They are a part of the structural framework of the language, and an extremely important part. They differ from content words in several important ways.

First, there are only a few function words. (Fries sorted out 154.) Consider what this means as you stand staring at the thirteen big volumes of the *Oxford English Dictionary* on the library reference shelf. At most a couple of hundred of the words in there are function words. All the rest are content words.

Second, the function words recur over and over and over. In the sentence we were playing with about the pretty girl or the belligerent sailor, there are fifteen words, of which seven are function words. Try marking all the function words in a sample paragraph of printed English and then determining what percent they constitute of the total. When I try this I come out with figures ranging between 35 percent and 45 percent. That this mere handful of perhaps 200 words should constitute such a percentage of the total wordage on a page means obviously that their recurrence is tremendous.

There is still a third important difference. We are forever making up new content words, or shifting them from one form class to another. (This is the basis of most slang.) As we devise new things and new concepts and new ways of doing things, we need more labels. So we invent them. How many words in tonight's newspaper do you think would have been completely unintelligible to Abe Lincoln's generation? But one thing we could bet on: those people would have understood all the function words. The high-schooler bending his ingenuity toward coming up with some fresh, attractive and preferably flip way of expressing something is very unlikely to invent a new preposition. He will not think of a groovy new way of saying "the." The limited list of function words is pretty well fixed. But the list of content words is practically limitless, and if you draw a limit it will be exceeded tomorrow.

When we set out a moment ago to consider some of the characteristic formal matters which would help us determine word classes (and let's start using that phrase instead of "parts of speech," so redolent of chalk dust), we got interrupted right away by having to note and describe content words versus function words. The reason for this is simple: certain function words have as one of their principal functions designating, marking off, the form classes of content words. For instance, take the skeleton sentence we looked at a while back:

The _____ _____-ed the _____ some _____-s.
(a)   (1)   (2)   (b) (c)   (3)   (d)   (4)

One big reason we could so readily identify (1), (3) and (4) as nouns is the presence of the function words (a), (c) and (d), because one of the principal functions of those words is to signal "noun coming." (This is true even though according to the traditional definition we would be compelled to detect meaning in the blanks.) So one thing we will have to direct our attention to as we attempt to sort words into classes is the presence or absence of certain function words.

A second kind of formal marker which will help us categorize content words into form classes is the kinds of inflectional suffixes they have (or can accept). For example, in the skeleton sentence above we are aided in deciding that (2) is a verb as we note item (b), which we accept as $\{-D_1\}$, the past tense inflection. We observe that certain kinds of inflections go with certain classes of words and not with others, and this will help.

We note too a somewhat similar scattering of derivational suffixes. In our chapter on morphemes, for instance, we noted that $\{-ment\}$ characteristically turns verbs into nouns, as *enjoy-enjoyment*. In other words, the presence of this bound morpheme on a word might quite likely tend to make us consider it a noun. Similarly, and as we also mentioned when talking about morphemes, $\{-ize\}$ might well indicate a verb. I am trying to pick words carefully here, for I don't want to give the impression that the whole business is very easy and we simply check some list of derivational suffixes and categorize a given word according to which suffix it bears. In the first place it might very well not have one. Second, the presence of a given derivational suffix might not necessarily indicate that a word belongs in a particular form class. This is why I use phrases like "might indicate" and "would tend to make us think," because the decision to pigeonhole a word in one category or another probably won't depend on the presence or absence of one formal indicator but on several. And in all truth there will be times when we can't make up our minds.

Another vitally important indicator is the position of the word in a construction. We have already talked about the major importance of word order as a signal in English, and this is one of the roles word order plays. It helps us sort words into categories. Just for example, let's stipulate that the following is a complete English sentence and is not a command.

_____ _____ his _____
(1)　　　(2)　　　　(3)

Would you have any hesitation at all in saying (2) is the verb and that (1) is a noun and the subject of the sentence? Or in adding that (3) is also a noun and the object? Of course you wouldn't. (And you're probably even refining it to the point of filling in blank (1) with a "proper noun" or a "personal pronoun"—"Geoffrey flipped his wig," "Rover bit his master," "He devoured his lunch," and like that. If you were told that the following represents an English declarative sentence:

$$(1) \qquad\qquad (2)$$

would you have hesitation in labeling the blanks as (1) noun and (2) verb? Certainly not. And this is what we mean as we say that word order plays an important role in helping sort out word classes.

Another signal, which would be more useful if we knew more about it, is intonation patterns. Remember how /ínsens/ and /inséns/ are differentiated by stress? We noted at the time that there are quite a few pairs of words like this and that those with stress on the first syllable are nouns, those with stress on the second are verbs (*ímprint-imprínt, áddress-addréss, ínsert-insért,* and others). It's perhaps true that this kind of stress contrast doesn't occur often enough to be a great help, but that it does occur occasionally deserves to be noted.

So to sum up, then, we have five kinds of signals which help us sort words into classes:

1. Function words
2. Inflections
3. Derivational suffixes
4. Word order (the slots a word can fill)
5. Stress patterns.

What good is all this? It's a good question and one which teachers should be prepared to answer, though unfortunately many of us are inclined to resent it, as though the student was not honestly asking a question but merely expressing contrariness and a general resentment at being asked for an expenditure of effort. (And in all fairness, this latter is sometimes the case too.) Well, at least part of the answer is that the student already knows this "stuff"—if he speaks English, that is. Because, you remember, we are simply at the moment trying to attach labels to features of the system. It is a fact of the language itself that words do relate to each other (modify one another, bear on one another, complete one another, or whatever you want to call it.) Our schoolchild friends, little Johnny and his sister Susie, understand this, though they are not consciously aware of it and they certainly don't know the labels until their teacher teaches them her kind of grammar, if then. But that we do know, and that we have to know, the relation of words to each other is perhaps made most clear on the occasions when communication breaks down, which is why linguists love to make collections of ambiguities. Sometimes more can be learned from a sample of language that is a "failure" than from any number of examples that are routine successes. Consider this one:

The ladies looked hard.

We can't tell what this means. It could mean that the ladies in question were a real tough looking bunch. Or it could mean that they looked and looked and looked and *looked*!

The reason we can't tell the meaning of this little sentence is that we have no way of knowing whether "hard" relates to "looked" or to "ladies." One way it means one thing, the other way something quite different. In traditional terminology we can't tell whether "hard" is an adjective (in which case it would go with, or "modify," ladies) or whether it's an adverb (in which case it would modify *looked*). Johnny and Susie wouldn't know the terms "adverb" and "adjective," but they would be just as stumped as you and me in interpreting the sentence and probably as aware as we are that it has two meanings, at least if they know the meaning of "hard" as "tough." So you see, knowing the classes of words *is* important if we are to understand the language—though I readily concede that knowing the terminology is of no consequence beyond making more convenient our discussion of these matters.

Incidentally, suppose the example sentence had been one of these:

The ladies looked tough.
The ladies looked painstakingly.

These have no ambiguity. We understand immediately and clearly what each means. What's the difference between these and the original version? It's simply that as we look at the way "tough," and "painstakingly" normally pattern themselves in the language we discover that "tough" consistently patterns itself with the adjective group (unless it has a noun marker as in "He's a tough") and "painstakingly" groups with those we call adverbs. Therefore in the slot "The ladies looked _____ " we know which classification to assign to each, which word each "goes with" or "modifies," and there's no trouble. "Hard," however, consistently patterns with *both* the adjective and the adverb groups, so in our problem sentence we don't know which way to jump. It could be either.

An example repeated and reprinted so often it's practically famous in its own right is Fries' famous telegraphic:

SHIP SAILS TODAY

Here again the problem is that we can't understand the word classes, though this time the trouble is with a noun-verb possibility rather than adjective-adverb as in our last example. If "ship" is a verb then "sails" is a noun, and the message might be a telegram directed to a sailmaker asking him to get on the ball and ship the sails. On the other hand, if "ship" is a noun then "sails" is a verb and the message is an announcement that some ship is sailing. Note how easily the ambiguity is cleared up with the addition of a simple function word:

SHIP THE SAILS TODAY
THE SHIP SAILS TODAY

We probably should note that Fries' example is a made-up one to illustrate a point and that in real life nine times out of ten the context would save the situation. Suppose, for instance, that you were a sailmaker and that you had an urgent order for sails from the people about to engage in the America's Cup race and that you'd been delayed in filling it. If you received a telegram saying "SHIP SAILS TODAY" would you think it was a piece of routine information that some ship was sailing? You would not. And so it is that context saves us all from making more bloopers than we otherwise would. (An interesting side-issue raises its head here. Would the fact that you were a sailmaker behind time on filling an order be a "grammatical fact"? We wouldn't want to say that, but certainly it would help repair some deficiencies in the sample construction, wouldn't it?)

Ambiguities crop up all the time. Newspaper headlines are a particularly fruitful source of them, obviously because of the headline writer's desire, and need, to cram much information into little space. If you laugh at his blunders, and we all do, you ought to try writing headlines sometime. Here are a few I've collected. See if in each you can not only spot the ambiguity, but can account for it in terms of the mix-up over which classes the words ought to be assigned to.

BABIES LIVE THROUGH TEAM EFFORT
IN LOCAL HOSPITAL HEART CENTER

SLANTED
OIL INQUIRY
TO RESUME

(You won't be able to "see" the real meaning of this one unless you are aware of the thieving practice of some oil well operators of drilling wells not straight down, as they should, but on a slant, so that they arrive at a pool of oil under a neighbor's property instead of under their own.)

COMMISSIONERS AWARD
PAUPER BURIAL CONTRACT

VISITING CAMEL DRIVER
SHOWS ANIMAL COMPASSION

(We'll talk about this one a little later on.)

CURSING CRYSTAL CITY MAYOR
GETS AUTO DEALER ARRESTED

JONES WILL FIGHT
HINGES ON BABY

LOS ANGELES
BRAKES SKID

Not all such errors occur in headlines, of course. Here are a couple from what newspapermen call "leads" (that's /liydz/), the opening sentences of news stories:

1. Political potshots ricocheted off the walls in the usually solemn Senate Monday during debate on the Governor's abandoned property bill. [I.e., had the Governor abandoned a property bill, or was it a bill concerned with abandoned property?]

2. The Soviet Union has its own sea monster with a taste for hunting dogs, Radio Moscow reported today. [Play with the stress patterns on "hunting dogs."]

Here is one that appeared as the "cutline" (the explanatory statement under a picture) in a magazine distributed nationally by a motel chain. The picture was of a couple of women fraudulently got up in colonial-type clothes, holding spyglasses and peering out over a large body of water:

Spotting ships on the Delaware River, perhaps carrying home their loved ones, was a pastime of the ladies of old New Castle.

[Maybe sailors then were as sailors now, and sometimes needed to be carried home?]

Believe it or not, students sometimes write this kind of howler. Here, for one example, is a quiz answer to a question on Tennessee Williams' *The Glass Menagerie:*

The mother cannot accept the fact that she has been deserted gracefully.

You might well say that this kind of thing is good fun, but what's the point of it all? The answer is simply this: if you can't tell just exactly how the words in a statement relate to each other you can't tell just exactly what the statement means. In other words, as we try to sort words into word classes, as we try to see how they work together, we are not merely indulging in idle sport, but we are trying to see, in focus and deliberately, what it is that we do all the time as we use, or mis-use, our language. This is not a mere game, then, but is for real and is simply an examination of what we engage in all day every day. The only difference is that at the moment instead of manipulating all these matters at a level beneath consciousness, as we usually do, we are taking a hard look at them.

Now let us see some of the criteria we have already listed as the linguist goes about trying to use them in his admittedly-impossible task of sorting out all the words into "form classes."

The Noun

Function words

You already have the idea, from our various examples, that there are certain function words whose primary role is to point out that there is a noun coming up. These are, generally speaking, words like "the," "a-an," "some," "his," "her," "two," and so on. We can say that they are words that will fit into the first slot in our first test, or frame, sentence: "*Her* foot was on the table." What we are saying is that these words can fill the same slot in the same construction, and maybe we need to pause for a moment to clarify what we mean by that.

Since "construction" is an important term, and one that we've bandied about loosely without defining it, we need to take a look at it, but at the same time we have to recognize that we're in one of those awkward situations where the terms needed in our definition haven't themselves been adequately defined. However, we've got to begin somewhere, and you'll have to be patient and assume that everything will come out all right in the end. We'll say that two constructions are the same when the classes that comprise them are the same and are in the same order. (We'll clear this up practically right away.) Conversely, we will say that two constructions are different when: (1) they are made up of different classes or (2) when the classes that make them up occur in different order.

When the definition talks about "classes" it means "word classes." That is, *noun, verb, adjective*, etc. (We haven't even named them all yet, let alone defined them.) If we have two constructions made up of "Noun-verb-adverb" (whatever those terms might turn out to indicate) we would say they were the same. Thus:

James choked agonizingly.
Birds fly high.
Hell erupted suddenly.

These are all the "same construction" because they have the "same classes" in the same sequence. However:

Hell suddenly erupted.

is different, a different construction, because while it has the same classes they are in a different arrangement. Similarly,

Helen looked foolish.

is a different construction because instead of N-V-Adv. it has N-V-Adjective. It has the same sequence but it is made up of different classes. Now is it becoming a bit more clear? Let's repeat the definition then:

Two constructions are the same when the classes that comprise them are the same and are in the same order.

Conversely, they are different when they are made up of different classes or when the same classes are in different sequence.

Now then, back to the problem we were working on. "Her feet were on the table." Let's describe it arbitrarily, in the absence of real definitions of form classes, as:

_____ Noun—Verb—Prepositional phrase.

Thus we can have:

Her feet were on the table.
Some fish were in the lake.
Two dogs were in the classroom.
The champion was at the plate.
A lady was in the doorway.

At the moment we appear to be going in a circle, because while what we're trying to define is the *noun*, what I seem to be defining is these little function words which serve to indicate the noun. But what I'm *really* pointing out is that when you see one of these words you know that there is a noun coming—or a word functioning like a noun, which point we'll take up a bit later. I think from the examples already given you know perfectly well the kind of words being talked about, but here are some more:

several	every	both
enough	our	each
its	my	this-these
some	their	that-those

The most usual function of these words is to signal "noun coming," and as speakers of English we have *conditioned* ourselves to expect a noun (or a word of the class we are trying to get labeled as nouns) when we hear or see one of these words. Even if the word is not one that we usually think of as belonging to this class, the presence of one of these words, in the right construction, will make us convert the word into a noun. Thus:

Her immediately was always later.

Though this is not conventionally punctuated ("Her 'immediately' was always 'later.' ") you understand it, and of course in speech you don't hear the quotation marks anyhow.

This exceedingly common function word is most often called a "noun marker" or "noun determiner" and in most of the books it is symbolized with a D or a T. We'll use the D. That is, a construction of determiner—adjective—noun would be represented as *D-Adj-N.*

Note that as the paragraph above indicates, while the noun marker or determiner always means "noun coming up" it might not necessarily mean right this instant. Thus we have not only "the dog" and "the girl" but "the ugly dog" and "the incredibly beautiful small blonde girl."

Incidentally, it is irrelevant that some of these words just cited as determiners are words which you might have grown used to calling "pronouns." We are now defining our own terms in our own way, and we choose to call them determiners. Thus in "Her cigar was on the bureau," the word filling the first slot is a determiner. Determiners are the most frequent and the most conspicuous indicators of the form class we are going to call nouns. But there are of course others.

Inflections

A very satisfactory help in creating our "noun class" is that while some words can be pluralized others can't. As we put it earlier, some can accept $\{-Z_1\}$. It is also true that some words can accept $\{-Z_2\}$ and others cannot. Those that can accept these inflectional suffixes we are going to include in our noun class. Thus if a word can be pluralized or if it can take a possessive (either or both) we are going to toss it into the noun box. Though it's perhaps anticipating a little bit, we can surely point out at this time that you can't pluralize an adjective (or what we're going to call adjectives) nor an adverb. Nor çan you pluralize a verb, not really, in spite of the fact that we traditionally call "they drink" a verb in the "third person plural." It doesn't mean *plural* in the sense that "some drinks" means more than one drink. "They are drinking" doesn't mean a lot of times. (The plurality occurs in the noun—or "pronoun," if you wish.)

Since you have been reading alertly, you might have just caught me in a little contradiction. Here is the problem I think you might have noted: We just stipulated that words that fill the first slot in a construction like "Her hat was on the table" are noun determiners. We also said that the only class of words that can accept $\{-Z_2\}$ are nouns. What about:

Dorothy's hat was on the table.

We've got to reconcile the thing somehow or else leave it as a hole in our system. I think *what* we call it doesn't really matter much. Maybe we need simply say that "nouns in the genitive (that is, with $\{-Z_2\}$) often function as determiners." The only thing wrong with that is that it implies that once we get words sorted into classes they aren't going to necessarily stay put, but might shift from class to class—and as a matter of fact, this is precisely what happens anyhow. If, for instance, you look at a list of the 500 most common words in English, such as the Thorndike-Lorge list, you find many entries like *fly, break, walk, wait, talk, play, bite, blow, catch, cut, drink, drive, fall* . . . Are they nouns or verbs? You can't tell, of course. Perhaps you can't tell the word class of any word unless you see it in context, in a frame. Some astonishing shifts occur, and of words you might think rather fixed in one class or another. For example, one of the local sportswriters was complaining that the university football team wasn't "scholarshipping" enough athletes. As neat a verb as you ever saw. Another sportswriter, referring to a no-hit baseball game, wrote:

It was a Day of Infamy for the hitters. They were Pearl Harbored.

A cartoon from last Christmas season shows two ladies looking at a department store Santa Claus. One of them is saying:

Let's steer clear of Santa today. I'm in no mood to be HO-HO-HOed!

Keep your ears and eyes open and in no time you can have a great collection of similar items (should you have any desire to). The point is, of course, that almost any word in any word class seems capable of being transferred, under some set of circumstances or other, into a member of some other class. If we want to say that "Dorothy's" in "Dorothy's hat was on the table" is a determiner, though it's *really* a noun ordinarily, we're not kidding anybody, least of all ourselves, for we know that in reality there is no such thing as either noun or noun determiner except as we choose to give certain words one label or the other. Notice, by the way, that the answer to "Whose hat was on the table?" might well be:

Dorothy's was on the table.

And now the big question is, do we have a determiner filling in as a noun? Or was it the other way around all the time? Since we see clearly enough that "Dorothy's" will function in either way, all we really need do probably is decide which to call it. And it really doesn't matter which.

A problem is created by the suffix $\{-ing_2\}$ since it also serves to mark both verbs ($\{-ing_1\}$) and adjectives ($\{-ing_3\}$), for discussions of which see below. We do find frequent occurrences of forms like this:

His wailings were most annoying.

"Wail" is clearly a regular verb, and "wailing" is a regular inflection of it. Yet here it is not only set off with a noun determiner but has the plural inflection $\{-Z_1\}$. It seems in many ways easiest to call it a noun and to call $\{-ing_2\}$ a derivational suffix of nouns, though let it be noted quickly that this is not the solution everyone arrives at. (See later for a discussion of "nominals," "adjectivals," etc., which is merely another way of tackling this same problem of what is, after all, merely nomenclature.)

Derivational Suffixes

As a third criterion in helping set up a class of words to call nouns, we note that we have certain characteristic derivational affixes that will go with the words that noun markers indicate and that will fit on many of the words that accept the inflectional endings we were just talking about. We've noted in an earlier chapter that the bound morpheme $\{-ment\}$ often indicates these words we're going to call nouns. (Unfortunately you can't just assume that any time you see "ment" you're dealing with a noun: "We segment utterances," "The space was compartmented," "He fragmented the mirror.") With this caution in mind, though, it is still true that many derivational suffixes will signal "noun" to us. Here are just a few:

{-ism}	{-er }	{-ster}
{-ist }	{-ian}	{-ness}
{-ance}	{-ee }	{-ity }

As in *patriotism, violinist, attendance, fighter, parliamentarian, absentee, punster, illness, rarity.*)

Word Order

Perhaps in talking about the general principle of word order we've already said enough so that you can see how it's going to apply in helping sort out the noun. You already know that nouns occupy certain slots in sentences. If you were given this skeleton sentence:

_____ hit _____.

you would assume that blank one is to be filled with a noun, and very possibly blank two, though it could be something else. Notice that in this sentence there are no noun markers, no inflections, no derivational suffixes to help decide how to fill the blanks. We do it on word order alone. With, to be precise, a little help from the nature of the verb, for with a verb of a different kind our choice in the second blank might also be different, as in:

_____ looked _____.

In this case we would be much less likely to select a word from our noun class to fill the second blank. Doubtless, therefore, if we were making a complete and careful grammar, instead of merely taking a quick look at some of the principles involved in constructing one, we would have to go on and separate verbs into lists and note that some of them tend to indicate "noun following" and others don't. We won't, however.

The whole point, then, is that English sentences occur in a certain few, familiar patterns (which we'll look at more closely when we deal with transformational grammar), and these patterns occur over and over and over again so that they are ingrained in us. Following these patterns, which have somewhat the force of linguistic straitjackets, we anticipate that certain kinds of words, and not others, will occur at certain slots in them. And they do. If we foul up the pattern we foul up the meaning, and as often as not it is through creating confusion in the classes some of the words belong to.

Stress

As for stress patterns, we've already noted one that differentiates certain nouns from certain verbs: /ínsens/—/inséns/. There is a noun vs. adjective stress that we'll note later on. In the meantime it is safe to say that the role of stress in sorting words into classes is not sufficiently understood.

For right now, let's conclude that we've listed the features that will characterize the class of words we're going to call nouns: noun markers; inflections {-Z₁} and {-Z₂}; certain characteristic derivational suffixes; word order; and, occasionally, a distinctive stress pattern.

These features do not "define" the noun, but rather they comprise a list of noun characteristics. We could probably do a better job of pinpointing the noun by extending this list of characteristics, but that would be the best we could do. It is in this sense that Gleason observed that "many" linguists are dubious about the feasibility of *defining* parts of speech.

Finally, please observe that in citing these characteristic features of the class of words we will call "noun," nowhere did we consider meaning, that least satisfactory and least reliable of all tools of analysis.

Before going on to another major form class, I'd like to call your attention to a feature of language that linguists call "redundancy." Redundancy is a built-in feature of all languages, and it means, in essence, that many more language signals are used than are "really needed." We are very prodigal with signals which indicate how a construction is put together. Consider this example:

His illnesses were very frequent.

We would undoubtedly call "illnesses" a noun. Why? Well, let's look at it. First of all it's marked as a noun by the determiner "his." Second, it's in a characteristic noun slot between the determiner which opens the sentence and the verb. If the determiner means "noun coming," there isn't any other word available to be the noun. Third, we know we have "illness" as well as "illnesses," so this word is clearly bearing {-Z₁}, which we've seen occurs only on nouns. Fourth, "ill," ordinarily an adjective, has here been converted by the addition of the derivational suffix {-ness}, characteristic of nouns. So we have not *one* signal that we're dealing with a noun, but four.

Actually, there's even a fifth one, which lies in the fact that if we change "illnesses" into the singular, "illness," we also have to change "were" to "was," and since this "agreement" exists between subject and verb, and since the subject is usually a noun, we have a fifth clue to the noun-ness of "illnesses."

This is "redundancy" in spades. Clearly it is considered important, in the fabric of this language, that the role played by individual words in constructions must be clear. It's as though the language said to us, "Now listen, it's important that you get these form classes straight, so I'm going to give you every opportunity." It is this redundancy which enables us to understand spoken messages even where there is a high level of interference or "noise." With a poor phone connection, for instance, or in a radio conversation hampered by static, some of the signals are going to be blotted out. But chances are there will still be some which get through, so that communication can take place under very poor conditions. Some linguists have observed that there is less redundancy in written English than in speech. It makes sense that there might be, doesn't it?

The Verb

Our discussion of the verb can be considerably shorter than that of the noun, not that the verb is any less important, which would be ridiculous, but that by this time we have so many of the principles under our belts. It turns out that the signals that indicate verbs are similar in principle to those which set off nouns.

Function Words

The conspicuous function words which serve as verb markers are those little words we were taught to call in school "helping verbs" or "auxiliaries." "I *can* go," "I *will* go," "I *might* go," "I *may* go," "I *should* go," and so on. These words are italicized here merely to call attention to them, not to indicate any special stress. In fact, these markers are usually unstressed. Thus we say /ayl+gow/ instead of /ay+wil+gow/. Many of these words lead a double life and serve not only as verb markers but frequently are independent verbs in their own right. One way we often tell which is which is the lack of stress when the word is a verb marker. Thus:

1. I /kɨn/ go. But
2. I /kæn/ frúit.

Or, if we put them both together:

   3. I /kɨn kæn/ frúit.

You would never say: "I /kɨn/ frúit," and if you did you'd be turning "fruit" into a verb, with what meaning I can't imagine. But the lack of stress on "can" would turn it into a verb marker, and hence "fruit" into a verb.

We put these markers together into some rather fancy combinations at times to create certain subtle refinements in the verb. Thus we have not only "I eat" and "I'm eating" and "I'm going to eat," but such strings as "I must have been going to eat" and "I should have been about to eat" and "I ought to have been going to eat." But they all serve the function of indicating: "verb coming."

(Parenthetically, the lack of stress on "have" when used as an auxiliary is responsible for a fairly frequent error in writing:

I should of gone.

What is needed here, assuming for some reason the writer is attempting to catch the flavor of spoken English, is of course: "I should've gone." Since we can hear no phonemic difference we have to say it's merely a spelling error and not some ignorant confusion between a verb auxiliary and a preposition.)

Inflections

Perhaps indicating its vital role in the message of the sentence, the verb is marked by four inflections, three of which we have already noted in another context. They are: {-Z_3} (the inflection on the third person singular, he walk*s*), {-D_1} (the past tense, he walk*ed*), and {-D_2} (the past participle, he had flow*n*). The verb inflection we have not so far discussed is {-ing$_1$}, the present participle (he is walk*ing*).

Since the verb is the only word class that carries the idea of tense and since this tense is indicated by inflectional suffixes, these inflections are very useful in helping us set up the verb class. But suppose the verb is without one of these inflections—suppose, that is, it's in what we call "present tense" (even though it often signals past or future):

Susannah and I stroll in the corridor.

We ask ourselves, could "stroll" accept {-D_1}? Would it still be English if we said "Susannah and I strolled in the corridor"? Obviously it would, so we put a verb label on "stroll." The test, then, is not merely whether the word in question has a verb inflection but whether it *could* take one.

The regular English verb has only four forms, including the base or uninflected form:

> walk
> walks
> walking
> walked

Since the past participle is the same form as simple past (I have walk*ed*), we need {-D₂} only to take care of a handful of irregulars that have a fifth form.

One comment remains to be offered about a special "verb"—*to be.* Many linguists today don't consider "to be" a verb. (Whether it really *is* a verb is a meaningless question.) This word comes in eight different forms: *be, am, are, is, was, were, been, being.* Almost every time you make a statement about English verbs you have to make an exception for "to be." It turns out therefore to be more convenient, more expedient, not to include it with the verbs. So what does the linguist call it? He calls it simply "to be." (It would seem to make as much sense, really, to call it "am" or "is," but it has to be called something and the label "to be" seems universal.)

Derivational Suffixes

There are a few derivational suffixes which are characteristic of the verb. One of these we have already seen: {-ize}. Like *fictionalize, rubberize, brigandize.* This is a very live suffix. You will find firms willing, for instance, to "concrete-ize" your patio, "winterize" your car, and to "-ize" this and that until you are yourself "pauperized."

Another common suffix is {-fy}—/fay/, as in *electrify, solidify, verify, putrify.*

Still another is {-en}, such as in *hasten, lighten, fasten.*

Another would be {-ate}, like *calumniate, asphyxiate, hyphenate, radiate, implicate . . .*

There are some typical verb prefixes, too. *Enlighten, enable, enmesh* exemplify one. *Bewail, berate, bemoan* illustrate another.

These are not all the affixes that serve to help us sort out verbs, but they serve as an indication of what we have in mind.

Word Order

There are two most characteristic slots for verbs. The slot following the subject, is, of course, the first—or between subject and object,
or complement, if the sentence has one. Thus:

Children _____ .

The man _____ the rats.

The lady _____ beautiful.

George _____ his girl a corsage.

The team_____ beautifully.

There is another very characteristic slot at the beginning of a
pattern. Try these out:

_____ the door.

_____ your mouth.

_____ your dinner.

This same pattern is often prefaced by words like "please" or "let's,"
or by a name followed by double bar juncture:

Please _____ to the dance.

Let's _____ a coke.

Henry,_____ the dishes.

Stress patterns

There isn't much to say about special stresses marking out verbs,
because they don't seem to, but we should note that the nouns we
saw earlier that were indicated by stress have verbs as their opposite
numbers—/ímprint/—/imprínt/ and others.

Before leaving the subject of verbs, we need to note a group of
them that are called "two-part verbs" (or sometimes "separable
verbs"). As the name implies, these verbs are made up of two words
instead of just the usual one, and as the alternate label "separable"
suggests, the two parts can often be separated. Here, as an example,
are two sentences, one with a separable verb and the other without.

The wind blew down the house.

The wind blew down the street.

Superficially these look very alike, and yet we have an instinctive
feeling that they are very different. A closer look reveals that they
are indeed very different, and that the difference is that the first one

has a two-part verb. We can say "The wind blew the house down," but we can't say *"The wind blew the street down," not and retain idiomatic standard English, that is. Another test is what we might call "one word substitutability." That is, for the two-part verb in the first sentence we can substitute a one word synonym: "The wind demolished the house." We haven't changed the sentence very much. But if we substitute for "blew down" in the second sentence, we might get something like "The wind demolished the street," which isn't the original meaning at all.

There are quite a few of these two-part verbs in English. Though traditional grammar usually considers them verbs plus adverbs (or "adverbial particles"), it would seem easier and neater to consider them simply as verbs which happen to be in separable parts, especially since they can be so neatly substituted for by similar verbs that are indisputably single words. As often as not, by the way, the awful "preposition at the end of a sentence" is analyzable as part of one of these split verbs, as in:

> I told him to set the targets up.
> (I told him to set up the targets.)
> (I told him to erect the targets.)

Some two-word verbs are not "separable," really. "He gave in quickly" doesn't idiomatically become *"He gave quickly in." That "in" is really part of the verb, however, is demonstrated by substituting: "He surrendered quickly."

Adjectives

In sorting out the adjectives we will use the same kind of criteria as for the noun and verb, but we'll take them up in a different order, one more convenient for the problem posed by the adjective.

Word Order

The adjective fills two characteristic slots, one between a determiner and a following noun, and the other following a few special verbs (which you probably learned in school to call "linking verbs"). In the first position the adjective is often called an "attributive adjective," in the second a "predicate adjective." The following test frame demonstrates both positions:

> The _____ girl seems _____ .

You will appreciate, of course, that this frame is a *construction,* and that other words of the same class in the same order will not change the construction. Thus:

His _____ dog is a dog that seems very _____ .

We will say that a word that can fill *both* blanks in this construction is an adjective.

In terms of traditional grammar we get some "odd" results this way, but you will remember our earlier observation: if we establish criteria we must either accept the results or change the criteria. There is no honest alternative. Besides, if we don't come out with the same results as traditional school grammar, we won't necessarily wind up in Leavenworth. As we compare what we produce with what school grammar has produced we will not be asking ourselves which is "true," but which is neater, more systematic, and more convenient. Let's look briefly at some of the results of using the frame we have just established. Let's try it on the words "beautiful" and "telephone." (Even before seeing these words in the frame you might be saying to yourself that that's an odd pair to choose, and if so you are helping establish the validity of our frame right off the bat.)

1. A beautiful girl is a girl who is very beautiful.
2. *A telephone girl is a girl who is very telephone.

Obviously the first one is permissible in English, the second one is not. Therefore, "beautiful" is an adjective and "telephone" is not, in spite of the fact that in "a telephone girl" *telephone* clearly modifies *girl.* The necessary conclusion, then, is that we are saying that a word that modifies a noun is *not* necessarily an adjective. Now, what we might want to call "telephone" in that situation is another problem but, if we are going to stick with our test frame it cannot be an adjective because it won't fit.

What a word like "telephone" in this slot is most usually called is an "attributive noun" because it's in the "attributive adjective" position between determiner and noun, and seems to be a noun in all respects other than its position. Different people have different names for it, but the label doesn't matter much and "attributive noun" seems as good as any. At least it's descriptive, if you remember what "attributive" means, the slot between D and N. So we have a noun modifying another noun, "telephone" modifying "girl." Let us remember to note, as we continue our consideration of the adjective, whether we are merely splitting hairs or whether the adjective and what we are going to call the attributive noun really do act in different ways.

Interestingly, if we use both of these modifiers together, both modifying "girl," they occur in a rigidly fixed order: the adjective comes first and then the attributive noun, and it has to be this way. Thus we can say "She's a beautiful telephone girl" but we cannot say *"She's a telephone beautiful girl." It always works like that. For illustration, let's try another couple of pairs:

> A good driver is a driver who is very good.
>
> *A taxi driver is a driver who is very taxi.

"Taxi" would seem to be another attributive noun, wouldn't it? If we put the two modifiers together in the same phrase we can have "He's a good taxi driver" but not *"He's a taxi good driver."

> A white house is a house that is very white.
>
> *A beach house is a house that is very beach.

Again: "A white beach house" but not *"A beach white house." (Note that the President of the United States could have, if he wanted, "a beach White House," but then the stress pattern on /hwayt haws/ changes so that it is no longer an adjective modifying a noun but a compound noun which is being modified by the attributive noun "beach." That is, a /hawyt háws/ is one thing but the /hwáyt hâws/ is something else again.)

Inflections

The most characteristic adjective inflections are {-er} (which should, no doubt, have a sub-number to distinguish it from the noun derivational suffix as in *farmer*), and {-est}, as in *sweet, sweeter, sweetest*. These are of course the traditional "comparative" and "superlative." Though it is characteristic of adjectives that they can be thus "compared," many of them do not take {-er} and {-est} but instead use "more" and "most," as in "more beautiful" and "most beautiful." Though the "more and "most" work exactly like {er} and {-est} in the effect they have on the sentence, and though you often find the two kinds of comparatives alternated (as when people say "more sad" and "most sad" instead of "sadder" and "saddest"), it would probably be stretching things a bit to try to call "more" and "most" inflections, so we will instead list them under function words, simply observing that they parallel {-er} and {-est}. Let's consider them so noted.

Derivational Suffixes

There are a number of derivational suffixes which serve to help us mark out the adjective. In fact, they are so common that they help mark off two classes of adjectives, the so-called "base" and "derived" (from "derivational" suffix) adjectives. Generally speaking, the base adjectives are one-syllable, rock-bottom, hard-core adjectives: *sad, sweet, dumb, weird, poor,* and so on. (Not all of them are of one syllable, just most of them: *pretty, happy, clever.* None of them are of more than two syllables, unless they tack on a prefix: *unhappy.*) *Derived* adjectives, on the other hand, are made-up by adding affixes to other stems. There are many of these, so many that most adjectives are derived. *Gusty* ({-y} added to "gust"); *reputable* ({-able} added to "repute"; *wishful* ({-ful} added to "wish"); *traditional* ({-al} added to "tradition"); and many others too numerous to list here. You know them all anyhow, and I wouldn't expect you to memorize a list of them—but I *do* want you to get the idea. There are a couple of others, though, that you need to look at. These are {-ing$_3$} added to verbs, and {-D$_3$} also added to verbs. These might quite easily be confused with the verb inflections if it were not for our test frame. Thus we can say:

An interesting girl is a girl who is very interesting.

but not

*A marching soldier is very marching.

So with the {-D$_3$} suffix. We can say

The hated woman was very hated.

(though many would vastly prefer . . . "was very much hated"), but we cannot, in English idiom, say

*The drowned woman was very drowned.

So we do seem to have to differentiate {-D$_3$} from the verb inflections {-D$_1$} (past tense) and {-D$_2$} (past participle).

Function Words

We have already seen that "more" and "most," as comparatives, serve to mark off adjectives, though as always we must be cautious and we cannot assume that any time we see one of these words the following word will be an adjective:

I want more potatoes, please.

I want the most ice cream, mommy, please.

However, it is in truth easy enough to tell when these words are being used as comparatives and superlatives, and when they are marking out nouns.

Another kind of function word that appears with the adjective is generally called the "intensifier" from the fact that it seems to "intensify" the meaning of the adjective. Thus we can not only say "she's beautiful" but

> she's very beautiful
> she's quite beautiful
> she's rather beautiful
> she's damn beautiful

and so on. One thing we must be careful of is that nearly all, if not all, intensifiers will also go with certain adverbs, so that they are useless in distinguishing our adjective class from the adverb class. But at least the intensifier won't go with a noun or a verb,[3] so when we find that an intensifier will fit we know we're not dealing with a word from one of those classes. You might have noticed that we thought to include an intensifier in our test-frame sentence for the adjective:

> A beautiful girl is a girl who is *very* beautiful.

When we try an attributive noun instead of an adjective (*"A deep-sea diver is a diver who is very deep-sea") at least part of the un-English result is caused by the intensifier, *very*.

This, too, helps convince us of the reality of the distinction between attributive nouns and adjectives. The adjective will accept an intensifier; the noun won't.

There are others of these intensifiers besides those listed here, but they are perfectly familiar to you, so we'll not list them. We do need note, though, that adverbs will also fit into the slot where these intensifiers regularly go, as in the preceding sentence where I said "they are perfectly familiar . . . " That could as easily have been "they are very familiar . . . ," but it wasn't. The adverb in this slot, fortunately, is usually marked with a characteristic adverb inflection ($\{$-ly$_1\}$) so it is not likely to be confused with the intensifier. Note

---

3. Note that the *very* in a pattern like "That's the very girl I was talking about" is not the intensifier. (Remember back on p. 88 we discussed different words that happen to sound alike?) We would not say that one person is a girl and another is a very girl. Thus, that the *very* which on occasion appears before the noun is not the intensifier is demonstrable by varying the pattern slightly. However, should you insist that the differentiation between what we might call *very*$_1$ and *very*$_2$ verges perilously close to depending upon shades of meaning, I would have to agree with you.

that though the adverb shares *this* slot with the intensifier, it will fill others which the intensifier can't, so we do want to differentiate it.

Stress

The attributive adjective has a characteristic stress pattern which sets it off from the attributive noun. Thus you are quite likely to say:

He's a splêndid mánăgèr.

but you will also say:

He's a básebàll mânăgĕr.

You will say "She's a swêet gírl," but "She's a bár gìrl." This is an intricate little pattern which you have known and used all your life, but probably never consciously thought about before. It seems to me more than anything else to demonstrate the reality of the distinction between the adjective and the attributive noun: we don't even pronounce them alike in our daily speech.

It is true, of course, that in the example sentence just above you could, if you wanted to emphasize the girl's sweetness, put the stress on the adjective: "She's a swéet gìrl!" But observe that you still couldn't say: "She's a bàr gírl." If you did you would sound foreign, for the simple reason that speakers of other languages have a terrible time learning to hear and make these very subtle stress shifts that you and I make all the time as a matter of course.

Here's another pair that someone dreamed up to demonstrate this shift in stress that distinguishes the attributive noun from the adjective:

That's an àntîque váse.
He's an àntíque dêalĕr.

If we said

He's an àntîque déaler

we might be talking about a card table man at Las Vegas who had grown old and grey in his profession.

While we're discussing this business of distinguishing the attributive noun from the adjective let's go on to note one other fact of possibly some interest. This might at first seem to verge perilously close to using meaning as a yardstick, but we'll avert that danger at the last moment by showing how essentially it's a matter of patterning. The adjective seems to designate some quality inherent in the noun it's modifying. Thus in "the white house" the whiteness is a quality in the house itself; in "the big man" bigness is in the man; and in "the beautiful girl" the beauty is in the girl. However, the attributive noun seems to show how the word being modified is related to something *outside* itself. Thus "the dog trainer" doesn't possess "dogness" but is somehow related to dogs; "the beach house" isn't filled with "beachness" but has some connection with the beach. As we pursue this further, and try to get away from the semantic implications, we see that always the attributive noun is used as a kind of short way of expressing an idea that could "normally" be expected to be put in a phrase. A "radio station" is a station for transmitting radio broadcasts; a "camel driver" is a man who drives camels; a "telephone girl" is a girl who answers telephones; and a "table radio" is a radio that is set on tables. An adjective is not, like this, a shorthand way of saying a phrase. (Observe how the attributive noun often pluralizes when put into the phrase construction.)

This use of the attributive noun, by the way, is a comparatively modern trend. You will find many more such nouns in modern writing than you will in Shakespeare. We use them routinely, normally, as a compact way of saying something. Because they are so compact they are beloved of headline writers, who would never think of writing "a talk on the television" when they could write "a television talk"—or, more likely, "a TV talk." This sometimes leads to confusion, when we are not able to see clearly and immediately the underlying phrase construction. For instances, the headline quoted back on page 119:

VISITING CAMEL DRIVER
SHOWS ANIMAL COMPASSION

Here is a momentary confusion over whether it's compassion *to* an animal or compassion *like* an animal, and since either is a clear possibility, ambiguity results.

Another of the headlines on the same page is now more clearly explainable:

JONES WILL FIGHT
HINGES ON BABY

We see now that "will" is an attributive noun, and that the underlying phrase is "the fight over Jones's will." But since "will" is also a common verb marker, and since "hinges" could just as easily be a plural noun as a verb with $\{-Z_3\}$, great confusion results. A funny thing I've noticed: if you get started wrong on reading one of these

ambiguous things it's sometimes almost impossible to make yourself
see the intended meaning.

As for the difference between the attributive noun and the adjective, we have noted the following:

1. The adjective will fit into both adjective slots in the test
    frame, but the noun won't.
2. The adjective will take an intensifier but the noun won't.
3. The adjective will "compare," but the noun won't.
4. The adjective and the noun have different stress patterns.
5. The noun is related to a phrase construction, but the ad-
    jective isn't.

All of these things seem not only true but readily demonstrable—
and if you have been testing them out on your own knowledge of
English as we've gone along, I hope you will agree. Now, doesn't it
seem to you that any grammar with any pretensions to accuracy and
completeness would note such an obvious, such a real, difference?
Yet school grammar completely ignores it. In the school grammars
with which I am familiar, "the faithful herder" and "the sheep
herder" are the same construction. Well, they aren't. It makes no
difference what you decide to call "sheep," attributive noun or whatever: but the difference between the two constructions certainly
would seem demanding of notice, at least.

Adverbs

The adverb is a considerably tougher nut to crack than the three
form classes we have dealt with so far, and as a consequence grammarians, including linguists, have done a much less satisfactory job
with it. The reason is that the various "sub-classes" of adverbs frequently act so much unlike each other that it is hard to see why
anyone would want to put them in the same class. There is a strong
temptation to remark that the adverb has been less happily treated
than any other of the "parts of speech" and let it go at that. However, we owe it to ourselves at least to take a look at what recent
efforts at classifying this form class have been like, for the fact that
the problem is difficult doesn't make it any less real. We can see after
considering the three major classes we've already examined that there
clearly does seem to be another large class of words undescribed, and
effort needs to be made to create some sort of description of them.

Perhaps the easiest approach would be the one actually used by
many schoolchildren. I did it myself. It's a simple process of subtrac-

tion. Your teacher has given you the task of identifying the parts of speech in an involved sentence. What you do is identify everything you can: nouns, verbs, adjectives, prepositions, conjunctions, etc.—and every word that you simply can't otherwise account for you hopefully label "adverb." This often produces pretty good results, but it doesn't cut the mustard as a definition.

One thing we are not going to do is follow the traditional definition: an adverb is a word that modifies a verb, an adjective, or another adverb. This leads us to such a motley array of words, some of which function like others and have similar forms, and others which neither work alike nor are formed similarly, that it is practically useless. Further, many times words which in most circumstances seem to be adverbs will be found modifying nouns, as in "the weather *outside* was cold." "Outside" won't pass our adjective tests. So what is wrong with saying that it's an adverb modifying a noun? Nothing is wrong with it, of course. Of more relevance is the consideration whether it's going to help us establish and (try to) define the class of words we will call the adverb. That's another question, and a harder and mooter one.

One of the most satisfactory ways of trying to identify this slippery customer, the adverb, is with a test frame or frames. A very useful frame is a construction with subject-verb-indirect object-direct object-slot. Here is one:

The sharp character told me his lie _____.

We can put quite a few different kinds of words in this slot: *again, twice, there, anyhow, outdoors, eagerly, convincingly, abroad, yesterday, backwards, crook-wise, upstairs,* etc. Even though there are discernible differences among these words, we can—and will—say that they are all adverbs because they fill that particular slot. Further, we will say that any word that will fit that slot is an adverb. This, then, is a test frame.

Unfortunately, this doesn't always help us to pin the label "adverb" on a given word, because as we have seen, words in English have a tendency to shift from one form class to another. That is, the adverb in *this slot* may be defined, but how about when it occurs somewhere else in the sentence? Can we as easily identify it? This is a particular problem with the adverb because it occupies so many different positions in the sentence that one English grammarian simply called it "the movable." When, therefore, a word that will easily fill our test slot pops up somewhere else in the sentence we might want to call it an adverb and we might not. Thus:

He sold it to me *yesterday.* (adv.)
. . . all our *yesterdays* have lighted fools the
way to dusty death. (noun)
Her hair *yesterday* became brunette. (adv.)

There are other slots which are generally considered to be occupied only by adverbs. One such occurs in the midst of a cluster formed by a verb and its markers or auxiliaries:

He could have done it.
He could *easily* have done it.
He could have *easily* done it.

Another characteristically adverbial position is between a noun (pronoun) or a verb and a following preposition:

The nice girl *there* in the convertible . . .
He ate *upstairs* in the mornings.

Still another slot is between the whole subject and the verb, as in:

His griping in the morning *almost* made me sick.[4]

Something of the extreme mobility of the adverb is indicated by the following, clipped from the Fort Stockton (Texas) *Pioneer:*

Why things get a little confusing around the office sometimes: Some guy has discovered a sentence that can have eight different meanings by placing the word "only" in all possible positions in it: "I hit him in the eye yesterday." Try it.

(A question for you: Is *only* an "adverb" in all the slots?)

We could do worse than follow the lead of some who have made this very kind of mobility one of the tests for adverbs. Certainly the other form classes are much more rigidly positioned in patterns.

Fortunately, the class we are seeking to establish is often marked by certain derivational suffixes, the most common of which, by far, is the bound morpheme $\{-ly_1\}$. In English class we always greeted this with a sigh of relief, for we knew all words ending in "ly" were adverbs—and we occasionally get shot down by finding out that there is a handful of adjectives that end in "ly" too. The difference is that

---

4. For an interesting discussion of adverb positions, though with somewhat different terminology from what we are using, see Brown, Brown and Bailey, *Form in Modern English,* Oxford University Press, pp. 110 ff. Be careful to note, though, that they include among the adverbs the class of function words we have been calling "intensifiers."

the {-ly$_1$} which marks the adverb is attached, most often, to derived adjectives to convert them into adverbs, like *angrily, conditionally, laughably, derisively, beautifully, wickedly, expeditiously,* and *ordinarily,* from *angry, conditional, laughable, derisive, beautiful, wicked, expeditious* and *ordinary* "respectively." These are representative only. There are others.

Most derived adjectives can thus be converted into adverbs. Also, many base adjectives can accept this suffix: *sweetly, prettily, sadly,* and so on. If we identify these words as adjectives first, through other tests, then we can be pretty sure that when we add {-ly$_1$} we have adverbs. What we have to look out for is {-ly$_2$}, which is added to some nouns to form adjectives, such as *queenly, friendly, brotherly,* and some others. (There are also a few adjectives that will add "ly" and remain adjectives, such as *goodly.* One can only note them and despair.)

A derivational suffix which marks adverbs, and which has popularity in certain circles today, is {-wise}. "Today is a scorcher, not so much temperature-wise as humidity-wise." Many people with "a feeling for the purity of the language" find this suffix particularly hateful, but, alas, such people are not always heeded. Anyhow there are a few common vocabulary items which use this morpheme, as "He sawed it in two *lengthwise.*"

Another suffix that marks adverbs is {-ward}, or, more surely, {-wards}. *Backward, inward, outward, upward, downward, heavenward.* Without the final /-z/ these words are often adjectives, but they are easily told from the adverb on other grounds, such as position. Example:

> He suffered an inward agony. (Adj.)
> His examination then turned inward. (Adv.)

There is also one prefix which helps distinguish a few adverbs: {a-}. This is seen in words like: *aground, afoot, apart, astir.*

There are a few other affixes which mark some adverbs, but we need not list them here. More important, perhaps, is to note that there are also adverbs which, like some cops in patrol cars, go about unmarked. We call them adverbs because they are always turning up in adverb slots, such as those in our original test frame: *there, anyhow, outdoors, yesterday, upstairs.* These are adverbs by courtesy of their consistent patterning in adverb positions.

As for function words which mark adverbs, we have already seen, in our discussion of the adjective, that the intensifiers work with certain adverbs as well as with the adjective. They are not thus much help in differentiating the two classes, though they certainly do serve to distinguish them from nouns and verbs.

Adverbs do, generally speaking, sort themselves into three large groups which correspond to the traditional categories of adverbs of place, adverbs of manner, and adverbs of time. However, in arriving at these types the linguist operates in a different fashion from the traditionalist, for the traditionalist looks at the word, asks himself what it means, and then proceeds to pigeonhole it accordingly. The linguist, wanting to deal with meaning only as little as possible sets about the problem differently, by determining which of three key adverbs (*there, thus, then*) will substitute for the word in question without fundamentally changing what the sentence says. (This of course skirts perilously close to asking about meaning, but to be technical we can ask our old friend and informant, the native speaker, whether after the substitution has been made the sentence is approximately the "same" as before or whether it's radically "different." This is all we care about, and not really what it "means." Is this fudging?) For example:

He ate it *outside.* (*There* substitutes, so we have an adverb of place.)

He ate it *greedily.* (*Thus* substitutes, so we have an adverb of manner.)

He ate it *yesterday.* (*Then* substitutes, and we have an adverb of time.)

An alternate way of arriving at the same result is with three key question words: *where, how,* and *when.* Thus in the example above we might ask of *outside,* does it answer the question *how? when?* No, it answers the question *where,* so we have an adverb of place. If it answered *how,* of course, we would have an adverb of manner, and if *when,* one of time.

Oddly enough, several things indicate that these three kinds of adverbs are not just a grammarian's nitpicking but honestly do seem to reflect a reality in the language. For one, if we use three adverbs together, to modify the same word, they will most likely occur in the order *place, manner, time.* (One does *not* say of adverbs that they must appear in certain slots or in certain orders, for as we have already seen the adverb is slippery. However, we can say that this order is "most likely.")

Nor do we use two adverbs of the same type to modify the same word unless we connect them with *and* or *but* or some word of that sort. We would not say *"He ate it slowly greedily," though "slowly but greedily" would be all right. Even the adverb, then, flexible as it is, has certain limits to the way it can pattern.

We have looked, very broadly and more than a little superficially, at the direction of some of today's efforts at trying to describe the four major form classes. As we observed at the outset, most linguists today are willing to concede that these four huge form classes probably cannot be satisfactorily defined. The effort therefore is not to create a precise definition, but rather to list "characteristics" of the form classes which, while certainly not airtight, are nevertheless generally usable and workable. If we wind up unable to confidently pin a label on every word in every sentence anyone can produce, we still can feel that all is not necessarily lost. We are playing percentages, and if we can set up logical categories that work most of the time, even nearly all the time, we can feel that we have accomplished a lot. And at least what we have established will be demonstrable. It will not have to rely on the trickiness of trying to show that a color is a "quality" and therefore must be a "thing." This is to live in a world of make-believe.

Some of the troubles that we get into, as we try to apply the criteria sketchily outlined above for sorting words into classes, spring from the fact that these broad, open form classes are not comprised of words that always operate exactly like each other. We find that they have what we might most easily call "sub-classes." By way of illustration, and without trying to solve anything, let's look at a few of them.

Consider the difference between "water" and "book" in the way they function as nouns. You can say:

> I'd like a little more water, please.

or

> I'd like a few more books, please.

But not:

> *I'd like a few more water, please.

or

> *I'd like a little more books, please.

You have *a few* of some nouns and *a little* of others. Which would you use with *sugar, ink, coffee, sand, steel, beer, coal, gasoline?* Which with *coin, hat, rug, pencil, fan, typewriter, gun?* Which group patterns with "I don't want so much _____"? Which with "I don't want so many _____"? Is there a real and demonstrable difference in these kinds of nouns? Obviously. Yet, like some other differences, it is one that nearly all school grammars ignore.

Linguists call nouns of the "book" type "count nouns" or "countable nouns," indicating that generally they refer to things that are countable. The others, nouns of the "water" group, are referred to as "mass nouns," or often "non-count nouns" to indicate that they refer to "uncountable" items. (Like so many things in language analysis, this is a bit of a fiction, for quite often the things designated by a mass noun really *are* countable. This is some more of the arbitrariness of language, that's all. And mass and count nouns vary from one language to another, like so many other things.)

The mass nouns don't ordinarily have plurals, one of the hallmarks of the noun. We don't ordinarily say "I'd like some more waters, please." But observe that we *can* pluralize these nouns, and sometimes do. When we do we change their meanings somewhat, though. Look at these:

I need three more waters. (Waitress setting a table. She means, of course, glasses of water.)

They have very good sugars. (You might be referring to a company that sells different types of sugar, and you mean all of them.)

Blank Co. sells very fine steels.

And so on. Already we see that some of the general statements we made about nouns are perhaps not true of all nouns.

Here is another kind of noun. We said that nouns take determiners and that in fact the determiner is the principal marker of the noun. Yet some don't. How about *Charlie? Mr. James? New York?* We call them "proper nouns," of course, and we have to note that in several ways they are special. Perhaps we could set them off as a sub-class of nouns which do not ordinarily take determiners. They can, as in "I met your Mr. James yesterday." And consider these:

He sailed on the *Texas.*

He stayed at the *Pennsylvania.*

This particular kind of noun not only has to take a determiner, but it never takes any other one than "the." Some linguists try to regularize this kind of proper noun by insisting that the "the" is part of the noun itself and not a determiner. There is certainly nothing to prevent a man from classifying these nouns in this way, and it might make for an easier description of the noun. At least it would prevent one sub-sub-class of a sub-class of nouns.

Then there is the pronoun. Many scholars—I think most—prefer to think of the pronoun as a sub-class of nouns. Morphologically (that is, in its shape) there appears to be little reason for this, for pronouns don't look like nouns and they don't act like them, except for certain features of patterning. "We" is not the plural of "I" in the same sense that "books" is of "book" clearly. It does not mean "more than one *I*." Nor is "hers" made out of "she" in the way "Gwendolyn's" is made out of "Gwendolyn." Nor, again, do pronouns regularly pattern with determiners.

On the other hand, they do regularly pattern in noun slots, and many linguists obviously feel that this is a powerful enough characteristic to justify calling pronouns a sub-class of nouns. A word of caution here: remember that some pronouns have *homophones* (other words that sound exactly the same) that are noun determiners. Which is which can easily be told from the position in the pattern. For example:

Henry stole her purse. (determiner, patterning like "the")

Henry stole her. (pronoun, patterning like "Heloise")

Verbs, too, are not all alike. Here is a pair, for instance, which show a considerable difference:

Virgil became a man.

Virgil killed a man.

In the second of these, "Virgil" and the "man" are different people. In the first, "Virgil" and the "man" are the same. "Become" has the power of making the noun in front of it and the noun following it refer to the same thing in this fashion. There are not many verbs that can do this. These are the so-called "linking verbs." If a verb can pull this little stunt it's a linking verb.

"Killed," on the other hand, has a noun following it with a different "referent" (the thing a noun refers to) from the noun in front of it. Further, the "Virgil killed a man" construction can be changed into this construction: "A man was killed by Virgil." (This is of course the"passive.") These two possibilities determine what is called the "transitive" verb.

Contrast this one: "Allen died." There's no noun following it. Allen didn't die anyone, for instance. Nor would we say that someone or something was died by Allen. Thus "died" has nothing following it and it can't be made into a passive construction. This characterizes that we call the "intransitive" verb. (It is risky to say that any verb—or any word, for that matter—is *always* something or other.

For instance, we could say "Allen died a horrible death," and then "died" is transitive.)

These are the three principal kinds of verbs. Though there are others, we'll not look at them right now but defer that until we consider *syntax,* or how words operate together in larger constructions.

For the time being the main point is that separating words into word classes is by no means easy. If all nouns (or verbs or adjectives or adverbs) invariably operated in the same way and were even marked all with the same affixes (as they are in some of the *synthetic,* or "made-up" languages like Esperanto) there would be no problem at all, but in real languages it's a very complex matter. What we have been doing is looking at some of the complexities. This is a far, far different thing from providing solutions.

Now we need to spend a little time considering those plain, unglamorous, but absolutely indispensable items in English: the function words. You already have a good idea of what function words are, and how they differ from the major form classes. Fries (in *The Structure of English,* Chap. VI) lists fifteen kinds of them, designating them by letter names: Group A, Group B, Group C, and so on. We'll not look at all of them, nor even list them, but will instead discuss briefly some of the more conspicuous types. Also, we will not use the letter names. What Fries calls "Group A," that is, we will continue to call determiners.

Some of the groups (or classes or "families") of function words are relatively large; others are so small they have in them only *one word.* (You will recall that all the function words taken together are an insignificant percentage of the total words in the language, but that their frequency is tremendous.) Consider "there" in "There is a man in the house." No other word patterns like this one. It is literally unique. It isn't the same word as "there" in "She stayed there three weeks," because we can say "There is a man here" and if the "there" meant the same as the "there" in pointing, the statement would be ridiculous. All that the "there" we're talking about does is introduce one familiar sentence pattern in which subject and verb are reversed. Instead of "A man is in the house" we reverse them: "There is a man in the house." Also the function word "there," unlike the adverb, is always unstressed.

If some function word classes are small, others are large. There may be seventy or so of the function words we call "prepositions." Their principal function is to relate a word, usually a noun, to another word or words in the construction

Thus:

The girl_____the yellow convertible smiled at me.

What sort of word would fill this slot? Words like *in, on, with, near, under, by*. Prepositions. Some prepositions, like separable verbs, are written as two or even three words. In the slot above, we could put such things as "in front of," for example. It would seem easiest simply to label this a preposition and note that it's made up of three words. If this offends your sense of propriety you could work out some other name for it. But you can't throw it out of the language.

In this preposition test frame we could fill the blank with something like *who was driving*, or simply *driving*. Does this mean that *who was driving*, or *driving* is a preposition? No. Clearly *was driving* is recognizable as a verb, and *who* doesn't pattern with *in, on, at*, and the others we've listed. What does it mean then? It simply means that we haven't devised a very good test frame and need to make a better one. Doesn't this imply that we already have in the back of our minds a list of prepositions and that we want to devise a frame that will let them in and keep other words out? I hope not. If so, we are wasting our time. But we do want a test frame that will exclude something like *who was driving*, which is clearly demonstrable to be something other than the class we're trying to establish. Perhaps we should, as Fries does, use more blanks. Here are his test sentences:

> The concerts *at* the school are *at* the top.
> The dress *at* the end is dirty *at* the bottom.

And he says that prepositions (though he doesn't use the label) are the words that can stand in those various positions.

Admittedly this quick sketch does not delineate the preposition very satisfactorily, but remember that we are not trying actually to do that difficult job but rather to observe the direction modern efforts are taking. The "test frame" approach is one of the principal methods. Clearly the trick is to tinker with possible test frames until one is devised which produces satisfactory results. We could say that the frames are satisfactory when they produce a group of words that function consistently like each other. Clearly my test frame doesn't do this, and neither, I think, does that of Fries.

Conjunctions are another kind of function word. Generally, they're words that pattern like *and*. The usual ones are *and, but, or, nor, yet, not*. They are often called "co-ordinating conjunctions" because they serve to connect equal elements in a construction, but we can get away with calling them simply conjunctions, having junked a couple of other terms from which they ordinarily need to be distinguished. The words in this list nearly always serve as conjunctions, and other words hardly ever do. Even so, the situation is not one that will permit us simply to use a list as a definition, saying that *these and no others* are what we mean by "a conjunction," for the fact is that there are occasionally others. So the easiest thing to do is stick with "words that pattern like *and.*"

There are two more kinds of function words whose primary function is to make connections between other items in the construction: these are the subordinators and the sentence connectors. Loosely, but usefully, we can say that subordinators are words like *because, who, which* in these patterns:

> I was late *because* I overslept.
> He's the one *who* is my friend.
> The jalopy *which* I owned was a real headache.

You'll notice that the function of these words is to take what would ordinarily be an independent utterance—"I overslept." "He is my friend." "The jalopy I owned."—and subordinate them to another construction. Hence the name, subordinators. Some of them simply hook two structures together by being added (like "because" in the example sentence). Others function by replacing an element of the subordinated construction, as "who" replaces "he" in "He is my friend." Sometimes the subordinator can actually be omitted, and then what holds the whole construction together is word order, as well as familiarity with the pattern that does include the subordinator. Thus, more normal in speech than the example given above would be:

> The jalopy I owned was a real headache.

(Tip: more often than not when you can't decide between "who" and "whom" as subordinators you can resolve the problem by just omitting them.) Sentence connectors are words that pattern like

Sentence connectors are words that pattern like *therefore* and *moreover* and *however.*

> We were late; however, dinner was still hot.
> We were late; therefore, dinner had been thrown out.
> We were late for class; moreover, we were denied admission.

There are some interesting differences in the way conjunctions, subordinators and sentence connectors pattern. For instance, the sentence connector is moveable within the second element: it can occur at the beginning, as in the examples just given, or in the middle or at the end:

>We were late; dinner, however, was still hot.
>
>We were late; dinner was still hot, however.

The conjunction won't do this. It will go at the beginning of the second element:

>We were late, but dinner was still hot.

but not in the middle nor at the end:

>*We were late, dinner was still hot but.
>
>*We were late, dinner but was still hot.

The position at the beginning of the second element is shared by the sentence connector and the conjunction. Because *however* occurs in this position so frequently, and because it means more or less the same as *but,* students frequently punctuate it with a comma, as they would do with *but,* and they cause their teachers to requisition red pencils by the gross in order to put angry red circles around the resultant "comma splices" (or "comma faults" or "comma blunders").

The subordinator patterns differently still. It too can go in the middle:

>I was late because I overslept.

But unlike either of the other two it can go on the front of the whole shebang:

>Because I overslept I was late.

(Note: this is *not* to say that conjunctions cannot begin sentences. They often do. But they can't begin a sentence that doesn't refer back to a preceding one. And that's obvious, I suppose.)

Still another function word is the one often called the "question word"—*what, why, when, how*. These words are most often used to introduce "information questions" and serve as a signal to the listener that a question is coming.

There are other function words that are important—all function words are important, really, for they serve to make the language hang together—but we observed at the outset that we weren't going to try to discuss, or even list, all of them. Anyhow, by this time you surely have the general idea.

There is just one other little matter involving this business of labeling that we need to devote a few paragraphs' attention to and then we'll have done with it. The following sentence will serve us as an introduction to the problem:

The poor are always with us.

What form class is *poor*? Would it surprise you to learn that many linguists call it an adjective? But, gasps the outraged schoolmarm, *it's serving as the subject of the sentence*!!! Indeed it is. So what the linguist is suggesting is that there's no reason you can't have an adjective as the subject of a sentence. Or, for that matter, a verb. As for *poor* in the example sentence, it can take adjective inflection ("The poorest have already gone"). On the other hand, it surely doesn't act like a noun. So we might most reasonably call it an adjective.

What is being introduced here is that there is a difference between form and function, and that we need to keep that difference in mind. We not only have noun, verb, adjective, and adverb but we have subject, predicate, complement, object, and so on. They are not the same. To say "subject" is not to say "noun."

It is, however, true that the subjects of most sentences are nouns, and that the noun occurs in this position with such regularity that we have a feeling that the subject position is a "noun slot." Perhaps we need a name for the words that can fill the various slots usually occupied by nouns. Such words could be called *nominals*.[5] A nominal, then, is any word occupying what is characteristically a noun position. Thus *poor* in our example sentence is a nominal at the same time it remains an adjective. This seems to me a neat way around the problem posed by words which are clearly of one form class but which occupy positions in a construction usually reserved for words of another form class.

This system has, as you are perhaps expecting, not only nominals, but *adjectivals* (words or phrases occupying slots usually filled by adjectives), *adverbials* (words or constructions filling adverb slots), and *verbals* (words or larger units filling positions characteristically filled by verbs).

As the repeated *words or constructions, words or larger units,* implies, these *-als* are not restricted to single words. Thus the subject of the following sentence is a nominal:

---

5. For a full and intriguing presentation of this appraoch see James Sledd, *A Short Introduction to English Grammar,* Scott Foresman, 1959. Or the forthcoming *An Introduction to English Linguistics for the Teacher of English* by Rudolph Troike.

That the idiot was going to break his neck became apparent.

But, you might object, isn't all this simply a matter of creating and applying more labels? It is, of course. At the same time it's a way of describing neatly the manner in which words clearly belonging to one form class, and which we are quite content to have in that form class, occasionally will pop up in a situation where we would expect a word of another class. But, you might urge: isn't it only some kind of device? A gimmick?

Let me remind you once more. Speakers of English have for a long time been saying things like "The poor are always with us," and presumably will go on saying such things for a long time to come. That is reality. All the grammarian, or the linguist, is trying to do is to create some sort of systematic description of that reality. In this very real sense, then, *all* grammatical description is a tissue of devices, of gimmicks. And, you will remember, whether one grammar is to be preferred to another depends simply upon its usefulness.

In this chapter we have not solved any problems involved in classifying words into "parts of speech," to use the old term. But we have looked fleetingly at what some of the problems are, and at what efforts scholars are taking today to solve some of them.

So we'll pass on to a discussion of other matters. We need to take a look at how these words of the various form classes, and the function words which glue them together, work with each other as they go to form larger constructions.

SUGGESTED READING

Fries, Charles. *The Structure of English* (chapters 5-7). New York: Harcourt, Brace & World, 1952.

Gleason, H.A. Jr. *Linguistics and English Grammar* ("Parts of Speech," chapter 6). New York: Holt, Rinehart & Winston, 1965.

Laird, Charlton. *The Miracle of Language* ("The Speech that Blooms on the Tongue, Tra-La, Has Little to do with Case" and "More Leaky Grammars," chapters 11-12). Cleveland: World Publishing Co., 1953. Paperback edition, Fawcett (Premier R271).

CHAPTER 6

SYNTAX I - WORDS IN BUNCHES

Perhaps you will recall the old gag about the girl who upon first hearing of syntax said, "Gosh, are they going to tax *everything*?" Such a tax might not be a bad idea. It could even reduce the incidence of sin, but more likely would come close to wiping out the national debt. Unfortunately this intriguing line of speculation has nothing to do with the syntax we are about to consider, which is defined in Webster III as a "connected system or order: orderly arrangement; harmonious adjustment of parts or elements." A second definition, perhaps more relevant here, is simply: "sentence structure." Words as individual items are pretty helpless; they take on real power only when they are combined into larger constructions. What we are to consider now is how they do this. How are the constructions made? What kinds of them are there? What do they do? First we need to define our area of concern. We aren't here taking on the whole English language but only a particular aspect of it: the sentence and its constituent parts.

It would be a good idea at the outset to try to define what we mean by "the sentence." Like the definitions of some other familiar things, this isn't easy. One of the definitions we were given in school is that "a sentence is a group of words containing a subject and a predicate." The main trouble with this is that it isn't true. Lots of sentences lack one or the other. For instance, if I say to someone, "Shut the window," that is clearly a sentence and equally clearly it has no subject. The usual schoolbook answer to this problem is to say that the subject is "*you* understood," but as a method of procedure this business of imagining things is not satisfactory. We could imagine almost anything. Suppose somebody hollers "FIRE!" What do we imagine?

1. (The building is on) FIRE (and we'd better get out).
2. (Number two turret is ready and you should) FIRE (the guns).
3. ("Did you say *friar*?" "No, I said) FIRE."

This is a great game and could provide a measure of sport (How many contexts can you imagine for "fire"?), but it hardly gets down to grammatical brass tacks. Of course, in real life the situation would determine the meaning the hearer would derive, but the fact that you might be on the rifle team awaiting the signal to start shooting is hardly a *grammatical* fact.

What the traditional definition does is first set up a definition and then warp and twist the facts of the language to make them fit. It would seem preferable to observe the language in action and *then* concoct a definition that would fit the facts. Without "imagining" things—"*you* understood" or anything else—we would have to account for dialogues like the following:

> Claude: "What's doing?"
> Marie: "Nothing much. A little studying."
> Claude: "Tired?"
> Marie: "Some."
> Claude: "Interested in a movie?"
> Marie: "Most emphatically."
> Claude: "Great. The Palace?"

A lot of talk is like this. If these exchanges are not sentences then we'll have to recognize that a great deal of our communication is in something other than sentences. But it might be possible, and make more sense, to create a definition of the sentence that would include the individual utterances in such a dialogue.

Another definition of the sentence that you might remember having run across in school is: "A sentence is a group of words expressing a complete thought." The trouble with this is that it seems to assume that thoughts come like sausages on a string, each neatly separate and observable. What is a "complete thought"? Look at the sentences so far in this paragraph. Are they sentences? I'm sure you will feel they are. Are they complete thoughts? Well, for instance, the second sentence is not understandable without the one that precedes it. And that preceding sentence, beginning "Another definition . . . ," isn't "complete," certainly, unless you know what the definition(s) is (are) that have gone before. Just standing by itself it isn't complete. Perhaps to get the "complete thought" you need the whole chapter, or even the whole book. Most sentences are like this, you'll find. Open any book at random and examine the first sentence you put your finger on. Is it complete, really? I try it with a book on my desk and come up with this:

> Similarly, you may want to illustrate your article by clipping from magazines and newspapers one or more appropriate cartoons.

Can you tell me what that's all about? We would deduce that it's most likely from a book telling someone how to write articles, or at least how to illustrate them. But what about the "similarly"? What does it refer to? In other words, is the sentence a "complete thought"? Obviously it isn't.

Having found fault with the two most common textbook definitions, can we come up with anything better? I think so. Look at this:

> Irma said the dance was a ghastly flop for one thing a lot of the boys drank too much several fights broke out she said she got a headache and went home early.

If this was turned in as part of a composition, any English teacher receiving it would first flip and then reach for the old red pencil, writing angrily in the margin something like "This is not one sentence but four. Why don't you punctuate it as four?"

The question is: How does one know it's four sentences? Does he go through it matching up subjects and predicates to see how many pairs of them he can find? Does he examine it carefully for "complete thoughts"? You know he doesn't, and neither did you when you read it. What he does, and what you did, is read it, listening in the mind's ear to see how it sounds. He determines the sentences by listening for certain intonation features.

Of course with the example given it is impossible to tell exactly where the sentence breaks occur, for there are alternate possibilities. The phrase "for one thing" could go either with the sentence preceding it or the one following; so could the "she said"—and from the cold print there's no way of telling. Suppose we rewrite it indicating some of the features of how the author might have spoken it:

> Irma said the dance was a ghastly flop#for one thing ‖ a lot of the boys drank too much#several fights broke out#she said she got a headache and went home early#

If we could have heard those double-plus junctures we'd have *known* where the sentences ended—and if the author, who certainly heard them, at least in his mind, as he wrote them, had appreciated their significance he would have punctuated them properly and saved himself an angry blast from his instructor.

Here is another example:

Yesterday I went downtown.

Is it a sentence? You might answer that it is, quite properly interpreting the period as representing double-plus juncture. But suppose it doesn't have that juncture. Suppose that instead of falling, the voice holds level, as though you were going to add "to buy some shirts."

^{2}Yesterday I went downtown^2

Now is it a sentence? Clearly not, and yet it has subject and predicate, and it's perhaps as nearly a "complete thought" as the first version. Or maybe it isn't. Perhaps we arrive at a "complete thought" when we use double-plus juncture.

Anyway, we can proceed to define a sentence as a word or group of words ended with double-plus juncture. Or, for a written sentence, a word or group of words ended with a symbol intended to represent double-plus juncture. These would of course most often be: . ? ! This kind of "definition" is not one to which nobody can possibly take exception but at least it's a working one, and it's better than the "subject-predicate" or "complete thought" type.

One thing observable about the sentence is that it's a construction. Even when it's only one word it's a construction, for it is always and inevitably accompanied by an intonation pattern, but we are more interested now in sentences built up of more than one word. The first thing we note is that words combine into constructions, word clusters, and that these then often combine into larger constructions, which in turn combine into still larger constructions until we have the complete sentence. Of course we have sentences of differing degrees of complexity, like:

He died.

and

The wizened little whisky-drinking old man who used to live on the floor above us when we were attending the University of Pennsylvania in Philadelphia died agonizingly of cancer a week ago Wednesday in a down-at-the-heels charity hospital in New York.

There is really no limit to the expansion a sentence can be made to undergo, except the very practical one of how much you think your listener (or reader) can absorb. It is often better to break huge, complicated sentences into bite-size chunks, but there is nothing in grammar that puts a limit on sentence length or complexity. It's a matter of style—and of practical common sense.

What we must note at the moment, though, is that these sentences are not made simply by putting one word after another, like freight cars in a string, but are instead composed of constructions, fitted together in one way or another. We need to consider some of the more common constructions.

Let us stipulate first that the largest units we are going to talk about are sentences, and that the smallest are morphemes. Every construction is made up of contributing parts which we will call *constituents*. Thus for us, a sentence is a construction but never a constituent, and a morpheme, conversely, is a constituent but never a construction. What we are doing is setting limits to what we are going to consider. It is obviously true that sentences are constituents of paragraphs, but we are not going to consider how paragraphs are constructed. The upper limit of our concern right now is the sentence. Similarly, the morpheme is, as we have seen, constructed of phonemes, but we are not now interested in that. The morpheme represents the bottom level of our present interest. So we can say (to repeat) that the morpheme is a constituent but not a construction, and the sentence is a construction but not a constituent. This defines the range of syntax, our immediate concern.

What is a construction? We may come up with a firm definition and we may not, but we do want to understand what it is we're talking about. We observed earlier that we speakers of English somehow feel differently about *the boy* and *boy the* even though *boy the* does occur in English and in that sequence, as in:

I gave a *boy the* tickets.

We say that *the boy* "makes sense," while *boy the* doesn't. The difference is that *the boy* is a construction, and *boy the* is not. In the above example we have two constructions next to each other, *a boy* and *the tickets*. We can thus say that while *boy the* does occur in English it is not a construction but happens only inadvertently, and without significance, at the boundary between constructions. We see too that in the example sentence *a boy* has a grammatical role to play (indirect object), as does *the tickets* (direct object), and since they are constructions perhaps we have found a clue that will help us define what it is we sense when we observe that constructions have a unity about them which is totally lacking in *boy the.*

Let's say, then, that a construction is two or more morphemes which can either function independently or work as a grammatical unit in a larger construction. To simplify things a bit, let's talk about words, though keeping in mind that our smallest constituents of constructions are indeed morphemes. Constructions are very often referred to as "word groups" or "clusters," and we will often use these terms.

So we say that a construction, or cluster, can operate independently or can function as a grammatical unit in a larger construction. An illustration might be useful. "Dogs bark" is a construction, standing independently as a sentence, but in "We heard dogs bark" the same two words are functioning as the complement, a grammatical unit.

Constructions, or clusters, come in two major types: endocentric and exocentric. You can forget those fancy words right now. Simpler terms for these two kinds of clusters, which we will use, are "headed" (for the endocentric) and "non-headed" (for the exocentric). Now we need to understand what these terms mean.

Headed clusters, or word groups, are those in which one word can fulfill the grammatical role of the whole group. The word that can do this is called, appropriately enough, the "headword." For example:

Some beautiful, red American Beauty roses were on the desk.

Some beautiful, red American Beauty roses is a cluster, functioning as subject, and *roses* is the headword. *Roses* can take the place, grammatically, of the whole cluster:

Roses were on the desk.

Of course *roses* doesn't say everything that the whole cluster does, and we're not insisting on that—after all, those other words have their part to contribute too or it would be a wasted effort putting them in the sentence in the first place. But *roses* functions as subject just as well as *some beautiful, red American Beauty roses,* and that's what makes *roses* the headword and makes *some beautiful, red American Beauty roses* a headed cluster.

On the other hand, in a non-headed cluster there is no word that can fill in for the whole cluster. Let's look at this sentence:

Mary saw the cat on the roof.

Mary saw is a cluster and so is *on the roof.* (So is *the cat,* but we'll ignore that for now.) You can't say *Mary* and have it operate like *Mary saw,* nor can you just say *saw* and expect it to take the place of *Mary saw.* Similarly with *on the roof.* There is no word in the group that will fill in grammatically for the whole group. You can't just say *Mary saw the cat on.* Nor *Mary saw the cat the roof.* These, then, are non-headed groups.

There are four principal kinds of headed groups, and only two of non-headed groups. (There are some others, but we're not trying to be exhaustive here.) The four kinds of headed groups turn out to break down into two of one kind and two of another; a nice symmetry to help the memory. We'll look at the kinds of headed clusters first and then at the non-headed.

Headed clusters are named after the form class of the word that serves as headword. Thus the one we were looking at a moment ago, *some beautiful, red American Beauty roses,* is a noun cluster because its headword, *roses,* is a noun. The rest of the cluster, besides the headword, also has a name. It's called the "tail." These tails sometimes precede the headword, as in *some beautiful, red American Beauty roses.* In this case the cluster is described as "tail-head." It's a simple matter of sequence. Sometimes the head comes first and the tail follows. If so, it's a "head-tail" cluster. As it turns out, we have two kinds of tail-head clusters and two kinds of head-tail clusters. They add up to the four kinds of headed groups.

One of the tail-head clusters is the noun cluster, which we just considered. Here are a few more noun clusters:

> *The wonderfully trained cutting horses* were sensational.
> *His old red brick house* crumbled away.
> *That long downhill putt* really boogered me.

These happen to be noun clusters functioning as subjects, but that's irrelevant. They would still be noun clusters were they functioning otherwise:

> We loved *the wonderfully trained cutting horses.*
> He lost *his old red brick house.*
> I was scared of *that long downhill putt.*

The second kind of tail-head cluster is the verb cluster or verb group. This consists of the main verb with all its markers, or auxiliaries, and included adverbs if any. Thus in:

> Mr. Smith should have been busily building houses.

the verb group is the italicized portion, with *build* as the headword and *should have been busily* the tail. It is not important that if we want to use the headword alone, to take the place grammatically of the whole cluster, we may have to alter its form:

Mr. Smith *builds* houses . . .

Obviously as we add or take away auxiliaries the actual form of the base verb has to change, but it is still the same word and in our present frame of reference we count such changes irrelevant. So we have

Mr. Smith *builds* houses.

Mr. Smith *can build* houses.

Mr. Smith *ought to build* houses.

In all of these verb groups the headword is *build* in one disguise or another.

The two types of clusters, or groups, just discussed, then, are the two tail-head kinds of headed groups: the noun cluster and the verb cluster.

The two kinds of head-tail clusters are the verbal cluster and the modifier cluster.

A word of caution is needed as we undertake to describe the "verbal-headed cluster." "Verbal" here is *not* being used in the sense in which we used it in the last chapter, a word of another form class functioning in a slot characteristically occupied by verbs. Rather we use the word now in its traditional sense, a word made from a verb but fulfilling a function more like that of a noun. You may think this is a shifty business, this changing of the meaning of a term, and I must say I agree with you. But it seems to be a sad fact of life among the linguists that we must always be on our toes to see what terms (and symbols) mean, and it is true that from time to time—and especially from book to book—they change. For instance, in our next chapter we will be using the term "auxiliary" in a sense totally different from what it means in this chapter. I think probably no harm is done by this if we cooperate—you to stay alert and I to remember to comment on any shifts in meaning that might occur.

The verbals that will head verbal clusters are almost always either verbs with $\{-ing_2\}$ added (which we've observed makes them nouns, but nouns of a special sub-class we're right now calling "verbals") or with "to" and the base form of the verb. In other words, the infinitive. Here are some examples which, let's hope, will clear the air a bit:

> *Dancing* is good exercise.
> *To play* was all he wanted.
> *Smoking* gave him pleasure.
> *To drive* was his ambition.

These are what we are calling verbals. They very frequently serve as the headwords in verbal clusters, as in the following:

> *Dancing with Elena* is good exercise.
> *To play football on the varsity* was all he wanted.
> *Smoking big black cigars on airplanes* gave him pleasure.
> *To drive racing cars professionally* was his ambition.

Again, as with the noun clusters, the position of these in the sentence makes no difference:

> For good exercise try *dancing with Elena.*
> All he wanted was *to play football on the varsity.*

The modifier cluster, the other kind of head-tail group, has as its headword a modifier, usually, but not inevitably, an adjective.

> The co-eds looked *strange.*
> The accounts *payable* were overdue.
> Our new dorm is *beautiful.*

As headwords of clusters these would shape up like this:

> The co-eds looked *strange as Martians.*
> The accounts *payable to the old skinflint* were overdue.
> Our new dorm is *beautiful beyond belief.*

We have examined, very briefly to be sure, the four kinds of headed groups: 1. The noun cluster (tail-head), 2. the verb cluster (tail-head), 3. the verbal cluster (head-tail), and 4. the modifier cluster (head-tail). We need to take a look at the non-headed groups, of which there are principally two.

The first of these is called the "subject-predicate group" and is exemplified in its simplest form by skimpy sentences like these:

> *Eggs break.*
> *Scholars plagiarize.*
> *Markets crash.*

In none of these could one of the words grammatically fill the place of both, so they are non-headed. We'll refer to them as S-P groups (for "subject-predicate," of course). They need not, naturally, always be as minimal as these three examples. Here's one of them pumped up a little:

> Nearly all distinguished scholars plagiarize from one another under the name of "research."

This is simply a longer S-P group.

The second kind of non-headed group is always introduced by a preposition which often, but not always, relates it to a preceding word or cluster. For this reason they are called "prepositional groups" and are referred to more simply as "P-groups (or clusters)." An example: "I took a bottle *of pills.*" *Of pills* is a P-group, and neither *of* nor *pills* can function grammatically in the place of both.

The clusters we have looked at so far could be displayed, as a memory aid, in a branching diagram like this:

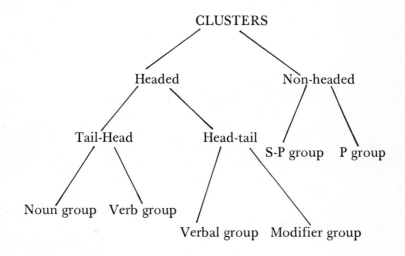

Now that we have that exercise in terminology out of the way, and we understand what these various kinds of clusters are, we come to the payoff: how these clusters work together, fit and fuse together, as we form sentences. Let's take a fairly simple sentence to start with:

> The pretty blonde girl in the choir is a cousin of mine.

The first thing we note is that it's an S-P group, with *the pretty blonde girl in the choir* as one element and *is a cousin of mine* as the other. But *the pretty blonde girl in the choir* is obviously not exactly like *birds* in *birds fly*. It is itself a fairly elaborate construction. If I were to ask you to divide *the pretty blonde girl in the choir* into two parts, two more-or-less logical parts, where would you divide it? Between *girl* and *in,* surely. Thus we find that the "subject" element of the whole sentence (the S-P group) is itself a construction, consisting of *the pretty blonde girl* as one part (or constituent) and *in the choir* as the other. We see immediately that *the pretty blonde girl* is a noun cluster with *girl* as the head and *the pretty blonde* as the tail. Also we see right away that *in the choir* is a P-group, with *in* as the preposition and *the choir* as the rest of it. Clearly, too, *the choir* is a noun cluster, with *choir* as the head and *the* as the tail.

Turning our attention to the "P" of the S-P group (*is a cousin of mine*) we find that it too is a construction. It would seem obviously to have *is* as one element and *a cousin of mine* as the other. And *a cousin of mine* is clearly made up of two clusters: *a cousin* as a noun cluster and *of mine* as a P-group with *of* the preposition and *mine* the rest of it.

Let's look at this kind of grouping in a more elaborate construction:

To act such a fool before an audience comprised of deans would have been a stupidity I couldn't have committed.

Split it into two parts. Where do you divide it? You probably have no hesitation in saying between "deans" and "would," and I would agree. What we have, again, is nothing more than a sizeable S-P group, both elements of which are themselves constructions. Let's look at the "S" element and the "P" element one at a time and see what they're made of. We'll take the "S" part first.

To break the "S" part into two constituents you'd probably select the point between "fool" and "before." The two parts, therefore, are *to act such a fool* as one and *before an audience comprised of deans* as the other.

Looking at *to act such a fool* we see that it is a verbal group with *to act* as headword and *such a fool,* a noun cluster, as tail. (Of course within the noun cluster *fool* is the headword and *such a* is the tail).

The other element, *before an audience comprised of deans,* is a P-group with *before* as the preposition. The rest of it is, as you have already come to expect of what follows a preposition, a noun cluster— but it is more than that. It is a noun cluster with *audience* as the headword, but *audience* itself is being modified by a modifier group with *comprised* as headword and the P-group *of deans* functioning as tail.

Now let's turn our attention for a moment to the "P" element of the original S-P group: *would have been a stupidity I couldn't have committed.* Again I ask you to break the construction into two parts, and again probably (but by no means certainly) we agree that the break would occur at one most logical point: between "been" and "a." If you agree (and please do for the moment), we have two clusters, *would have been* and *a stupidity I couldn't have committed.* *Would have been* is of course a verb cluster with *be* as the headword. The rest of the construction, *a stupidity I couldn't have committed,* is usually called the "complement" (that which completes or rounds out the predicate or "P" half of our S-P group). More to the point right now, however, is that it is a construction. Surely if I were to ask you to break it into two parts you would come up with *a stupidity* as one and *I couldn't have committed* as the other. That is, you would produce *a stupidity,* a noun cluster, as one element and *I couldn't have committed* as the other element. What kind of cluster is *I couldn't have committed?* Without looking at the next line or so of text, see if you can provide the proper label. It's an S-P group, with *I* as one element and a verb cluster, *couldn't have committed,* as the other, with *commit* as headword. The tail in this tail-head group is of course *couldn't have.*

Here is the way the sentence we have just taken apart would look laid out in a sort of graphic representation.

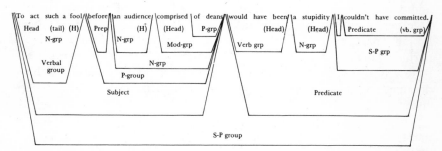

Having studied the "graphic representation" carefully and seen that you understood it all easily enough, you well might at this moment be pretty indignant. "Isn't this," you ask, "just another kind of sentence diagram, only more of a pain than the ones we made in school?" I'm with you. I sympathize. Diagrams never exactly enchanted me either. However this one has a couple of differences. The first is that we're not going to make any more of them—not like this one, anyhow, and not in this book. The second difference I'd like you to prove for yourself. Find some friend, and, without tipping him off to the kind of thing we've been discussing, ask him to read to you, out loud, the sentence we've just been tearing apart. Here: I'll reprint it to make it easy:

To act such a fool before an audience comprised of deans would have been a stupidity I couldn't have committed.

Listen carefully as he reads it (or as she reads it, for that matter). Then ask him to read it again. *Are there not clear intonation boundaries between the clusters we have painfully separated out?* Of course there are. Try it on another friend, and another. Don't push them too hard, though. You don't want the mere pursuit of grammar to leave you friendless. But you'll find it works every time.

And, indeed, why shouldn't it? It's one of the built-in, basic features of our English language. Words issuing forth in sentences do not come one at a time but in clusters, in bunches. We actually talk in these word groups. They are far from some grammarian's imaginings, you see. They're for real.

We begin to see something of how the complexity of English is developed out of a few simple structures. We have an assortment of patterns which we hook up, or embed in each other, and then insert the new construction into still a larger one until we have wheels within wheels within wheels.

We need to notice, too, that we have not dealt here with yet another important group of function words: the conjunctions. These add yet another dimension to the possibilities of putting clusters together. For instance, the rather long S-P group we've just been taking apart ended with the word "committed" followed by a period. There is no reason why "committed" shouldn't have been followed by a comma and then *and*—as in "and I wouldn't have dreamed of doing it in the very worst nightmare I've ever experienced."

Also, headwords can be doubled (or tripled or quadrupled or more), as the following example:

> all the beautiful little girls in the room

can easily become:

> all the beautiful little girls and boys in the room

Or, we could have two clusters:

> all the beautiful little girls and all the handsome big boys in the room . . .

In short, if we were to describe carefully all the types of clusters in English, and if we were to describe also all the mechanics for fitting them together, we would have a pretty fair description of how the language operates. That is, at least we would have pretty well described its syntax.

We're not going to attempt that, you will doubtless be relieved to hear. This is not just a matter of being lazy. It's a big order, so big that no one has adequately done it yet. And what we're interested in here is the principle underlying it. With just the few clusters we've looked at, though, you can create a pretty good variety of fairly elaborate sentences. Adding one more would extend our range greatly: this one is known as the "S-group" after the fact that it is introduced by a subordinator. Here's an example. Let's start with this sentence:

> He was a big slob.

Now let's preface it with a subordinator:

> That he was a big slob

The subordinator has, you might say, destroyed the sentence's independence *as* a sentence. It now needs something to be attached to:

> That he was a big slob was no news to me.

The S-group, which has the subordinator as one element and the rest of it, usually an S-P group, as the other, is still another device we have for fitting clusters together. Oddly enough, the subordinator itself sometimes doesn't have to be present, in which case we rely on word order, and our familiarity with the pattern when it does have the subordinator. An illustration:

> I found out that she was honest and upright.

This would just as likely be:

> I found out she was honest and upright.

Now let's spend a little while considering this business of the syntax of English from a somewhat different, though basically similar, angle. We will talk about what has the formidable label of "Immediate Constituent Analysis," usually referred to by linguists as "IC" analysis. In spite of its imposing name the whole matter turns out to be fairly simple.

I remember some years back watching Leonard Bernstein deliver one of his marvelous TV lectures on music. The subject of the one I'm recalling at the moment was "Rhythm." He said that rhythm in music always comes in two's, and he traced this to the fundamental beat of the human heart: THUMP, thump; THUMP, thump; THUMP,

thump. Always, he said, in two's. So with music: BOOM, boom; BOOM, boom; BOOM, boom. He called this "duple," a word I thought he had invented on analogy with "triple" until I checked it in the dictionary. It means just what you would think, too.

The thought occurred to me that this would not apply to the waltz, and just as this objection was taking shape in my mind, Mr. Bernstein said something like, "You might object that in the waltz the beats come in three's." Presumably he didn't read my mind half way across the continent, so my profound observation turned out to be routine and foreseeable. Indeed he immediately went on to demolish it. If you have something like lah-dee-DAH, in an ascending phrase, he said—with the entire New York Philharmonic illustrating his argument for him—then it must immediately be followed by a balancing phrase, perhaps a descending lah-dee-DAH, and you are right back in the old ONE, two; ONE, two; ONE, two. So he made his point.

I wonder if Mr. Bernstein would be irked to know that as he worked so hard explaining rhythm in music, at least one listener was speculating on how his thoughts would apply to language. I was wondering whether, if Mr. B. is correct, and the rhythm of music really does trace back to something as fundamental as the human heart beat, this might not apply to language also, and perhaps account for the fact that English too is "duple," or as the linguist calls it "binary." It is a fact that in English most things come in pairs. That is, most sentences have two parts. Each part, if it is a construction, will have two constituents, and they in turn will have two, until we get down to the last, or "ultimate" constituents. Of course, to make anything out of the theory that this might be due to something as basic as the heartbeat one would have to show that this "binary" quality, this "dupleness," is true of *all* languages, for no doubt the speakers of Quechua and Tagalog have hearts too.

Anyhow, the nature of English has made possible an analysis of it in terms of what are called "immediate constituents." Right now we need to see how this works.

Let's start with a very simple sentence.

Most puppies will chew slippers.

The "constituents" of this are the parts that it is made of. We could list them:

slippers	puppies
chew	most
will	

(For the sake of simplicity and speed of discussion we're ignoring, for the moment, that some of these words are of more than one morpheme. We're also ignoring intonation patterns.) We might say, then, that we have five components or "constituents" of that sentence. Obviously they all have some relation to each other, or they wouldn't be—couldn't be—functioning together in the same sentence, but the connection between "most" and "slippers," say, is rather hard to state. They are both constituents of the construction but they have no *direct* bearing on each other. On the other hand, now that we have looked at the way words bunch into clusters and the way clusters fit and function together, we can see that there is no need to state how "most" and "slippers" work together. We see that they fit into clusters, each with its role to play, and that then the clusters of which they are parts work together. Further, we can state that a "constituent" need not be a single word but can itself be a cluster. Then we can, and do, say that the constituents that bear directly on each other are the "immediate constituents" of a construction. Thus, what are the immediate constituents of our sample sentence?

Most puppies will chew slippers.

Let's put it this way. If you had to divide it into two parts, where would you most likely make the division? (Recognizing it as an S-P cluster, you would probably have no hesitation.) As the linguists say, you would "make the cut" between "puppies" and "will." We would write it like this:

Most puppies / will chew slippers.

It is immediately apparent that these two immediate constituents are themselves constructions. This means that they have constituents. What are the immediate constituents (IC's) of "most puppies"? Clearly:

Most / puppies

(And, again, we can note that the IC's of "puppies" are *puppy* and $\{-Z_1\}$, but let's stop at the word level.)

Similarly, "will chew slippers" is obviously a construction. It's IC's are:

will chew / slippers

And "will chew" is itself a construction, the IC's of which are "will" and "chew," thus:

will / chew

So getting back to the idea of what we mean by an "immediate constituent," we can make an example of "will" in the above sentence. Is "will" an immediate constituent? It depends. In the whole sentence

Most puppies will chew slippers

"will" is a constituent but not an *immediate* constituent. Just so, in the predicate

will chew slippers

"will" is a constituent but not an immediate constituent. But in the verb cluster, *will chew,* "will" *is* an immediate constituent. Whether a given word or word group is an IC, then, depends upon the construction you happen to be talking about. And what is a construction on one level can quickly become a constituent on another. Consider this:

If not carefully watched, most puppies will chew slippers.

What would be the IC's of this one? (If not carefully watched / most puppies will chew slippers.) And the construction which we were dissecting into constituents a moment ago has become an IC in a larger construction. We always have this possibility, and it is one of the things that help account for the complexity of English. At the same time, oddly enough, it helps account for its simplicity.

Let's pursue this IC business a bit further. The sentence we have been operating on is a very simple one. Here it is blown up a little:

Most pedigreed poodle puppies that I have known will chew bedroom slippers if they have the opportunity.

But again (wheels within wheels), these IC's are themselves constructions. What are the IC's of the subject? of the predicate? Is there any doubt? Of course not. It's obvious, and I'm certain that you did it, mentally, like this:

1. Most pedigreed poodle puppies / that I have known
2. will chew bedroom slippers / if they have the opportunity

And each of these constituents is a construction which itself has IC's, which are themselves constructions with IC's, and so on down to the individual words and morphemes which are known, fittingly enough, as *ultimate constituents.*

It is not only true to say that as English speakers we have a "feel" for these immediate constituents but we can go further and state that if you don't know what the IC's are you can't understand the construction. Here is a simple example:

old men and women

The constituents of the phrase could be either of these:

old / men and women

old men / and women

This principle is what underlies the argument about the placement of "only" in a sentence like: "Reginald only had five bucks." The purists, backed up by most school grammars, insist that the cut has to be made this way:

Reginald only / had five bucks

(Reginald was the only one with five dollars.)

You and I, on the other hand, along with some 99+ percent of American speakers of English, understand the cut to be like this:

Reginald / only had five bucks

We understand it immediately to mean that Reginald didn't have $5.49. The point here is that where you make the cut—what you determine the IC's to be, in other words—makes a big difference in what you understand.

Normally we don't have this kind of trouble, and it's a good thing or our communicating would be badly fouled up. We know instinctively what the IC's are. Let me give you some examples. I'll write each one as a normal construction first and then rewrite it indicating where I think the cut should be made.

The blonde on the beach was sunning herself.
The blonde on the beach / was sunning herself.

The blonde was sunning herself on the beach.
The blonde / was sunning herself on the beach.

The profs I like give reasonable assignments.
The profs I like / give reasonable assignments.

I like profs who give reasonable assignments.
I / like profs who give reasonable assignments.

All the barking dogs on our street at night keep me awake.
All the barking dogs on our street at night / keep me awake.

Luckily, the problem was an easy one.
Luckily / the problem was an easy one.

The man who annoyed the women fled.
The man who annoyed the women / fled.

I'm sure these gave you no trouble at all. As we said, it's almost instinctive. Take the last one, for instance. Suppose we made the cut somewhere else:

The man who annoyed / the women fled.

This obviously gets us nowhere. On the one hand we have a statement which doesn't seem to mean much of anything, *the man who annoyed.* If you were to hear someone say something like that, you'd stand there waiting for him to finish what he was going to say. On the other hand we have the statement *the women fled,* which isn't what the sentence had in mind at all, because it was the man and not the women who did the fleeing.

Did you note that, with one exception, all the sentences we just cut were simple S-P groups, and we cut the subject as one element and the predicate as the other? Where the S-P group itself has a modifier, we cut so that the modifier is one IC and the S-P group the other:

Luckily / the problem was an easy one.

Then the S-P group is cut like any other: *the problem / was an easy one.*

Naturally, the cuts we have been making are only the first ones made as we begin to dissect whole sentences. Each of the immediate constituents is likely to be a construction which in turn needs to be cut into *its* ICs, and so on. For practice, let's try this on a rather longish sentence. Let's use the one we already took apart in order to see the different kinds of clusters it was made of. Here it is again:

To act such a fool before an audience comprised of deans would have been a stupidity I couldn't have committed.

Since this is, as we have already seen, only a fairly sizeable S-P group, we make the first cut between the "S" element and the "P" element:

To act such a fool before an audience comprised of deans / would have been a stupidity I couldn't have committed.

For the moment let's forget the predicate half of that and look at the constituents of the subject:

To act such a fool before an audience comprised of deans

What are the IC's of this? When we were dealing with it earlier we felt it should be:

To act such a fool / before an audience comprised of deans

This still looks good. There isn't any other place, really, where you could cut it and have two parts, each with a sort of unity.

To act such a fool gives us little trouble, either. We would surely agree that its IC's are:

To act / such a fool

Cutting these further we get:

To / act   such / a fool
                a / fool

We have broken that verbal cluster down to its ultimate constituents. Now let's look at the P-group:

before an audience comprised of deans

Where do we cut this? The usual procedure is to consider the preposition as one part and all the rest of the group as the rest. Like this:

before / an audience comprised of deans

This would leave us a noun cluster and a modifier cluster, *an audience comprised of deans,* which we can separate rather easily:

an audience / comprised of deans

Then:

an /audience   comprised / of deans
                    of / deans

However, suppose you want to argue. You might feel, and insist, that *before an audience comprised of deans* should be cut this way:

before an audience / comprised of deans

Perhaps you would point out that there we have two IC's, each a unit and each making perfect sense. In rebuttal I could urge that the "before" doesn't just apply to "an audience" but to the whole noun cluster. It's before *an audience comprised of deans,* that's what it's before.

Perhaps I could convince you. You might even convince me. But the trouble is there's no way of *proving* that one way is the better way, that it somehow accords better with the reality of the language. As I observed above, we feel almost instinctively where the cuts should be made, and probably on most of the key ones we'll be in agreement. But the trouble with relying on our feeling about our language, our intuition, is that the correctness of a feeling cannot easily be demonstrated. Suppose I feel strongly one way, and you feel equally strongly in a different way? How resolve this? Maybe we could flip a coin, but that would shoot our image as "scientists."

In short, in cutting constructions up into their constituents, the experts often disagree. Now, it is possible to set up certain arbitrary rules to follow. Thus, in a P-group the preposition is to be one part and all the rest of it the other. This seems reasonable. Certainly I find nothing to object to in the procedure. At the same time it is difficult, and probably impossible, to demonstrate beyond cavil that the stipulated procedure is *the* correct procedure.[1]

It all relies on intuition, feeling, and when the going gets sticky in handling certain problems, this intuitive base is revealed as one of the fundamental weaknesses of IC analysis.

With that off our chests, let's look at how our subject got cut up finally. (This kind of diagram is one we haven't used before, but I think it should be perfectly clear.)

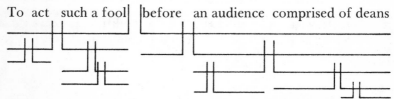

Now, let's go back and pick up that predicate we left lying around. It was:

    would have been a stupidity I couldn't have committed.

What is your feeling about this construction? Where do we cut it? Doesn't it seem that there really is one place preferable to all others? Suppose we cut it after "stupidity," thus:

    would have been a stupidity / I couldn't have committed

---

1. For carefully worked out rules for making cuts, the interested student is referred to C.C. Fries, *The Structure of English* or to Paul Roberts' *Patterns of English.*

Surely that isn't right. *Would have been a stupidity* is possible, but the *I couldn't have committed* seems now somehow to be hanging loose. It's the "stupidity" I couldn't have committed, not the *would have been*. That is, *I couldn't have committed* seems to work directly on "stupidity," not the verb. So let's try it like this:

would have been / a stupidity I couldn't have committed

That seems better surely. The spot after *would have been* is undoubtedly the place for the cut. Now we have to look at each of the IC's, to determine what *their* IC's are. Let's take the "complement" first:

a stupidity I couldn't have committed.

Again I imagine there is little doubt in your mind:

a stupidity / I couldn't have committed

What couldn't I have committed? A stupidity, of course. So the two parts of the construction seem in perfect balance. Now, since there is only one possible way to cut *a stupidity*, let's look at *I couldn't have committed*. The merest glance will serve to convince us that it's nothing but an S-P group, and that therefore it should be cut this way:

I / couldn't have committed

The "I" is an ultimate constituent already, which is to say there's no way to cut it further, so we turn our attention to the predicate, and immediately we find ourselves in a mess of trouble. We have several possibilities:

could / n't have committed
couldn't / have committed
couldn't have / committed

A good argument could be put up for the logicality of any of the three, and it's hard to see any compelling reason why one is better than another. (By "better," remember, we still mean more fruitful, more productive, in our analysis of English.) You might well feel that it doesn't matter much which way we do it, that it's hardly a vital issue. If so, I'm with you. And we're in good company. At least one distinguished linguist has pointed out that these places where the cuts get difficult to discover and easy to argue about do not seem to be "structurally significant."[2] If our feeling is right, that it really

---

2. H.A. Gleason, Jr., *Linguistics and English Grammar*, p. 162.

doesn't matter much—or show us much—however we make this cut, the only sensible thing to do would seem to be forget it. There is no point in nitpicking over matters that are inconsequential.

We find ourselves in very much the same sort of situation as we turn back to one construction we left unexamined, the *would have been* in *would have been / a stupidity I couldn't have committed.* Again we have options:

would / have been

would have / been

And again we conclude that the problem is not very interesting, in the sense in which the mathematician uses that term. That is, it's not likely to produce significant results. You may feel that the problem is not very interesting in the more usual senses of the word too, and again I'd have to say you have something there. So let's drop it at this point.

Using the kind of diagram we used a few pages ago to show how we had hacked up the subject element of our sentence, let's now take a look at the whole big S-P group and the way we have searched out its constituents, being somewhat arbitrary (as we have to) about where to cut the verb clusters:

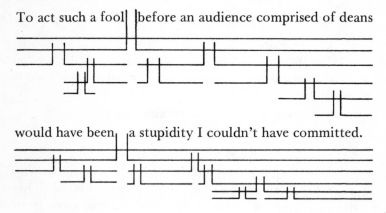

Analyzing English structure by IC's has certain weaknesses. As we have just seen, you arrive at a point in your analysis where this approach doesn't seem to come up with anything very helpful. Also, as we saw earlier, a possible (and even likely) flaw in the IC approach is that it is based on the analyzer's intuitive feeling about his language. Or if he should consult other informants ("Say, chum, if you had to break this construction into two parts, where would you break it?"), then he is relying on *their* intuition. Any way you do it, it can't be brought down to something whose essential rightness can be demonstrated. And if you get into an argument with someone over where a cut should be made there's really no way to settle it. It's your feeling against his, and you could quickly get into one of those "It *is*"—"It *isn't*" arguments that settle so little. It is noteworthy, too, that in the course of arguing that one place and not another is the proper place to make a cut, you have to deal with how elements are modifying each other and it is difficult to avoid getting mired in the morass of meaning. Not that the sentence (or construction) doesn't have meaning, of course, but remember that as we are trying to explain how the meaning is made from its constituent parts we can hardly legitimately use the meaning itself as a tool of analysis.

There is one other place where IC analysis falls down. As long as the sentences we are analyzing are of a pretty simple, straightforward kind (the kind we are going to call "kernel" sentences in our next chapter, to anticipate a little), as long as the sentences have a simple, basic structure, all goes well. At least up to a point. But change this structure a little bit and trouble erupts. Consider this sentence, for example:

Has our cute little baby been naughty?

What are the IC's of that? Well, we want to say that they are *our cute little baby* for one and *has been naughty* for the other. So where do we put our cut sign: "/"? One linguist uses what his colleagues call "Chinese boxes." For instance, to show the IC's of "The man bit the dog" he would have an arrangement like this:

Then to show the IC's of "Has our cute little baby been naughty?" he would come up with something like this:

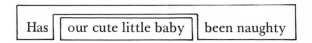

This is all very well, aside from the fact that by the time he has finished reducing an elaborate sentence to its ultimate constituents

he has created boxes within boxes within boxes until the dizzied
reader, eyes red from strain, is ready to flip right out of his mind, but
the main question remains: *How do we know* that *"Has"* at one end
of the sentence and *"been naughty"* at the extreme other end are
one IC and everything in between is the other? We just know, that's
all. Intuition again. And of course we *do* know—you have had to
"underline the whole subject once and the whole predicate twice" in
countless drillbooks, and so have I, and we can do it without a fluff.
But *how*? What is it that enables us to do this so unerringly? This
question the analyst doesn't ever answer finally. And that lessens, it
seems to me, the value of the whole analysis.

Nevertheless the development of the IC approach, the "structural
linguistics" of the popular mind, has been of tremendous service to
us as language students. If it doesn't ultimately answer all our questions about English—well, what does? For one thing, IC analysis
turned our thoughts away from the prescriptiveness of earlier grammars and made us realize that what we need to study is not what the
language "should be" but what it *is*. For a second thing, it insisted
upon what Jesperson and some of the great scholar-traditionalists
had observed but that school grammar had ignored, that the language
is basically speech, not writing. Third, it emphasized and re-
emphasized that meaning is determined by structure, rather than the
other way around, and that as we attempt to study a construction we
must leave it as it is and not arbitrarily change the order of the parts
every which way, as in traditional diagramming for instance. (Too,
we must explain a construction like "Leave that cat alone" without
"understanding" a word that actually isn't there.) And fourth, IC
analysis does reveal clearly some of the structural facts about English. An example: Remember when we were talking about two-part
(or separable) verbs in the last chapter? We had a pair of sentences
something like these:

1. The wind blew down the street.
2. The wind blew down the house.

We observed that they are clearly different, and that the difference is
in the verbs. Let's now take a look at them through the IC apparatus.
With each sentence the first cut is in the same place and tells us
nothing to answer our problem:

1. The wind / blew down the street.
2. The wind / blew down the house.

But now let's look at the IC's of the predicates:

1. blew / down the street
2. blew down / the house

And we see clearly that the two sentences have different meanings, the parts relate differently to each other, because they are different constructions.

It is basic that different constructions will produce different meanings and it is helpful to be able to show by means of IC's how constructions do differ so that we can see something of how these different meanings are produced.

That is something of what grammar is all about.

SUGGESTED READINGS

Francis, W. Nelson. *The Structure of American English* ("Syntactic Structures," chapter 6). New York: Ronald Press, 1958.

Fries, Charles C. *The Structure of English* ("Immediate Constituents: Layers of Structure," chapter 12). New York: Harcourt, Brace & World, 1952.

Roberts, Paul. *Patterns of English* ("How Sentences are Built," part 5). New York: Harcourt, Brace & World, 1956.

CHAPTER 7

SYNTAX II - WORDS IN FORMULAS

Transformational—Generative Grammar

Isn't this chapter heading impressive? Lovely, mouthfilling phrase! Formidable and scientific-looking, too. But lots of things with frightening labels turn out to be simple enough when examined patiently and carefully, and so it will be with transformational-generative grammar. We're not going to be like those social scientists (including, alas, some linguists) who retire into their hogans after having erected a wall of formidable jargon at the entranceways to make sure that outsiders stay out while the priests of the science perform their mystic rites. We'll need a mere handful of technical terms, and they will become comfortable and familiar with use. And we'll occasionally throw around some wonderfully awe-inspiring phrase just to impress the unwashed. However, in sober fact, the term is quite literally descriptive of the kind of grammar we are going to explore, as you will see. Explanation, while having the advantage of making the phrase clear, will unfortunately ruin its impressiveness. But, we can't have everything.

In the last chapter we saw how analysis by means of IC's can explain the underlying difference between:

> The wind blew down the street.

and

> The wind blew down the house.

But, as we also saw, there are serious limitations on what IC analysis can do. What we need is a more "powerful" grammar, one that can break through these limitations. Such a tool is provided us by transformational-generative grammar. Consider these two sentences:

> The snow was piled up by the wall.
> The snow was piled up by the man.

These happen to have the same constructions. The IC's show us nothing. Yet we sense that the sentences are clearly quite different. In the first one the snow, piled up by the wind or some unstated agent, happens to be near the wall. In the second one we don't know where the snow is but we do know that "the man" piled it there. Underneath their superficially identical structures these sentences are certainly different. Transformational-generative grammar explains the underlying difference *in terms of other sentences to which these sentences are (or are not) related.* Thus we can have:

> The snow was piled up by the man.
> The man piled up the snow.

The second retains the same sense as the first version. (Ask any native speaker of English.) But we cannot have:

> The snow was piled up by the wall.
> *The wall piled up the snow.

Perhaps I got too quick with that asterisk, since "The wall piled up the snow" certainly is a possible English sentence. But equally certainly it doesn't mean what we were thinking of as we read "The snow was piled up by the wall."

We can create a quite similar sentence that is perfectly ambiguous:

> The snow was piled up by the machine.

However, we can explain why this sentence is ambiguous, again in terms of other sentences. On the one hand we can say "The snow was piled up near the machine," and on the other, "The machine piled up the snow." The sentence is ambiguous because *it can relate* to *both* of the other versions.

Here is another pair—phrases this time—which have identical structures:

> the raising of flowers
> the roaring of lions

Looking at constituents won't explain how these identically-constructed phrases are basically so different. But relating them to other structures outside themselves will explain it:

> somebody raises flowers
> lions roar

Again we can create an ambiguity by dreaming up a phrase that will relate to both of the other constructions. For instance:

> the hunting of lions

This could relate to either of these structures:

> somebody hunts lions
> lions hunt

It is therefore completely ambiguous—and we are able to explain why.

We should observe that we very often get help from meaning in resolving what might otherwise be an ambiguity. (No, we're not going to use meaning as a "tool of analysis," but rather observe merely that it's always there and that sometimes the speaker of a language does rely on it to help ferret out what an utterance signifies. It's one of the facts of language life.) Suppose this construction, for instance:

> the hunting of sportsmen

Most likely we would *relate it to* "sportsmen hunt." Of course, it's *possible* that somebody is hunting sportsmen but it is what linguists call a "lexical improbability," which is to say it isn't likely. Thus it is true that as we search for the meaning in something we hear (or read) we play the odds, as it were. If a structure can relate to two (or perhaps even more) structures outside itself, we tend to choose the most likely as the intended meaning.

What we have actually been playing with the last few paragraphs are "transformations." That is to say, there are "transformational" grammars and "generative" grammars, and when we talk about a "transformational-generative grammar" we are simply talking about a grammar that combines elements of both. Both terms will need to be explained. We'll start with "transformational."

We've been tinkering with transformations in the last few paragraphs. A transformation is, of course, a change. That's all. A transformational grammar is based on the theory that a language has essentially only a few simple sentence types (called "the kernel") on which the speakers of that language work a number of standard, patterned changes, or transformations. These changes, which all speakers of the language of course know, are so regular and so patterned that they can be (and are) reduced to formulas and stated in symbols. In essence, that's it. That's all there is to transformational grammar. However, to make it really clear, really understandable, we're going to have to provide and work with examples and illustrations, and basically that's what we're going to be doing the rest of this chapter. Let's have a simple example right now, to illustrate this point about changes being worked on simple sentence patterns. We'll start with this sentence:

<blockquote>My cousin is stupid.</blockquote>

Suppose we want to make it into a question:

<blockquote>Is my cousin stupid?</blockquote>

How did we do it? Simple. Ignoring the change in intonation pattern, which doesn't really appear here on the printed page anyhow, all we did was reverse the first and second elements. Suppose now we choose certain symbols to represent the elements of that sentence. We'll represent "my cousin" by *NP* (noun phrase); "is" we'll represent by *be* (since *is* is a form of *to be*); and "stupid" we'll represent with the symbol *Adj* (adjective). We can now write the sentence, the statement version, as:

<blockquote>NP + be + Adj</blockquote>

We can also make a generalization about the symbols: we can say that *NP* represents not merely "my cousin" but any noun phrase (i.e., noun or noun cluster) and that *Adj* represents any adjective, and not only "stupid." *Be* remains, of course, some form of "to be." Can we now say that any time we have a sentence of this pattern:

<blockquote>NP + be + Adj</blockquote>

we can convert (transform) it into a question by swapping the first two elements? Thus:

<blockquote>be + NP + Adj</blockquote>

I think we can. Let's try a few:

NP + be + Adj	be + NP + Adj
My grandmother is ugly.	Is my grandmother ugly?
George was darling.	Was George darling?
The old man was generous.	Was the old man generous?
His parents were irate.	Were his parents irate?
We're pugnacious.	Are we pugnacious?

Those cats are cool.	Are those cats cool?
Y' all are intelligent.	Are y'all intelligent?
These scridgins are grue.	Are these scridgins grue?

And so on and on and on. If we bent our best efforts to the task, how many millions of pairs of sentences like this could we create? Undoubtedly the number would be astronomical. But we don't have to state them all. Or perhaps another and better way of saying it is that we *can* state them all, like this:

$$NP + be + Adj. \Longrightarrow be + NP + Adj,$$

where the symbol $\Longrightarrow$ means can be changed into" or, more simply and more in keeping with our terminology, "transforms into."

It might well be that as we explore the language and its possibilities further we will find that that switch works both ways. That is, not only is any *NP + be + Adj* transformable into *be + NP + Adj*, but also any time we find *be + NP + Adj* we can turn it back into *NP + be + Adj*. We can state the relation between the two sentence patterns this way:

$$NP + be + Adj \Longleftrightarrow be + NP + Adj.$$

The double-headed and double-shafted arrow signifies that the change works in either direction. Thus we can easily change:

Is Genevieve ungainly?

into:

Genevieve is ungainly.

One thing I should call to your attention before we go on. That is that it's the *statement* that is basic. It is one of the so-called "kernel" sentences. The question form is a transformation, which is to say that it derives from the statement. Strictly speaking, we do not turn this around. We don't say that the statement derives from the question. In fact it doesn't derive from anything except the basic nature of the language itself. If someone asks you, "Why, in English, when you wish to attribute beauty to George, do you give it the peculiar structure of 'George is beautiful'?"—well, there isn't any answer to that except to say that that's the way speakers of English put those words together. But the question form can be explained, as we have seen, as a transformation of the statement. As an analogy, you can think of the kernel sentences as being like the primary colors, which are called primary because they cannot be made from any other colors. All other colors are produced from (we could say, analogically, "transformed from") the primary colors.[1]

Anyhow, that's the basic idea of the "transformational" aspect of transformational-generative grammar. Now for the space of a few lines we'll turn our attention to the "generative" part of the term.

We might say that the generative grammarian views a grammar as a sort of language-producing machine. Essentially the machine is a set of sentence-producing rules. These rules give instructions which if followed exactly will produce sentences in whatever language they are set up for. Of course our concern will be with English, but you might want to remember that generative grammars could be set up for Spanish or Hindi or Tarahumara or Language X.

The term "generative" seems to be borrowed from mathematics, in which a person might say of the formula $2\pi r$ that it will generate all possible circles. No matter how tremendous, no matter how tiny, any circle can be generated by $2\pi r$. Note too that it generates only circles. No ovals, no triangles, no squares. Just circles.

Just so the linguist wants his generative grammar to produce all the possible sentences in a language, but no sentence that is impossible. That is, the grammar could produce:

The girl danced a hula.

But if it were to turn out this:

Girl the hula a danced,

then back to the old drawing board to design a new grammar.

All that is required of our sentence-producing generative grammar machine is that it produce *grammatical* sentences. The assertions they make do not have to be true. Consider these sentences:

Water freezes at 212° Fahrenheit.
Tomatoes are delicious.

The first one is untrue; the second is a matter of opinion and is at least debatable. But are they good English? Certainly. Impeccable. Any English speaker would agree. So our generative grammar would be quite correct in producing sentences like these. All we require of them is that they be grammatical.

---

1. Recently a number of transformationalists have been failing to make this distinction between kernel and derived sentences, or at least have not been making it in this way. However, it seems to me still a useful distinction to make, particularly in an introduction to transformational theory.

Similarly, it could quite conceivably turn out sentences which are nonsense, like:

Fricasseed prunes are clumsy dancers.

What does it mean? I'm not sure. It may be avant-garde poetry, or something from a weight-watcher's nightmare. But is it recognizably English? Obviously.

It might interest you to know that in the thinking of transformational-generative linguists *you* are a transformational-generative grammar. That is, you are a sentence-producing machine, and you produce tremendous numbers of sentences and you do not produce non-sentences. You needn't get too puffed up about it, though, because everybody who speaks a language is such a machine—you and I and our friends in English, and other people in other languages. The theory is that as we learn our language, as infants, we somehow grasp a few simple structures—perhaps the kernel sentences?—and we learn the standard ways of manipulating them. (How old were you when you learned *NP + be + Adj* $\Longleftrightarrow$ *be + NP + Adj*? I don't mean the formula of course, but the transformation it represents. Look around you at three and four-year old kids. Can they make statements on the pattern of *NP + be + Adj*? Can they transform them into questions? You bet they can.

When we have learned these few simple structures, and a relative handful of standard, patterned changes we can work upon them, we suddenly are able to produce perfectly acceptable English sentences that we have never heard before and which, possibly, nobody has ever said before. If you were to record all the sentences you utter in a day, it's quite likely that some of them have never before been said in just the way you said them. And yet you produce them as English and your listeners accept them as English.

How many sentences can be produced in English? It's impossible to say, of course, but if it isn't an infinite number it will do until an infinite number comes along. Watch:

This morning when I stood on my head in front of my typewriter I saw little pink-striped worms dancing a tango on the keys.

The point is that I doubt very much that in all the long history of English anybody ever spoke or wrote that exact sentence before. I want to ask you one serious question about that sentence: asinine though it is, is it English?

Let me ask you one more question about that same sentence: if it had never before been spoken or written by any one of all the millions upon millions who speak and have spoken English, how come I was able to produce it? And, for that matter, you to understand it? In a sense, it's because we're both machines with the same set of rules programmed into us. What are those rules? Transformational-generative grammar provides us with a theoretical, sample set. It isn't necessarily the answer. But it's a suggestion of what the answer might be like when we do learn it, if we ever do.

Transformational-generative grammar is a fairly recent development in language study. It is by no means the *most* recent development, for just as transformational-generative grammar sprang into being because of dissatisfaction with the inadequacies of earlier grammars, so other linguists are dissatisfied with certain features of transformational-generative grammar and are creating new grammars of quite different kinds. No doubt it's all very healthy and the more theories and even, perhaps, "truths" we can produce about the way language operates the sooner we will be able to explain exactly what it is that a five year old child has mastered which enables him to use his language so fluently.

The linguists of the transformational-generative persuasion, however, have been an eager and industrious lot—often quite arrogant in presenting their revelations to lesser linguists—and their doctrines, not to say "findings," have been spreading far and fast. It all started with a book entitled *Syntactic Structures* by Noam Chomsky, published in 1957. It is a little book, only 118 pages from cover to cover, but it is packed. Graduate students quickly learn to beware courses where the only text is one of these skinny books, especially if it has in the title *An Introduction to.* I'm surprised Professor Chomsky missed the chance to entitle his book *An Introduction to Syntactic Structures.* Then it would have had everything. Indeed, within the relatively narrow field of linguistics, this book changed the world.

At first, of course, it was read and appreciated only by other linguists. Then it got into the graduate schools. And then many, many other linguists got caught up in the excitement of this new kind of grammar and began making their own contributions until now there is a substantial bibliography of transformational grammars. There is not only a good text on transformational grammar, a sort of self-teaching book, for the high school level[2] but there are in print several such grammars for elementary school. Nor are these feeble or tentative efforts, but full-blown multi-volume series intended to be used through several grades. In short, this grammar is

2. Paul Roberts, *English Syntax.*

with us, and will probably be around a long time, and it behooves us to know something about it. Who can tell? You might wind up on a school board some day and have to sit in judgment of somebody's "grammar."

It should go without saying—but I'll say it anyhow—that as you go from one to another of these various transformational grammars, you find a number of differences. They don't all use the same symbols, and of course don't all use them in the same way. They don't all arrive at identical results. Some are highly abstruse and difficult to read; others are clear and easy for the reader to follow, if he's at all patient. But they all have the same underlying, basic philosophy—and principles—and it's that with which we are concerned here.

Generally, to the uninitiated these books look forbidding. Riffle through a few pages of one and you might get the impression that you've stumbled across an algebra text or a book on symbolic logic. But really they are not math books, though it is true that advanced language study today is being infiltrated by mathematicians and that sometimes they make their books unnecessarily difficult by bringing their math jargon with them. (It is not true that because a man is a brilliant linguist he can therefore write well any more than it is to be expected that the speech teacher will deliver a good speech.) These transformational-generative grammars have a strange, and perhaps even forbidding, appearance because they deal with language by means of symbols in an effort to make statements as general—that is, as widely applicable—as possible. This is neither more nor less difficult than the simple rule we set up a few moments ago: NP + be + Adj $\Longleftrightarrow$ be + NP + Adj. That is a simple, symbolic statement of a fact about English, and it surely is not difficult. It is, however, efficient. Notice how much simpler and more economical a statement it is than saying something like "When you have in English a statement consisting of a noun phrase, which is a noun or noun substitute or noun cluster, followed by some form of *to be,* followed by an adjective, it is possible always to make a question of it by reversing the order of the first two elements, the noun phrase and the form of *to be.*" The symbolic statement is much simpler, and we have observed a number of times that in creating a grammar simplicity is one of the goals.

Transformational grammar is utterly simple. Understanding how it works and why it works, and judging how well a particular transformational grammar is functioning, is quite a different matter and we're going to be involved in that, too. Quite literally, anybody or anything that can follow very explicit instructions, could use such a grammar. Remember that a machine can produce perfectly acceptable English if the rules of a transformational-generative grammar are fed into it. The things that computers can do are fantastic. They perform complicated computations at incredible speeds with an accuracy beyond human skill—but they do *not* think. They follow instructions. A friend of mine who is a computer expert calls his machine a million dollar moron. If an idiotic mistake is programmed into the machine it produces an idiotic answer. Once, he told me, a complicated problem was put into the computer, with all necessary instructions for working it out, but without the instruction that the machine should print the answer. So the machine buzzed and hummed and solved the problem and swallowed the answer and sat there, probably grinning inwardly at its frustrated operator. Such a machine can produce perfectly good English by means of transformational-generative grammar. In fact, such machines are writing some rather interesting poetry nowadays, and we'll take a look at some of it a little later.

It should be obvious from the above that a transformational-generative grammar must be *explicit.* Nothing must be left to the imagination. Could you reasonably expect a machine, for instance, to weigh the problem of whether a word like "yellow" is properly "a person, place or thing" and hence should be treated like a noun in "That's a pretty *yellow*"? But you could expect the machine to follow instructions, and merely *using* such a grammar requires no more than following instructions. This is one of the grammar's great advantages: nothing can be left unstated, nothing can be left to the judgment of the user (which might well be a computer), nothing can be less than perfectly explicit.

An "investigation" of this grammar is what we're setting out on. This chapter doesn't pretend to be "a transformational-generative grammar," but rather a look at the kind of thing that goes on in such grammars. We want some kind of clear picture of how they operate. If we can get that, we'll at least have done something. And it's always possible for anyone interested to go on and look at books that do give an extended treatment. (There has not been produced, of course, a "complete" transformational-generative grammar of English.)

The kind of grammar we are contemplating proceeds through the application of several different kinds of sets of "rules," though the term "rules" means something different here from what we have long been used to, as in "It's a rule that you shouldn't split an infinitive."

In transformational-generative grammar "rules" might better be called "specific instructions." However, since the term "rules" is consistently used by transformational-generative grammarians we will use it too. These rules are of four types, each of which will become familiar to us, however strange they might sound right now: (1) P-rules; (2) T-rules; (3) L-rules; and (4) M-rules.

All of these are what are called "rewrite rules," which means that they operate on a very simple principle. When you see a symbol (any symbol) followed by an arrow pointing to another symbol, it means that the first symbol is to be rewritten as the second. Thus, this could be a rewrite rule:

$$X \longrightarrow y + z$$

Never mind what the symbols "stand for." (The machine doesn't care about that, remember?) All this rule says is that if you have a string of symbols and there is an "X" among them you are to rewrite that "X" as "y + z." For example, suppose you have a string like this:

$$A + B + X + C + D + X + E$$

Applying the rule just given we would rewrite it like this:

$$A + B + y + z + C + D + y + z + E$$

Surely that is simple enough. And, essentially, that's the method of procedure of transformational-generative grammar. It's the basic instruction of each rule: rewrite something as something else. If you have firmly in mind the meaning of that arrow you've got one of the keys to this whole system.

We will have a couple of modest refinements to this rewrite rule but they won't change the nature of things at all. For instance, we might have this rule:

$$X \longrightarrow \begin{Bmatrix} y \\ z \end{Bmatrix}$$

In this grammar, braces indicate an option. (They do not indicate morphemes, as they did a couple chapters back.) Thus, we would read this rule to say that *X* is to be rewritten *either* as *y* or *z*. And the string of symbols we rewrote a moment ago could quite properly come out any of these four ways:

$$A + B + y + C + D + z + E$$
$$A + B + z + C + D + y + E$$
$$A + B + y + C + D + y + E$$
$$A + B + z + C + D + z + E$$

Another slight refinement is in the use of parentheses, which mean that the symbol enclosed may be used or not. Either way is acceptable. Thus we could have:

$$X \longrightarrow y\ (+z)$$

According to this, wherever we find an *X* we are to rewrite it either as *y* or *y + z*. It makes no difference. Either follows the rule.

"P-rules," which will be the first ones we'll experiment with, are the familiar label, the nickname, for "phrase structure rules." Don't worry about what *that* phrase means—we will simply call them P-rules, and they are the ones that will produce our basic sentences. "T-rules" are the rules, or instructions, which govern "transformations" or changes we may wish to make in the structure of the sentence; like changing a sentence to a question (NP + be + Adj $\Longrightarrow$ be + NP + Adj). "L-rules" are the comfortable name for "lexical rules," by means of which we convert abstract symbols (NP) to "lexical items," or actual *words*. Finally, "M-rules" are the convenient label for what goes by the wonderful name of "morphophonemic rules," and all they are is the set of rules by which we convert morphemes into phonemes. It would be, for instance, a morphophonemic rule which would tell us that "cat" plus $\{-Z_1\}$ is to be /kæts/ and not */kætz/. For, you see, the symbols in these strings of symbols we'll be working with are morphemes, and we haven't done any sort of English-producing job until we convert them into something pronounceable, something recognizable as English.

For the moment don't worry about P-rules, L-rules, T-rules and M-rules. They'll all come clear pretty quickly. Right now, let's start out by creating a tiny—a very tiny—generative grammar.

First Model Grammar

We'll start with this symbol: *S*. Let's say that *S* stands for all the sentences that are producible by this grammar. Thus, if we were setting out to write a complete grammar of English, *S* would stand for all the sentences in English—*all* possible sentences. Our *S* at the moment, however, stands for the very modest assortment of sentences which this grammar will be able to produce.

Here are our very simple P-rules:

$$S \longrightarrow NP + VP$$
$$NP \longrightarrow D + N$$

What do they mean? How do we use them? Just exactly as we did above with X and Y. Whenever we want this grammar to produce a sentence we have to start with *S*, and whenever we see an *S* we're to rewrite it as *NP + VP*. As for what these symbols "mean," you can think of them as "noun phrase" and "verb phrase" if you wish, but what they really mean will be determined by the way they are in their turn to be rewritten. For instance, *NP* ⟶ *D + N*, which means simply that wherever the symbol *NP* crops up we are to rewrite it as instructed. Thus *D + N* can be said to be the real meaning of *NP*. (I do realize that it's easier to remember names for things than abstract symbols, so if you like, as a memory aid, you can think of *D* as "determiner" and *N* as "noun.")

What *D* is going to mean in this minuscule grammar is stated in this L-rule (lexical rule):

$$D \longrightarrow \left\{ \begin{array}{l} \text{some} \\ \text{the} \\ \text{all} \end{array} \right\}$$

That is, when you see a *D* you rewrite it as one of those three lexical items. If there are other determiners somewhere out there in the great world, that's irrelevant right now. They're outside the scope of this grammar, which provides us only with three ways of rewriting *D*.

Similarly, we turn to the "lexicon" (our set of words in the L-rules) and we find these rules for *N:*

$$N \longrightarrow \left\{ \begin{array}{l} \text{chickens} \\ \text{coeds} \\ \text{profs} \end{array} \right\}$$

Don't at this time bring up all the scads of nouns there are in English. This grammar, which is our immediate concern, has only these three.

In this miniature grammar we won't give any more P-rules. That is, we won't even define *VP* further, except to go right to the lexicon and find this rule:

$$VP \longrightarrow \left\{ \begin{array}{l} \text{eat worms} \\ \text{lay eggs} \\ \text{teach physics} \\ \text{dance waltzes} \end{array} \right\}$$

And that's all the rules we have in this grammar. Let's see how they work. We simply follow instructions, applying one rule at a time, and see what comes out. We start, of course, with S, and apply our first rule:

1. S ⟶ NP + VP

We are instructed by the rules not just to leave *NP + VP* standing there but to get busy and do some rewriting. So we take a second step:

2. D + N + VP

What did we do? We rewrote the *NP* of step 1 as *D + N,* just exactly as we were instructed to do. That's all. And we have exhausted our P-rules, so we turn to the L-rules, which we must also follow. Let's rewrite the *D:*

3. all + N + VP

That's the only change we made between the string of symbols numbered 2 and that numbered 3: we rewrote the *D* as instructed. (Of course, we had an option among three items; we were free to pick any one but we had to select one. The rules wouldn't let us skip it.)

Turning to the lexicon again, let's now rewrite the *N.* Here we have, again, three choices.

4. all + chickens + VP

It looks now as though the only thing we have left to do is go to the lexicon and rewrite the *VP* and we will have followed all the instructions given us. So:

5. all + chickens + eat worms

What hath our little grammar wrought? It hath clearly wrought an English sentence. It's a simple grammar—and a super-simple sentence—but the point is, at the moment: Do you see how it works? If so, you've practically mastered the technique of transformational-generative grammar, because from here on out all we are going to do is add refinements.

Some students find it easier to get the idea of what's going on in this kind of grammar if it's done with a diagram instead of the kind of "linear" step-by-step rewriting we just did, so let's try it that way. It's the same thing.

```
                              S
1.            NP            +            VP
             /  \                          |
2.        D  +  N           +            VP
           |      \                        |
3.       the  +    N        +            VP
           |        \                      |
4.       the  +    profs    +            VP
           |           \                   |
5.       the  +      profs  +          lay eggs
```

Here is a different version of the same diagram, without the
repetitions of the first version:

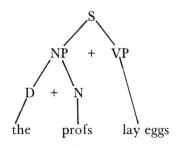

Clear enough? We'll try one more,

1. S ⟶ NP + VP
2. D + N + VP
3. some + N + VP
4. some + coeds + VP
5. some + coeds + eat worms

Ugly thought, but it's an *English* ugly thought.

This little grammar has some obvious shortcomings. It can turn
out only 36 different sentences, all on the same pattern. There is no
way for us to make it produce "The prof teaches physics," for all our
options in rewriting *N* are plural. There is no way for us to make it

turn out "Do the chickens dance waltzes?" for we have no apparatus for turning a statement into a question. Nor can we produce a passive: "Eggs are laid by some chickens." In fact, we have a lot more shortcomings than we do grammar. (But note that, even staying within this one sentence pattern, and still with only plural subjects, we could make our output of sentences vastly greater simply by adding to the lexicon.) All we've been trying to do is grasp some of the operating principles of this kind of grammar. Now all we need do is add refinements so that we can have either a singular or plural subject which agrees in number with its verb; so that we can produce questions; so that, in sum, we can produce something more like the variety and complexity of real English. To do this we are going to need to introduce, and use, T-rules and M-rules—and we're going to need more P-rules, for that matter.

One thing I must urge upon you, as strongly as I can, is that you actually *apply* these rules as we discuss them and make them produce sentences for you. You need a pencil and a supply of scratch paper, and you need to work these things out. It's really no good, with a subject of this nature, simply to read it, your head nodding sagely and you saying "I see! I get it!" Perhaps a reluctance to do this kind of pencil-and-paper busy work contributes something toward the resistance of English majors toward this kind of grammar.

Furthermore, let's face it, rewriting and rewriting, changing only one step on each rewrite, quickly gets tedious, especially as you're working out a long, involved sentence. It seems endless sometimes, and you might well wish you could do it with the speed of a computer. (Theoretically at least, it's possible that you *do* do something like this, subconsciously and with almost the speed of light, as you create sentences in your daily speech. But that's theory and undemonstrable, of course.) Remember, now, that our ultimate aim is not to produce sentences—we can already do that, and much more easily than with this rewriting process—but to gain an insight into the inner workings of the language, and an increased understanding of them. This seems maybe worth a bit of drudgery.

A while back we referred to "kernel sentences." We're now in a little better situation to understand what they are. Very briefly, they're the sentences produced by P-rules, with the subsequent application of the appropriate L-rules and M-rules. In other words, there are no T-rules involved in creating the kernel sentences. And so we come to the question, "How many of these kernel sentences are there?" This question is probably unanswerable. It depends not only upon how you set up your P-rules, but even to a larger extent on what you are going to consider "the same" and "different" as you compare sentence types. Look at these two sentences, for instance:

We elected Myrtle a cheerleader.
We considered Audrey a beauty.

In the second of these sentences there exists the possibility of changing the noun following the verb into an adjective:

We considered Audrey beautiful.

This possibility doesn't exist with the sentence about Myrtle's election as cheerleader. The question is whether we want, therefore, to figure that we're dealing with two basically different types of sentences or whether we want to figure that essentially we have only one sentence which, as we work out final details, can branch either of two different ways. It doesn't make much difference, really, which way we decide. What *does* make a difference is that when we get our grammar finished, if it is to be a complete one, it must be able to generate both kinds of sentences.

A factor involved here is what some linguists, following Chomsky's lead, call "elegance," again a term apparently borrowed from the mathematicians. It's a matter of achieving a precise, economical statement. Suppose, for example, you and I were both put to work demonstrating some proposition in geometry and I took fourteen steps to demonstrate it while you, with a proof just as conclusive, needed only eight steps. Your proof would be more "elegant." So a grammar that could ultimately produce all the sentences of English from only four basic sentence types (kernel sentences) would perhaps be preferable to one that needed ten or a dozen on the grounds that it was more elegant—"characterized by scientific precision, neatness and simplicity" (Webster's III).

Once again we must remark, as we did with other grammars, that the language itself remains unaffected by considerations like this one as to how many kernel sentences there might be. What is being discussed is not the language but the relative efficiency of different ways of describing it.

Now let's go on and set up a somewhat more elaborate grammar than the very simple one we created a few pages ago. With some modifications we'll follow, basically, the grammar first set up by Chomsky (as, indeed, all transformational-generative grammarians subsequent to him have done).

Second Model Grammar

To get started we need, just as we did in our primitive First Model Grammar, a set of P-rules. Again we start with $S \longrightarrow NP + VP$ and once again S means "all the sentences which this grammar can produce." Here are our P-rules, then, with comments deferred until after the rules are listed:

1. $S \longrightarrow NP + VP$
2. $VP \longrightarrow Verb + NP$
3. $NP \longrightarrow \begin{cases} D + N + \emptyset & \text{(i.e., a singular noun)} \\ D + N + Z_1 & \text{(i.e., a plural noun)} \end{cases}$
4. $Verb \longrightarrow Aux + V$
5. $Aux \longrightarrow C\ (M)\ (have + en)\ (be + ing)$
6. $C \longrightarrow \begin{cases} \text{s in the context NP singular, } N + \emptyset \\ \emptyset \text{ in the context NP plural, } N + Z_1 \\ \text{past} \end{cases}$

Also we will need, as we did earlier, some L-rules. Here they are:

1. $D \longrightarrow$ the, a, some, his, etc.
2. $N \longrightarrow$ man, boy, girl, dog, etc.
3. $V \longrightarrow$ sing, play, hit, chase, walk, etc.
4. $M \longrightarrow$ will, can, shall, may, must

We're going to need to add one more rule that will *always* apply after all the ones above, but we'll put off describing the rule until we have had a chance to discuss these. By the way, I certainly don't expect you to memorize these rules, so it might be a good idea if you keep your finger stuck in the book at this point so you can easily refer back here during the discussion we're about to get into.

First, some comments on the P-rules. Some of them seem pretty obvious, and I imagine you had no trouble with them at all. Others demand a bit of explanation. How to tell which is which? Maybe we better comment on each of them. You remember that we observed some pages back that if you are asked what a symbol means—say *VP*—the real answer is to be found in the way it is rewritten. Consider the following dialogue:

Bill: I don't get this stuff at all. What the heck does *VP* mean?
Susan: *VP* means *Verb + NP,* just like it says in the next line.

Bill: Thanks a lot. Now what does *Verb* mean?

Susan: That's easy. Verb is defined in Rule 4. It means *Aux + V*, that's all.

Bill: You're sure a real help. A real jewel. Now tell me what *V* means.

Susan: So look at the L-rules. *V* means *sing, play, hit, chase, walk*—like that. They do all seem to be ordinary verbs, don't they?

As dramatic dialogue, I guess that stuff won't drive Tennessee Williams out of business, but I hope its point gets through to you. It is simply that each rewriting *is* a definition, and we can follow through a number of them until we get down to the final rewriting. You might object, why don't you say in the first place that *VP* is a list of words like *sing, play, hit,* etc. and have it done with? But go back and look again and you'll see that *VP* is a lot more than that. In fact, if we were to diagram *VP* it would look like this:

$$VP$$
$$Verb \quad + \quad NP$$
$$Aux \quad + \quad V \quad D+N+\emptyset \ (\text{or } D+N+Z_1)$$
$$C \ (M) \ (have + en) \ (be \ + \ ing) \quad \text{the, a, etc.} \quad \text{man, boy, etc.}$$

play
sing
hit
run
walk
etc.

Obviously as Bill and Susan conducted their little discussion they were, each time, selecting just one of two alternatives.

In truth, then, the P-rules (and the L-rules, too) listed above already have in them all the definitions they need. But a couple of them are complex, and we might well pause to comment on them.

Consider *Aux.* You can think of it as meaning auxiliary, but you may remember that I cautioned you in the last chapter that in this one we would be using the term "auxiliary" in a way unfamiliar to you. Here the term does *not* mean quite what you have always meant by it, what we called in grade school the "helping verb." What does it mean? It means the string of symbols that Rule 5 says it means: *C (M) (have + en) (be + ing)*. And what does that string of symbols mean? Well, we need to press on patiently, looking for further rewrite rules.

C is rewritten, or in other words defined, as

$$\left\{ \begin{array}{l} \text{s in the context NP singular, N} + \emptyset \\ \emptyset \text{ in the context NP plural, N} + Z_1 \\ \text{past} \end{array} \right\}$$

That is, we get a *choice* as to how we rewrite *C*. (As a memory aid I always think of *C* as meaning "choice.") If *C* is in a string of symbols where the preceding noun phrase (NP) is singular, then we will rewrite it as *s*. On the other hand, if the preceding *NP* is plural—that is if it's $N + Z_1$—then we rewrite *C* as $\emptyset$. Not to be too mysterious about all this—after all, we're not involved in a mystery novel where giving away the ending would spoil things—let's see how this would work out if we were developing a sentence in this grammar. Let's take as noun phrase *the boy* and as verb *run*. Now the way the rule will work out is that if our noun phrase is singular, *the boy,* we will choose *s* in the *Aux.* Thus:

the boy + S + run = the boy runs

However, if our *NP* is plural, the boys, we will select $\emptyset$. Like this:

the boys + $\emptyset$ + run = the boys run

In other words, our *Aux,* which forces us to make a choice for *C,* far from being a "helping verb," is what governs the number and tense of the verb; that is, it provides for the *s* on "the boy run*s*" and leaves it off "the boys ru*n*."

Notice that we must always make this choice for *C*. You will perhaps remember that earlier in this chapter we said that parentheses in a rewrite rule would indicate that what is enclosed between them could either be included or left out. Look again at the rewrite for *Aux.* Here it is:

Aux⎯⎯⎯⟶ C (M) (have + en) (be + ing)

Since the other elements in the rewrite (whatever they may prove to stand for) are enclosed in parentheses they are optional, and can either be included or omitted in the rewrite. But the *C* is not in parentheses. We *must* include it in the rewrite. And, since it indicates the number of the verb, and since the verb has to have number (that is, it must agree with the subject) we can see why the inclusion of *C* is obligatory.

We still have a third choice with *C*, however. Regardless of whether the *NP* is plural or singular, we can as a third choice select "past." What this says, in effect, is that if the verb is in the past tense it makes no difference whether the subject is singular or plural. Is this right?

> The boy + run + past = The boy ran.
>
> The boys + run + past = The boys ran.

And this, of course, is proper English. In the past tense the verb doesn't have to "agree in number" with its subject. Or perhaps it would be better to say that the agreement doesn't show. Whatever you call it, the verb plus $\{D_1\}$ is the same in form with a singular or a plural subject. You might wonder why we're using "past" as a symbol instead of $\{D_1\}$. It is simply that most transformational-generative grammarians use "past"—though some do use $\{D_1\}$—and we are following majority practice. As we've observed before, the symbol doesn't matter as long as we both understand what we mean by it.

Now as to the other symbols in the rewrite of *Aux*. (M) is defined for us in the L-rules. (You can think of *M* as standing for "modal" if that traditional grammar term will help you.) Note that *M*, unlike other terms in the L-rules, means *only* the words that are in the rewrite rule. There is no "etc." following them. We must rewrite *M*, if we choose to have an *M* (remember it's optional in the first place), as one of these five words: *will, can, may, shall, must*. And that's what *M* means.

In addition to *(M)* in the rewrite of *Aux* we find *(have + en)* and *(be + ing)*. Those are easy, and will become even easier as you see them in action in a few minutes when we use them in building a sentence. Briefly, *have* is the verb "have" used as a "helping verb." (Let's use that schoolroom term "helping verb" in this chapter and save "auxiliary" for *Aux*. It might help us avoid some confusion.) The symbol *en* stands for the past participle morpheme, as in "I have eat*en*." True, we earlier called it $\{D_2\}$, but again, as with *past*, we are following general practice. The symbol *be* represents some form of *to be* used as a helping verb, and the *ing* is the present participle, both as in "He *is* walk*ing*."

All of that should clear up our terms. Now let's see how they operate as we use our P-rules and L-rules to construct a sentence. We start as always with *S:*

1. S———→ NP + VP

Our rules instruct us to rewrite both *NP* and *VP*. It doesn't matter which one we rewrite first, but we are going to do them one at a time. In fact, every rewriting which we do will change (rewrite) just *one* item in our string of symbols. Admittedly, this is a slow and plodding way to do it, and probably we *could* change two or more in a step, but one at a time will get us there in the long run and maybe serve to keep things clearer. What we need to do above all is keep things clear right now so that we can see and understand exactly what it is we're doing. If things seem too tedious to you, imagine these rules being fed through a computer, zippity zip, wham, and it's all finished. Unfortunately, or maybe fortunately, we're not computers. So this is going to take some time. Let's rewrite the *NP* first:

2. D + N + ∅ + VP

This is the same string (i.e., string of symbols) that we had in step 1, *NP + VP,* except that we have rewritten the *NP* as instructed in P-rule 3. Notice that the rule gives us an option: we can rewrite *NP* in either of two ways. We chose the singular, but we could as easily have chosen the plural. What we obviously couldn't do is choose both. Now let's rewrite the *VP* as instructed in P-rule 2:

3. D + N + ∅ + Verb + NP

Now we'll rewrite *Verb* according to P-rule 4. (It makes no difference that we are skipping around a little among these rules. We could take them in sequence, and in the next sentence we create we will.)

4. D + N + ∅ + Aux + V + NP

Is it perfectly clear what we have done so far? We have written down the whole string each step, each time rewriting (as instructed in the P-rules) just *one* symbol. We could represent what we have done so far in a branching tree type diagram, like this:

We could continue our rewriting with this diagram, but I think it will prove easier, and be just as simple, if we continue as we first started, rewriting each step on separate, numbered lines. So we'll go on to step 5, rewriting the *Aux.* Just for fun we'll take all the options offered us in *Aux.*

5. D + N + $\emptyset$ + C + M + have + en + be + ing + V + NP

You may be wondering what happened to the parentheses around *(M)* and *(have + en)* and *(be + ing)*. Those parentheses belong in the P-rule and signify to us that whether we include these items or not is optional. But we have decided to include them. They are in our string of symbols now. Since we are committed, we no longer need the parentheses. (Rewriting these strings is tedious enough without including symbols that we no longer have to have.) Now, applying P-rule 3 again, we'll rewrite that *NP* at the end of the string. Every symbol has to be rewritten just as far as the rules direct us to keep rewriting, and we are instructed to rewrite *NP* wherever it appears.

6. D + N + $\emptyset$ + C + M + have + en + be + ing + V + D + N + Z_1

This time we elected to rewrite *NP* with the plural morpheme. We didn't have to, of course. It could have been singular just as easily. Are there any P-rules still unapplied to that string? Anything that still needs to be rewritten? Yes. We still have to rewrite *C:*

7. D + N + $\emptyset$ + past + M + have + en + be + ing + V + D + N + Z_1

In rewriting *C* we had a choice, but only between two options. That is, we could not have rewritten it as $\emptyset$ because the rule says that that selection can be made only in the context of *NP plural* and we have already selected *NP singular.* (You will not fail to note that this rule implies that the rewriting of *C* can not be done until *after* the preceding *NP* has been rewritten, for otherwise we wouldn't know whether the context was *NP* plural or singular.) In the sentence we are developing, then, *C* can be rewritten as either *s,* since the context is *NP singular,* or *past,* which will go with either singular or plural. We chose *past* in this case.

We have now rewritten everything the P-rules have instructed us to, but we still have the L-rules to contend with.

8. the + N + $\emptyset$ + past + M + have + en + be + ing + V + D + N + Z_1

We simply rewrote the first *D* as instructed by L-rule 1. We'll now go ahead, without comment, rewriting one symbol each time as the L-rules tell us to, proceeding from the front of the string to the end of it:

9. the + man + past + M + have + en + be + ing + V + D + N + Z_1

(N + $\emptyset$, with "man" selected as the noun, will be "man," obviously. Had it been N + Z_1 it would have had to be "men." Actually, we need a set of M-rules to instruct us in this kind of conversion, and we may provide them later.)

10. the + man + past + may + have + en + be + ing + V + D + N + Z_1
11. the + man + past + may + have + en + be + ing + chase + D + N + Z_1
12. the + man + past + may + have + en + be + ing + chase + the + N + Z_1
13. the + man + past + may + have + en + be + ing + chase + the + boys

We have now done all the rewriting that the P-rules and the L-rules have instructed us to do. We can't go any further. We have produced what is called a *terminal string*, "string" because all we have is a string of symbols—no one in his right mind would call this a sentence—and "terminal" because it's as far as we can go.

We need now the one additional rule I spoke of a short time ago so that we can put this string into the order necessary for turning it into a sentence. This rule, which only superficially appears complicated, goes by different names in different grammars, but the name that appeals to me the most, because it is both simple and descriptive, is the "flip-flop" rule.[3] The rule works in three stages:

1. Go through the string and apply the symbol *Af* (standing for "affix," if you wish) to any *s, past,* $\emptyset$ (this is the *affix* $\emptyset$ on a verb), *en* or *ing.*
2. Also go through the string and apply the symbol *v* (a little *v*) to any *M* (modal) or *V* (verb) or *have* or *be.*
3. Then, any time the sequence *Af* + *v* occurs (without, that is, some symbol interrupting it), reverse it. That is:

    Af + v ⟶ v + Af# (Hence "flip-flop")

    (The symbol # stands for a word boundary, about which more later. We don't need it right now.)

Let's see how this applies to our string, which you can look back at as it stands in step number 13. Do we have a symbol *s*? No, we don't, so we do nothing about that. Do we have the symbol *past*? Yes, we do, so we write a little *Af* over it. Do we have $\emptyset$? Again, no. Do we have an *en*? An *ing*? Yes, we have one of each, so over each we write

---

3. A more formal term might be something like "the affix transformation rule" or "the affix positioning rule."

a little *Af.* And we have taken care of step number 1 of the flip-flop rule.

Now for step number 2. Do we have an *M*? Yes—it's been re-written and now stands as *may,* but it's there, so we write a little *v* over it. Do we have a *V*? Yes. It now stands as *chase,* and again we inscribe a little *v* over it. And since we have a *have* and a *be* we write our little *v* symbol over each of them. Our string now looks like this:

$$\text{Af} \quad v \quad\quad v \quad \text{Af} \; v \; \text{Af} \quad v$$
the + man + past + may + have + en + be + ing + chase + the + boys

Let's now go through it and link up the sequences of *Af + v:*

$$\text{Af} — v \quad\quad v \quad \text{Af—v} \quad \text{Af} —v$$
the + man + past + may + have + en + be + ing + chase + the + boys

That is *Af + v* occurs in that sequence and without interruption three times: *past + may, en + be,* and *ing + chase.* Following the third instruction of our flip-flop rule we reverse, or flip-flop, those occur-rences of *Af + v* as we rewrite the string one more time:

the + man + may + past + have + be + en + chase + ing + the + boys

We are now in shape to turn this string of symbols into a sen-tence, which is really to say, of course, into other and more familiar symbols. We need a few morphophonemic rules, like these:

1. may + past ⟶ might
2. be + en ⟶ been
3. chase + ing ⟶ chasing

Strictly speaking, and as you might already have realized, if we are to call these "morphophonemic rules" we should be dealing in pho-nemes. The rules would then look like this:

1. may + past ⟶ /mayt/
2. be + en ⟶ /bin/ ~ /bɨn/
3. chase + ing ⟶ /čéysiŋ/

Finally, then, if we wanted to present our sentence in conventional spelling these phonemes would have to be converted into letters, or "graphemes." If we wish to go directly from our string of morpheme symbols into words in orthodox spelling we would, technically, have to refer to "morphographemic" rules. This is a small point, but I thought you'd be enchanted to know. After all, it isn't everyone who can toss around nice big words like "morphographemics"—and know what they mean.

Anyhow, we've got our string in shape to apply the M-rules (whether we want to call them morphophonemic or morphographemic) and we apply them and come out with this:

the + man + might + have + been + chasing + the + boys,

or this: ðə+ mǽn + mâyt + əv + bɨn + čêysɨŋ + ðə + bóyz #

Knocking out the plus signs and writing it conventionally we obviously have:

The man might have been chasing the boys.

There are two questions I think you might well have:

1. How come *might* is the "past tense" of *may*?
2. Why go through this flip-flop routine? Why not put the silly affixes in the right position in the first place instead of putting them in front of the words they belong to and then reversing them?

As for the first question, *might* isn't really the "past tense" of *may* except that in transformational-generative grammar it is called so. Similarly:

$$can + past \longrightarrow could$$
$$shall + past \longrightarrow should$$
$$will + past \longrightarrow would$$

These are not, in any usual sense of the idea, "past tenses." We wouldn't say, certainly, that "I can go to the party" means right now whereas "I could go to the party" necessarily means at some earlier time. But the generative grammarian isn't interested in this matter. He is trying to devise a way of turning out acceptable sentences. Certainly both of these are all right:

The man may have been chasing the boys.
The man might have been chasing the boys.

And that's all the generative grammarian cares about. What exactly is the relation between "may" and "might" is not relevant at this point. The fact that the past tense morpheme, which works beautifully on a verb like *chased*, turns out "might" when applied to "may" is unimportant since in any event "The man might have been chasing the boys" is a perfectly acceptable sentence.

As for the second question—why the flip-flop business?—I'd like to defer answering that until we've constructed one or two more sentences.

This time we'll make it much like the first one but we'll take different choices where options exist. Perhaps it might be well to take the same lexical items so that the differences will stand out better. Again we start:

1. S $\longrightarrow$ NP + VP
2. NP + Verb + NP
3. D + N + Z_1 + Verb + NP
4. D + N + Z_1 + Aux + V + NP
5. D + N + Z_1 + Aux + V + D + N + $\emptyset$

Each step is a rewrite of one item only, and we have taken them in the exact order of the P-rules on page 195 except that, of course, to rewrite the second *NP* we had to go back and re-apply P-rule 3.)

6. D + N + Z_1 + C + be + ing + V + D + N + $\emptyset$

In rewriting *Aux* we must select the C, but we can choose any or all of the other items as long as we leave them in their proper order. For this sentence we have selected *C* and *be + ing*.

7. D + N + Z_1 + $\emptyset$ + be + ing + V + D + N + $\emptyset$

Be careful not to get the $\emptyset$'s confused. The first one is our rewrite of *C* and carries the tense and number of the verb; the second one indicates the absence of a plural marker on the noun, or in other words indicates a singular noun. Probably it would be a good idea, if we were going to go on and do very much with this grammar, to differentiate these symbols, perhaps as $\emptyset_1$ and $\emptyset_2$. But we're in no danger of confusing them right now so we won't bother.

8. the + N + Z_1 + $\emptyset$ + be + ing + V + D + N + $\emptyset$
9. the + men + $\emptyset$ + be + ing + V + D + N + $\emptyset$
10. the + men + $\emptyset$ + be + ing + chase + D + N + $\emptyset$
11. the + men + $\emptyset$ + be + ing + chase + the + N + $\emptyset$
12. the + men + $\emptyset$ + be + ing + chase + the + boy

At this point we have arrived at our terminal string. We have applied all the rules we have been instructed to, so now it is time to apply the flip-flop rule. (Check it again. It's on p. 201.)

Af — v   Af — v
the + men + $\emptyset$ + be + ing + chase + the + boy

Having distributed our *Af's* and *v's* according to the instructions of the flip-flop rule we find that we have two occurrences of the sequence *Af + v* and we must now reverse, or flip-flop, those elements so labeled.

the + men + be + $\emptyset$ + chase + ing + the + boy

Now to the M-rules. We will have to have one that says:

be + $\emptyset$ ⟶ are.

Is this right? What is the present plural of *be*? *The girl is, the girls are.* So the rule is presented as we want it to be. We already have an M-rule for *chase + ing.* So our sentence is clearly going to come out:

The men are chasing the boy.

It didn't take nearly so long to produce that sentence as it did the first one, largely because there was less need to stop and comment on rewrites as they were being made. Let's try one more. See if you can follow everything that happens, and remember: there will only be *one* change in each rewrite.

1. S ⟶ NP + VP
2. NP + Verb + NP
3. D + N + $\emptyset$ + Verb + NP
4. D + N + $\emptyset$ + Aux + V + NP
5. D + N + $\emptyset$ + Aux + V + D + N + Z_1
6. D + N + $\emptyset$ + C + have + en + V + D + N + Z_1
7. D + N + $\emptyset$ + s + have + en + V + D + N + Z_1
8. the + N + $\emptyset$ + s + have + en + V + D + N + Z_1
9. the + girl + s + have + en + V + D + N + Z_1
10. the + girl + s + have + en + chase + D + N + Z_1
11. the + girl + s + have + en + chase + the + N + Z_1
12. the + girl + s + have + en + chase + the + boys

This is the terminal string, so we turn now to the flip-flop rule:

Af — v   Af — v
13. the + girl + s + have + en + chase + the + boys
14. the + girl + have + s + chase + en + the + boys

Applicable morphophonemic rules would have to tell us that the third person present singular of *have* is *has,* and that the past participle of the regular verb *chase* is *chased.* Thus:

have + s ⟶ has
chase + en ⟶ chased

Actually, of course, we would have only one set of morphophonemic rules to cover all regular verbs + *en,* and only the relative handful of irregulars would need to be listed separately. Anyhow, we can see now that our sentence will come out:

The girl has chased the boys.

We can look now, in plain English, at other ways that sentence might develop depending upon the choices made in rewriting *Aux:*

1. The girl chases the boys.
    (terminal string) the + girl + s + chase + the + boys
2. The girl is chasing the boys.
    (t.s.) the + girl + s + be + ing + chase + the + boys
3. The girl has been chasing the boys.
    (t.s.) the + girl + s + have + en + be + ing + chase + the + boys
4. The girl may have been chasing the boys.
    (t.s.) the + girl + s + may + have + en + be + ing + chase + the + boys

Notice what happens to the *s,* the symbol that makes the verb agree in number with the subject. In sentence 1 it applies to *chase;* in sentence 2 it applies to *be;* in sentence 3 it is part of *has;* and in sentence 4 it applies to *may.* Let us see what enables this affix to be properly placed in the construction of *Aux,* which you will remember is *C (M) (have + en) (be + ing).* The *C* will apply to *M* if there is one, or to *have + en* if that is selected and the *M* is not, or to *be + ing* if neither of the first two options are selected, or to the verb itself if none of them are chosen.

We begin to see the answer to the question "Why the flip-flop?" It cannot be known ahead of time what the elements involved in the flip-flop are going to attach to, but it can be foreseen that they will fit appropriately on the items following them, whatever they might be. Thus in order to get the right morphemes matched up it is necessary to list them first in the order they have in *Aux* and then flip-flop them. Well, it might not be *necessary* to do it this way—doubtless other ways could be worked out—but this way seems both simple and economical.

The grammar we have just been working with is obviously much more productive than the miniature First Model Grammar which could turn out only a very modest set of sentences. Our Second Model Grammar will generate a great number. But even with our slight exposure to it you might have noticed some glaring deficiencies. For instance, the *NP* as subject, and its number agreement with the verb, is only for third person subjects. We have no way to produce "I was chasing the girls" or "You were chasing the girls." Also, if the *VP* has to be rewritten as *Verb + NP* how are we going to produce a sentence like "The lady sighed," in which there is no *NP* after the verb? If we wanted to handle this problem we could do something like changing the rewrite of *VP* to:

$$VP \longrightarrow \begin{Bmatrix} \text{Verb } + \text{ NP} \\ \text{Verb } + \text{ } \emptyset \end{Bmatrix}$$

This would, of course, involve us in differentiating different kinds of verbs, like those that take objects and those that don't (transitive vs. intransitive). In our Third Model Grammar, which we'll outline a little later on, we'll have to pay attention to some of these problems.

In the meantime, we can vastly extend the range of our present model grammar by the addition to it of some T-rules, which will enable us to make statements negative as well as affirmative, to convert statements into questions, to convert active into passive, etc. This would be a very great increase in the scope of our grammar.

T-rules differ from the other rules we've been using in several ways. For one thing, many of them are optional (there's no reason why you should *have to* turn a statement into a question), and the ones that are obligatory depend upon finding the string in a certain situation. That is, the rule reads in effect: *when a certain condition exists,* apply this T-rule. If the particular situation which calls for the application of the T-rule doesn't exist in the string, then forget it. Another thing about T-rules that differs from P-rules: with the P-rules there was only *one* item to the left of the arrow, which is to say that only one thing at a time was rewritten. With a T-rule, on the other hand, whole strings are rearranged, and items are added or deleted as the rule requires. But in one key particular the T-rule is the same as all the others: it is perfectly explicit.

Let's start with the transformation rule which permits us to make an affirmative statement into a negative. This rule is called *T-not* and it is, of course, an optional one. Let's see how it works. First we need to see where it applies. You remember the construction of *Aux: C (M) (have + en) (be + ing)*. What we need to do is add a *not* (or *n't*) to our string, and it turns out that we add it in the *Aux*. If the *Aux* has only one element (and that would have to be *C*) we add the *n't* after it. If Aux has two or more elements, we add the *n't* after the second one. Here are the possibilities:

	X	Y	Z
1.	NP	C	V
2.	NP	C + M	_____
3.	NP	C + have	_____
4.	NP	C + be	_____

You will note that in the second possibility, for instance, we could have *C + M + have + en + be + ing* but everything after the *M* is irrelevant as far as the application of this rule goes because it says if the *Aux* has two or more elements the *n't* is to be added *after the second one.* Therefore, if we ascertain that there are two elements we know where the addition goes and we don't care if there might be a hundred more tagging along later. Now, suppose we have a terminal string like the following (which I divide up with letters X-Y-Z like the chart above):

X	Y	Z
NP	C + M	(Immaterial)
the + friends + $\emptyset$ + can		+ be + ing + feud

The rule tells us that the *n't* is to be added after the second element of the *Aux.* This one happens to have others—*be + ing*—but they are irrelevant to this problem. The second element is *can,* so we add our new morpheme after it:

the + friends + $\emptyset$ + can + n't + be + ing + feud

We now have to apply the flip-flop, which is always the last move before applying the morphophonemic (morphographemic) rules and producing our end product:

Af—v   v   Af—v
the + friends + $\emptyset$ + can + n't + be + ing + feud

This then becomes:

the + friends + can + $\emptyset$ + n't + be + feud + ing

With the application of M-rules this will work out to:

The friends can't be feuding.

Let's try this T-rule on the last sentence we produced with our Second Model Grammar. The terminal string was this:

the + girl + s + have + en + chase + the + boys

To apply *T-not* we first need to see whether *Aux* in this case has only one element or two or more. It has three: *s + have + en*. *T-not* says we add *n't* after the *second* morpheme of *Aux*, so let's do that:

the + girl + s + have + n't + en + chase + the + boys

Now the flip-flop rule:

$$\text{Af———v} \qquad \text{Af———v}$$
the + girl + s + have + n't + en + chase + the + boys

Our string now becomes:

the + girl + have + s + n't + chase + en + the + boys

Since *have + s*———→ *has,* and the addition of *n't* to *has* produces *hasn't,* and since *chase* plus the past participle clearly produces *chased,* we come out with:

The girl hasn't chased the boys.

This one T-rule has tremendously increased the output potential of our grammar.

Let's look at another T-rule, the one which enables us to turn statements into questions. It's generally abbreviated as *T-q.* It applies to the same kinds of strings as *T-not,* i.e:

	X	Y	Z
1.	NP	C	V
2.	NP	C + M	___
3.	NP	C + have	___
4.	NP	C + be	___

T-q instructs us to reverse the first two elements (that is, X and Y). Again we are concerned only with the first two morphemes of the *Aux,* if it has two or more, and with only one if it has only one. *T-q* is also, of course, optional. Nobody says we have to make a statement into a question. Let's see how it works.

X	Y	Z
NP	C + have	Immaterial
the + children + ∅ + have		+ en + be + ing + play

To apply *T-q* we reverse the first two parts (X and Y):

∅ + have + the + children + en + be + ing + play

That's clear enough, certainly. Now we have to apply the flip-flop rule:

Af——v   Af——v   Af——v
Ø + have + the + children + en + be + ing + play

Making the flip-flop according to the rule, we get:

have + Ø + the + children + be + en + play + ing

This will produce:

Have the children been playing?

Again a simple T-rule has served to expand tremendously what our model grammar can produce. Now we can not only make affirmative statements but negative ones, and can turn both into questions.

Alas, all is not quite such smooth sailing as it appears, because we find that not all negatives and not all questions can be produced with these rules. For instance, for the negative of "Herman drinks" we certainly don't want *"Herman drinksn't." Similarly, for the question form of "His sister danced beautifully" we would disapprove of *"Danced his sister beautifully?" and would insist on "Did his sister dance beautifully?" We need some way of getting this common little English word *do* into constructions where it is needed.

There is a transformation rule to take care of just this problem. It is called, fittingly enough, *T-do*. We need to see how it works. First, I need point out that *T-do*, unlike *T-not* and *T-q* is *obligatory*. That is, when a situation crops up where *T-do* would fit, it *has to be* applied.

We will find that sometimes as we manipulate our strings of morphemes by applying different rules to them, the tense morpheme (*C* in any of its versions: *s*, Ø, or *past*) will wind up in a position where there is nothing for it to apply to, and we would be unable to apply the flip-flop rule because there is nothing to flip-flop with it. When this happens, the *T-do* rule steps in and says we must add *do*. Written out it would look like this:

Af # ————→ # do + Af

in which *Af* stands for our "tense affix" and the symbol "#" indicates a word boundary or the beginning of the sentence. Let's take a look at this in action and it will be clearer. Suppose we take our little sentence, "Herman drinks." The terminal string underlying it is this:

Herman + s + drink

As you can see, applying the flip-flop rule would give us our beginning statement. Suppose now we wish to make it negative. Our *T-not* rule says that if there is present only one morpheme of the auxiliary we add *n't* after it. This would give us:

Herman + s + n't + drink

This is exactly the situation that calls for *T-do*. Our tense symbol, *s*, "hangs" or "floats" with nothing to attach to. This won't make a sentence without the flip-flop, and if we do apply it, carrying *n't* with the *s*, we would get the impossible **Herman drinksn't*. We would be in trouble if *T-do* didn't come to the rescue. That rule instructs us to rewrite the string as:

Herman + do + s + n't + drink

Now you can see how this is going to develop:

Herman doesn't drink.

T-do helps us out of the same sort of jam with many kinds of questions. Let's look at a simple example. The terminal string underlying "Lolita slept" is:

Lolita + past + sleep

Suppose we want to apply *T-q* and make it a question. You will remember that the rule (pp. 209) instructs us to reverse the first two elements. We would get:

past + Lolita + sleep

Again we have an intolerable situation, one which is going to lead us no place. We have our tense morpheme out there on the front of the string with nothing to attach it to, and no possibility, either, of straightening matters out with a flip-flop. But this is precisely the situation where *T-do* applies, so we rewrite it this way:

do + past + Lolita + sleep

The past tense of *do* being *did* our sentence is going to come out:

Did Lolita sleep?

Notice how in the statement version the past tense in English is in the verb, "Lolita slept," and how in the question form the tense is borne by the "helper word," *do,* while the verb remains in its base form. Observe how neatly *T-do* provides for this.

Here's another handy T-rule. I'll write it in symbols first, and then we'll discuss it and try it out on a sample string:

$$NP_1 + Aux + V + NP_2 \longrightarrow NP_2 + Aux + be + en + V + by + NP_1$$

This rule is known as *T-passive* and it says that any time we have a string like the first one we can transform it into one like the second one. In other words, we can convert "active" statements into "passive." What's so great about that, you might say? You've always been able to perform this little trick, and without going through all this rigamarole of symbols. True. But did you know that the change is so absolutely regular that it can be reduced to a formula statement like this? Isn't it at least possible that this very regularity was what enabled you to learn the trick in the first place? In any event, let's see how it works.

Notice first that it only applies to a certain kind of string. That is to say, we can put "The boy ate the apple" into passive—"The apple was eaten by the boy."—but we can't do it with something like "The lady died." We couldn't come up with something like *"Died was by the lady." Which is only to state something that the rule already says for us: *T-passive* applies only to strings such as the one described. It is, of course, optional.

Notice that it has an *NP* before the *Aux + V* and one following it too, and that they are differentiated from each other by subscript numbers. These numbers are to enable us to tell which is which, for you will observe that while the string to which *T-passive* is to be applied leads off with NP_1 and ends with NP_2, the transformed string has these items reversed. Let's make a string on the model of the first one and see how this transformation works. Here's one:

$$NP_1 + Aux + V + NP_2$$

Applying P-rules, L-rules and M-rules to this string, it would work out like this:

1. $NP_1 + C + V + NP_2$
2. $NP_1 + past + V + NP_2$
3. $D + N + \emptyset + past + V + NP_2$
4. $D + N + \emptyset + past + V + D + N + \emptyset$
5. the $+ N + \emptyset + past + V + D + N + \emptyset$
6. the $+$ baby $+ past + V + D + N + \emptyset$
7. the $+$ baby $+ past + drink + D + N + \emptyset$
8. the $+$ baby $+ past + drink + the + N + \emptyset$
9. the $+$ baby $+ past + drink + the + beer$

Now labeling *past* with *Af* and *drink* with *v,* we flip-flop them and get:

10. the $+$ baby $+ drink + past + the + beer$

Since our M-rule is going to make *drink + past* ⟶ *drank,* we will get:

The baby drank the beer.

But suppose that instead of developing that string like that, we had first applied the *T-passive* transform and *then* developed it. (Remember, we need to keep the same lexical items, same tense choice, etc.) The string transforms into, according to the rule:

NP_2 + Aux + be + en + V + by + NP_1

1. NP_2 + C + be + en + V + by + NP_1
2. NP_2 + past + be + en + V + by + NP_1
3. D + N + $\emptyset$ + past + be + en + V + by + NP_1
4. D + N + $\emptyset$ + past + be + en + V + by + D + N + $\emptyset$
5. the + N + $\emptyset$ + past + be + en + V + by + D + N + $\emptyset$
6. the + beer + past + be + en + V + by + D + N + $\emptyset$

(Remember that the order of NP_1 and NP_2 was reversed, so that we have to put *beer* in here instead of *baby,* which is now at the end of the string.)

7. the + beer + past + be + en + drink + by + D + N + $\emptyset$
8. the + beer + past + be + en + drink + by + the + N + $\emptyset$
9. the + beer + past + be + en + drink + by + the + baby

We now have a terminal string, so let's apply the little *Af's* and *v's.*

Af——v   Af——v

10. the + beer + past + be + en + drink + by + the + baby

Next of course, the flip-flop:

11. the + beer + be + past + drink + en + by + the + baby

Let's say our M-rule stipulates that *be + past* ⟶ *was.* (Actually this is over-simplifying with *be* because if our subject was plural, *beers,* we would have to rewrite *be + past* ⟶ *were, the beers were.* This is easily done, but we needn't worry about it here.) Also, clearly, we will need an M-rule that instructs us to rewrite *drink + en* ⟶ *drunk.* Then our string will develop into:

The beer was drunk by the baby.

This T-rule needs a further refinement so that we can turn out not only the transformation we just did, but one in which "by the baby" is omitted, giving us "The beer was drunk." That's certainly correct

English, though it sounds a bit odd perhaps because it suggests another familiar pattern, "The man was drunk," which is something quite different. But we want our *T-passive* to change "The tornado destroyed the barn" into "The barn was destroyed by the tornado" and also into, simply, "The barn was destroyed." Perhaps we could do it like this:

$$NP_1 + Aux + V + NP_2 \Longrightarrow NP_2 + Aux + be + en + V + \begin{Bmatrix} by + NP_1 \\ null \end{Bmatrix}$$

in which "null" means "nothing," "zero," "blank." This, you can see, would enable our grammar to turn out "The barn was destroyed."

As a matter of fact, of course, we need many more transformations, and refinements on the ones we've already discussed, to enable our grammar to come closer to producing the complexity of English. For instance, from the statement

The baby drank the beer

we need not only to produce this question:

Did the baby drink the beer?

but also:

Who drank the beer?

and

What did the baby drink?

Simple transformations are at hand to enable us to construct such questions, and also many other "derived sentences." (Derived sentences, naturally, are ones "derived" from kernel sentences. In other words, the P-rules, L-rules and M-rules by themselves, with only the addition of the flip-flop, will produce our kernel sentences. The addition of T-rules enables us to turn out derived sentences, and makes our grammar immensely more powerful.)

However, we are not here and now going to run through any more T-rules. Instead, let us turn our attention to some of the other matters that would have to be considered in creating a grammar that would produce sentences more nearly approximating the variety that we have in our language. We'll start with a new (and our last) model grammar. Remember, though, that the principles in it will be exactly the same as the ones we're already familiar with.

Third Model Grammar

A good question at this point might be, "Why do we need a third model grammar? Can't the one we've been tinkering with be altered, or refined, to make it do more things?" And the answer is, yes it can. Essentially our Third Model Grammar is nothing but a refinement of the Second Model Grammar, just as that one was a further development of the rudimentary First Model Grammar we used merely to get a look at some basic principles. But a lot of things are more complicated than would appear from our Second Model Grammar. We did a lot of over-simplifying. For example, we treated the determiner rather cavalierly. We simply said $D \longrightarrow$ *the, a, some, his,* etc. And we had already rewritten *NP* as D + N + $\emptyset$, D + N + Z_1. But how about *NP's* that don't have determiners? Like:

Women are fickle.

Or, if you prefer:

Men are fickle.

We certainly need to make the possibility of this construction fit into our rewrite of NP. We can do it very easily by recalling a device that we used at the morpheme level some pages back, the concept of $\emptyset$. Thus we can remain consistent and say that indeed *NP* must include *D,* but that *D* may be rewritten as $\emptyset$.

But the addition of $\emptyset$ by no means resolves all the problems. We are certainly not going to attempt to resolve them here, nor even lay them out in the detail in which they are readily available in such transformational grammars as you will find listed in the bibliography in the back of this book. All we are going to do is indicate what some of the problems are, not only with determiners but with some of the other "parts of speech," and tentatively sketch out some possible ways of handling them.

If we set down a list of determiners and start experimenting with them to see how they function in actual sentences we find we have different kinds. We are not looking at what they "mean"—determiners have only minimum meaning anyhow—but at the fact that they operate in different ways. Some of them will go with certain kinds of nouns but not with others, some will go with singular nouns and not with plurals, and vice versa and etc. We seem to find three principal kinds. We sort them into classes and label them as in the following lists, which are not comprehensive:

Articles	Demonstratives	Possessives
a (an)	this	his
the	that	her
some	these	our
every	those	their
each		my
∅		Emily's
etc.		etc.

This would seem to indicate that we are going to have to rewrite D as:

$$D \longrightarrow \begin{Bmatrix} \text{Art} \\ \text{Dem} \\ \text{Pos} \end{Bmatrix}$$

This is, in fact, pretty standard procedure in transformational-generative grammars. However, this does not end the complications of the determiner. We find that we have not only sentences like

> The cats were in the kitchen.

but

> Several of the cats were in the kitchen.
> All of Madeline's cats were in the kitchen.
> Every one of those cats was in the kitchen.
> None of the first four cats was in the kitchen.
> A final few more cats were in the kitchen.

In some of these there seem to be words preceding the determiner; in others there are words following the determiner but before *cats,* the noun. How are these to be dealt with? The usual practice is to consider them as part of the determiner, and they are given the labels of *predeterminers* and *postdeterminers* depending on their position in relation to the article, demonstrative or possessive which might be considered the heart (or, perhaps, headword) of the determiner. Thus in the example sentences above, the determiners would be:

> several of the
> all of Madeline's
> every one of those
> none of the first four
> a final few more

Some of these have predeterminers (Pre-D) and some have post-determiners (Post-D) and one has both. (Can you tell which one it is? If not, never mind. We'll be discussing this a bit further.)

You will notice that in the first four of these determiners, each of which has a Pre-D, the little word "of" appears. Some grammarians call this a "marker" or "sign" of the predeterminer, differentiating it from the preposition "of." Most of the time the "of" has to be present in the Pre-D, but not all the time. Thus we can have both of these:

> All of Madeline's cats were in the kitchen.
> All Madeline's cats were in the kitchen.

However, any time this construction can appear without the "of" it also has a version with it, so probably in setting up our rule for constructing the determiner we would do best to set up this construction with the "of" in it and then concoct an optional T-rule which would provide for removing it when it *can* be removed. That is, you can have

> All Madeline's cats

but you can't have

> *several the cats
> *every one those cats
> *none the first four cats

There are also a very few words which will precede the determiner without the "of" and without being derived from a construction with it. They are words like *only* and *just* in:

> only these women
> just my luck

These words are often called "prearticles" (Pre-Art).

Taking into consideration the above observations, our rewrite of *D* would now look like this:

$$D \longrightarrow (\text{Pre-Art}) (\text{Pre-D}) \begin{Bmatrix} \text{Art} \\ \text{Dem} \\ \text{Pos} \end{Bmatrix}$$

You will remember that the parentheses signify that the symbols enclosed are optional, may either be included or left out. Thus the rewrite says that we may have a *Pre-Art* (or may not), we may have a

Pre-D (or may not), but we must choose among *Art, Dem,* or *Pos—* remembering that *Art* may be ∅.

We aren't through with this business yet, though. We saw earlier that there is also a postdeterminer, and we need to consider what it might look like. We saw one a moment ago in the sentence

None of the first four cats was in the kitchen.

Following the regular determiner *the* and preceding the noun *cats* we have *first four.* This is an example of a postdeterminer. We find as we experiment with the kinds of words that can function as post-determiners that there are three: ordinal (numbers), which we are going to symbolize *Ord;* cardinal (numbers) or *Card;* and superlatives and comparatives, *Comp.* Unlike the "headword" determiners, which come only one to a construction, we can have two or sometimes even three of these postdeterminers in the same determiner construction, but if we do, they have to occur in the same order in which they've just been presented: *Ord, Card, Comp.* Here are some:

Ordinals	Cardinals	Comparatives and Superlatives
first	one	more
second	two	few
third	three	most
etc.	etc.	fewest
last	few	least
next	many	less
		etc.

There are others, but these will do as a sample. Can you visualize contexts in which they might occur together? How about this one?

The *first few* questions were not too bad, but the *next three more* questions really stumped me.

Strained a bit, maybe, but is it English? Perhaps you'll agree that it is.

So now we have to rewrite *D* like this:

$$D \longrightarrow \text{(Pre-Art) (Pre-D)} \begin{Bmatrix} \text{Art} \\ \text{Dem} \\ \text{Pos} \end{Bmatrix} \text{(Post-D)}$$

This is obviously a far cry from $D \longrightarrow$ *the, a, some, his, etc.* But it is also obviously a more realistic description of what actually is involved in the determiner in English, and you will remember that several chapters ago when we said that one thing we would desire in a grammar was "simplicity," we also said that we would want the grammar to be as complete as possible. If it should prove that the above formula is a complete description of the determiner in English, I think we'd have to agree that it is, after all, fairly simple. For the construction of the determiner is, as we have been noting, pretty complicated.

To complicate things further, we have different classes of nouns, as we saw earlier. For instance, we noted that we have both "count" and "mass" (or "non-count") nouns, and we observed that they take different determiners. You would ask for "a" pencil and "some" water, but not vice versa. We have also, of course, proper nouns (and pronouns) which don't take determiners at all—or, more precisely, take the $\emptyset$ article. Thus you would say:

> Wilbur smelled bad.
>
> They eat grasshoppers.

You would not say:

> *The Wilbur smelled bad.
>
> *Some they eat grasshoppers.

On the other hand, you would say:

> The Queen Mary eased in to the dock.
>
> Huck and Jim floated down the Mississippi.

One linguist, to resolve this problem, has suggested that when we do use "the" with a proper noun in this fashion, it isn't a determiner at all but is part of the noun. Thus in this sentence:

> When in Pennsylvania he stayed at the Pennsylvania,

the is part of the name of the hotel. How about it? Does that sound like a reasonable way around this problem? We could still say, then, that one thing that characterizes proper nouns (and pronouns) is that they take the $\emptyset$ article, and the name of the hotel would be:

> Art + Proper noun
>
> $\emptyset$ + the Pennsylvania

Remember always that we're not looking for "truth"; we're simply seeking a convenient way of describing something that indisputably happens in English. As for me, I think I'll accept this kind of occurrence of *the* as part of the proper noun, at least until someone comes along with a better gimmick.

We also have "animate" and "inanimate" nouns—that is, nouns that refer to animate beings and nouns that refer to inanimate things. Consider:

> The burglar scared my grandmother.
>
> The noise scared my grandmother.

Burglar is animate, *noise* inanimate. Look at what happens when we transform them into what we call *Wh-* questions, questions that ask *who, what,* etc.

> Who scared my grandmother?
>
> What scared my grandmother?

We use *who* to ask about animate nouns and *what* to ask about inanimate ones, and before we can transform a statement into a *Wh-* question we have to consider what kind of noun we are dealing with.

Similarly, although we can correctly observe that English doesn't have a grammatical gender, in the sense that German and Spanish have, still nouns do have a sort of gender as we find when we substitute pronouns for them:

> He scared my grandmother. (The burglar)
>
> It scared my grandmother. (The noise)

And, if we had had a sentence "Margery scared my grandmother," the substitution would, of course, be:

> She scared my grandmother.

Finally, we must consider the distinction between "concrete" and "abstract" nouns. As an example of the difference, Webster's III says that "the word *poem* is concrete, *poetry* is abstract." The distinction between abstract and concrete is important in language style, of course, and you probably had composition teachers pointing that out to you. However, the difference is reflected in grammar, too, as in the way words of one class or the other go with cardinal numbers, or won't go with them. You can have one poem, two poems, three poems, and so on, but you can't have *one poetry, *two poetries, *three poetries. You can have one dollar, ten dollars, twenty dollars—but not *one wealth, *ten wealths, *twenty wealths.

Clearly all this has relevance to the construction of such a grammar as we are discussing, for all the subtle ways in which words of different categories mesh together have to be taken into account. If our grammar produces

> His first ten dollars were hard to earn

all well and good. On the other hand, if it turns out

> *His first ten wealths were hard to earn

all ill and bad. Such a construction is un-English.

Thus we should have some way to signal nouns of varying nature so that they can be fitted out properly with determiners. We could use a hyphen and an italicized abbreviation or label, thus:

> N-*mass* (mass noun)
> N-*count* (count noun)
> N-*fem* (feminine noun)
> N-*prop* (proper noun)

And so on.

Furthermore, we've already remarked that we're going to have to refine our rewrite of *VP*. As of now it reads

> VP ⟶ Verb + NP.

As we observed, not all verbs have *NP's* following them. For instance:

> Jerry drowned.
> The girls looked sweet.
> Uncle Thomas belched loudly.

Also, though we have dealt with *be* as part of *Aux* we have not yet allowed for the fact that *to be* regularly functions as the main verb in a sentence:

> That lady is my aunt.
> My dogs are intelligent.
> The plumber is here.

And so on. None of these sentences could we construct with our Second Model Grammar—and they're all extraordinarily common in English. It would be a sorry grammar indeed that couldn't provide for sentences like these. What we have to do is rewrite our rules for producing the verb (including *to be*) so that our grammar will produce such sentences. Let's start like this:

$$VP \longrightarrow Aux + MV$$

(You can think of MV as meaning "main verb.") Then:

$$MV \longrightarrow \begin{Bmatrix} be + Pred \\ Verb\ (+\ adv.) \end{Bmatrix}$$

Pred stands for "predicate," and means, not predicate in the usual sense, but only the objects, complements, or adverbial modifiers that can follow *be*. In the examples just above we had as *Pred*'s:

> my aunt (NP)
> intelligent (Adj)
> here (Adv)

So that the rule says that *MV* is to be one or the other: *be + Pred* or *Verb*, and it says further that an adverb may or may not follow *Verb*.

Now we need three more rewrite rules: one for *Pred*, one for *Verb*, and one for *Adv*. (Don't worry that these rewrite rules are proliferating all over the place. Just read for understanding. Later we'll gather them all up in a list, and put them through their paces, too.)

We'll rewrite *Pred* this way:

$$Pred \longrightarrow \begin{Bmatrix} NP \\ Adj \\ Adv\text{-}P \end{Bmatrix}$$

in which *Adv-P* is an "adverb of place." (That is, the kind of adverb which would be an answer to the question "where?") This rewrite will enable our grammar to produce sentences like those we were just discussing:

> That gentleman is our janitor.
> His fingernails were dirty.
> Your limousine is outside.

Our rewrite of *Verb* will be this:

$$Verb \longrightarrow \begin{Bmatrix} V_i \\ V_t + NP \\ V_c + Adj \end{Bmatrix}$$

The meaning of these symbols is as follows: V_i is an "intransitive verb," or a verb that doesn't have an object following it. (You will remember that our rewrite of *VP* is *Verb (+ Adv)*, so we have already stipulated that V_i may or may not have a following adverb.) Examples of V_i would be these:

> His writing stinks.
> Helene danced beautifully.
> Aunt Agatha snored.

V_t, of course, is a transitive verb; the kind of verb our Second Model Grammar featured, producing sentences like these, in which the verbs do have objects, or following *NP's:*

> Hilda's nephew eats birdseed.
> The pilot sank the battleship.
> The dean lectured the fraternity.

Finally, V_c stands for a "linking verb." This kind of verb is also known as a "copulative" verb; hence the little subscript "c." What kind of verb is a linking verb? For our purposes here it's a verb that can be followed by an adjective, like:

> The cook became sad.
> Eleanor appears healthy.
> The drinks tasted horrible.
> That pipe smells good.
> Their report sounded ominous.

There are only a few dozen of these verbs, but they are common enough so that we need some way for our grammar to produce sentences using them. (As a matter of fact, there *are* linking verbs which stand between nouns with the same referents—like "That sailor became a hero."—but since our grammar is to be only a sketchy one anyhow, we won't rewrite V_c to enable us to handle this construction.) Notice, by the way, that though *to be* is extremely common with an adjective following it ("They are sloppy") we do not include it in V_c but rather deal with that construction in our rewrite of *Pred.*

We still need to rewrite *Adv.* We do it like this:

$$\text{Adv} \longrightarrow \begin{Bmatrix} \text{Adv-T} \\ \text{Adv-P} \\ \text{Adv-M} \end{Bmatrix}$$

These are symbols for the traditional names of the three kinds of adverbs: those of time, place, and manner, which are as we noted earlier (p. 142) the adverbs which would serve as answers to the questions "When?" "Where?" and "How?" This rewrite will enable us to produce constructions like these:

> He ate yesterday.
>
> He ate upstairs.
>
> He ate noisily.

You might have noticed that so far nothing has been said about the adjective except the "predicate adjective," the one that can follow *to be* in *Pred* or that follows V_c. That is, we have not provided for the common adjective position preceding the noun, like "fat" in:

> My *fat* sister married his *fat* brother.

Nor have we provided for other extremely common constructions, such as this one:

> The girls *in the dorm* are lovely.

Nor this one:

> His father, *a judge,* is an alcoholic.

Nor other very common constructions, for that matter. Well, these three—the attributive adjective, the P-group, and the noun in apposition—we are going to handle with transformations, and we'll defer examining how we're going to do it until we need to describe the T-rules that produce them. But we are not going to try to produce all constructions, not even all very common ones. What we need—and *all* we need—is enough of a sample so that we can feel we understand something, at least, of how a transformational-generative grammar works. If you'll recall, that's all we set out to do in the first place, quite some few pages back.

Now, however, let's list the rules we've been busily writing, and rewriting, for this, our Third Model Grammar.

P-Rules

$$S \longrightarrow NP + VP$$

1. $NP \longrightarrow \begin{Bmatrix} D + N + \emptyset_1 \\ D + N + Z_1 \end{Bmatrix}$

2. $D \longrightarrow$ (Pre-Art) (Pre-D) $\begin{Bmatrix} \text{Art} \\ \text{Dem} \\ \text{Pos} \end{Bmatrix}$ (Post-D)

3. VP ⟶ Aux + MV

4. MV ⟶ $\left\{\begin{array}{l} \text{be } + \text{ Pred} \\ \text{Verb } (+ \text{ Adv}) \end{array}\right\}$

5. Pred ⟶ $\left\{\begin{array}{l} \text{NP} \\ \text{Adj} \\ \text{Adv-P} \end{array}\right\}$

6. Verb ⟶ $\left\{\begin{array}{l} V_i \\ V_t + \text{NP} \\ V_c + \text{Adj} \end{array}\right\}$

7. Adv. ⟶ $\left\{\begin{array}{l} \text{Adv-T} \\ \text{Adv-P} \\ \text{Adv-M} \end{array}\right\}$

8. Aux ⟶ C (M) (have + en) (be + ing)

9. C ⟶ $\left\{\begin{array}{l} \text{s in the context N } + \emptyset \\ \emptyset_2{}^4 \text{ in the context N } + Z_1 \\ \text{past} \end{array}\right\}$

10. Post-D ⟶ $\left\{\begin{array}{l} \text{Ord} \\ \text{Card} \\ \text{Comp} \end{array}\right\}$

L-Rules

1. N ⟶ man, boy, girl, child, Charles, he, she, water, etc.
2. V_i ⟶ die, sing, snore, sleep, etc.
3. V_t ⟶ give, throw, sell, chase, etc.
4. V_c ⟶ appear, seem, smell, taste, become, etc.
5. Art ⟶ the, a(n), each, $\emptyset$, etc.
6. Dem ⟶ this, that, these, those
7. Pos ⟶ his, her, Emily's, their, etc.
8. Pre-Art ⟶ only these, just my
9. Pre-D ⟶ all of, some of, most of, each of, etc.
10. Ord ⟶ first, second, last, next, etc.
11. Card ⟶ one, two, several, many, etc.
12. Comp ⟶ few, fewer, more, most, less, least, etc.
13. Adv-T ⟶ then, yesterday, today, etc.
14. Adv-P ⟶ there, outside, upstairs, etc.
15. Adv-M ⟶ thus, anxiously, hopefully, sweetly, etc.
16. M ⟶ may, can, shall, will, must

---

4. In these rules, unlike those of the Second Model Grammar, we will differentiate ϕ_1 (noun singular) and ϕ_2 (base form of the verb).

M-Rules

1. hat + Z_1 ⟶ /hæts/, etc. etc.
2. eat + past ⟶ /eyt/
3. eat + en ⟶ /íytən/, etc.

NOTE: These *M*—rules are so obvious, and you so surely have the idea from what we have already done, that we'll not list any more of them. It should be again pointed out, though, that the three rules above are morphophonemic rules (from morphemes into phonemes), and we will use here morphographemic ones (from morphemes into standard letters), which should be written:

1. eat + past ⟶ ate

and so on.

We also have a few T-rules that we used in our Second Model Grammar and which will be perfectly usable here too. We'll add a few more later, but we'll start with just these:

T-Rules

1. *T-not* (optional) applies to strings like these:

X	Y	Z
NP	+ C	+V
NP	+ C + M	_____
NP	+ C + have	_____
NP	+ C + be	_____

The rule says: X + Y + Z ⟹ X + Y+n't + Z
2. *T-q* (optional) applies to the same strings as *T-not*
The rule says: X + Y + Z ⟹ Y + X + Z
3. *T-do* (obligatory)
The rules says, when: #Af# ⟹ #do + Af#
4. *T-passive* (optional)
NP_1 + Aux + V + NP_2 ⟹ NP_2 + Aux + be + en + V + by + NP_1

Now let's go ahead and create some sentences with these rules. Remember that though we have a few more rules than we had in the Second Model Grammar, they still apply only one step at a time and as long as we follow the rules we can't get into much trouble. They may be tedious, but they are *not* difficult. Let's try one or two. On this first one we'll comment on the applications of the rules as we go along:

1. S ———→ NP + VP
2. D + N + Z_1 + VP

This is the rewrite of *NP* according to P-rule #1. Now we'll rewrite *D*, then *VP*, etc.

3. Pre-D + Dem + N + Z_1 + VP
4. Pre-D + Dem + N + Z_1 + Aux + MV
5. Pre-D + Dem + N + Z_1 + Aux + Verb + Adv

In our rewrite of *MV* we elected to have the adverb; but we didn't have to, since it's in parentheses.

6. Pre-D + Dem + N + Z_1 + Aux + V_i + Adv

We selected V_i merely because this will produce a sentence of a pattern we were unable to make with our Second Model Grammar.

7. Pre-D + Dem + N + Z_1 + Aux + V_i + Adv-P
8. Pre-D + Dem + N + Z_1 + C + have + en + be + ing + V_i + Adv-P

In rewriting *Aux* we have to select the *C*, you'll recall. We chose also *have + en* and *be + ing*, but omitted the *M*.

9. Pre-D + Dem + N + Z_1 + $\emptyset_2$ + have + en + be + ing + V_i + Adv-P

We have now followed the P-rules as far as they instruct us to. (Some books refer to the string in this condition as the terminal string; others apply the phrase to the string after L-rules have been applied, as we did earlier. The point is inconsequential, but I call it to your attention. We'll continue to mean by "terminal string" that string resulting from the application of both P-rules and L-rules.) So now we start substituting lexical items as instructed by the L-rules:

10. all of + Dem + N + Z_1 + $\emptyset_2$ + have + en + be + ing + V_i + Adv-P
11. all of + those + N + Z_1 + $\emptyset_2$ + have + en + be + ing + V_i + Adv-P
12. all of + those + child + Z_1 + $\emptyset_2$ + have + en + be + ing + V_i + Adv-P
13. all of + those + child + Z_1 + $\emptyset_2$ + have + en + be + ing + go + Adv-P
14. all of + those + child + Z_1 + $\emptyset_2$ + have + en + be + ing + go + outside

This, now, is what we are calling a terminal string. We need to mark the appropriate morphemes with *Af* and *v* and flip-flop them.

$$\text{Af} \underline{\quad} \text{v} \qquad \text{Af} \underline{\quad} \text{v} \qquad \text{Af} \underline{\quad} \text{v}$$

15. all of + those + child + Z_1 + $\emptyset_2$ + have + en + be + ing + go + outside

16. all of + those + child + Z_1 + have + $\emptyset_2$ + be + en + go + ing + outside

Now we apply the M-rules, which will tell us that *child* + Z_1 ⟶ *children*, *have* + $\emptyset_2$ ⟶ *have*, and so on. Clearly our string will develop into:

All of those children have been going outside.

Suppose we had elected to make a question of it. This would mean that we would have applied *T-q*, and we would have applied it after step 9 when everything was conveniently in symbols. Let's try it. Step 9 was this:

9. Pre-D + Dem + N + Z_1 + $\emptyset_2$ + have + en + be + ing + V_i + Adv-P

If you remember (or if you'll look back at the rule), *T-q* instructs us to reverse *NP* and the first two elements of *Aux* if it has two, or one if it has only one. In this case it has two. *NP* is represented in step 9 by:

Pre-D + Dem + N + Z_1

The first two elements of *Aux* which we have are:

$\emptyset_2$ + have.

All of the rest of the string is irrelevant to the application of *T-q*. So we rewrite the string, reversing elements as instructed to by the rule:

10. $\emptyset_2$ + have + Pre-D + Dem + N + Z_1 + en + be + ing + V_i + Adv-P

Now we simply go ahead and develop the string in what has become familiar practice to us:

11. $\emptyset_2$ + have + all of + Dem + N + Z_1 + en + be + ing + V_i + Adv-P

12. $\emptyset_2$ + have + all of + those + N + Z_1 + en + be + ing + V_i + Adv-P

13. $\emptyset_2$ + have + all of + those + child + Z_1 + en + be + ing + V_i + Adv-P

14. $\emptyset_2$ + have + all of + those + child + Z_1 + en + be + ing + go + Adv-P

15. $\emptyset_2$ + have + all of + those + child + Z_1 + en + be + ing + go + outside

Now the flip-flop:

Af—— v   Af—v   Af—v

16. $\emptyset_2$+ have + all of + those + child + Z_1 + en + be + ing + go + outside

17. have + $\emptyset_2$+ all of + those + child + Z_1 + be + en + go + ing + outside

Finally, morphophonemic/morphographemic rules will convert our string into:

> Have all of those children been going outside?

Thus the simple application of *T-q* at step nine has converted our statement into a question.

 Let's try developing another sentence, choosing different options where choices exist. This will probably go a bit faster since we'll need less commentary.

1. S $\longrightarrow$ NP + VP
2. D + N + $\emptyset_1$ + VP
3. Pos + Post-D + N + $\emptyset_1$ + VP
4. Pos + Post-D + N + $\emptyset_1$ + Aux + MV
5. Pos + Post-D + N + $\emptyset_1$ + Aux + be + Pred

(This time, instead of a verb we've selected *to be*.)

6. Pos + Post-D + N + $\emptyset_1$ + Aux + be + NP
7. Pos + Post-D + N + $\emptyset_1$ + Aux + be + D + N + $\emptyset_1$
8. Pos + Post-D + N + $\emptyset_1$ + Aux + be + Art + N + $\emptyset_1$
9. Pos + Post-D + N + $\emptyset_1$ + C + M + be + Art + N + $\emptyset_1$

(In the rewrite of *Aux* we selected only *M* among the options.)

10. Pos + Post-D + N + $\emptyset_1$ + s + M + be + Art + N + $\emptyset_1$
11. Pos + Ord + N + $\emptyset_1$ + s + M + be + Art + N + $\emptyset_1$

We have now applied all the P-rules, so we start with the L-rules:

12. Charlie's + Ord + N + $\emptyset_1$ + s + M + be + Art + N + $\emptyset_1$
13. Charlie's + first + N + $\emptyset_1$ + s + M + be + Art + N + $\emptyset_1$

14. Charlie's + first + child + $\emptyset_1$ + s + M + be + Art + N + $\emptyset_1$
15. Charlie's + first + child + $\emptyset_1$ + s + will + be + Art + N + $\emptyset_1$
16. Charlie's + first + child + $\emptyset_1$ + s + will + be + a + N + $\emptyset_1$
17. Charlie's + first + child + $\emptyset_1$ + s + will + be + a + girl + $\emptyset_1$

That is our terminal string, and we apply the flip-flop:

$$Af — v$$

18. Charlie's + first + child + $\emptyset_1$ + s + will + be + a + girl + $\emptyset_1$
19. Charlie's + first + child + $\emptyset_1$ + will + s + be + a + girl + $\emptyset_1$

Our M-rules will instruct us that the third person singular of *will* is *will*, which is to say *will* + *s* ⟶ *will*. So that we can see that our final product is going to be:

Charlie's first child will be a girl.

What a marvelous grammar this is indeed! It not only cranks out sentences but predicts the sex of unborn infants.

Let's create one more sentence, taking still different options, and then consider a couple of important transformations. We'll just run out this sentence pretty quickly:

1. S ⟶ NP + VP
2. D + N + Z_1 + VP
3. Pre-D + Art + N + Z_1 + VP
4. Pre-D + Art + N + Z_1 + Aux + MV
5. Pre-D + Art + N + Z_1 + Aux + Verb + Adv
6. Pre-D + Art + N + Z_1 + Aux + V_c + Adj + Adv

(We'll try the linking verb this time.)

7. Pre-D + Art + N + Z_1 + Aux + V_c + Adj + Adv-T
8. Pre-D + Art + N + Z_1 + C + be + ing + V_c + Adj + Adv-T
9. Pre-D + Art + N + Z_1 + past + be + ing + V_c + Adj + Adv-T
10. most of + Art + N + Z_1 + past + be + ing + V_c + Adj + Adv-T
11. most of + the + N + Z_1 + past + be + ing + V_c + Adj + Adv-T
12. most of + the + girl + Z_1 + past + be + ing + V_c + Adj + Adv-T
13. most of + the + girl + Z_1 + past + be + ing + look + Adj + Adv-T
14. most of + the + girl + Z_1 + past + be + ing + look + sweet + Adv-T

15. most of + the + girl + Z_1 + past + be + ing + look + sweet +
yesterday

$$\text{Af} \longrightarrow \text{v} \qquad \text{Af} \longrightarrow \text{v}$$

16. most of + the + girl + Z_1 + past + be + ing + look + sweet +
yesterday

17. most of + the + girl + Z_1 + be + past + look + ing + sweet +
yesterday

We will need an M-rule to tell us that *be + past* ⎯⎯⎯→ *were* when
it follows N + Z_1, or a plural subject. With other M-rules, which are
perfectly obvious, the sentence will come out:

Most of the girls were looking sweet yesterday.

By applying at the appropriate place in the process the T-rules we
already have we could have made this a question, or a negative question:

Weren't most of the girls looking sweet yesterday?

Could we have made it passive by applying *T-passive?* No, we could
not, because *T-passive* applies only to strings of a certain description,
and this string doesn't fit it. Our grammar is thus prevented from
producing some monster like:

*Sweet was looked by most of the girls yesterday.

We need to consider a few more transformations. We must first
figure how to provide for the placement of adjectives between the
determiner and the following noun. As it stands, our grammar can
produce:

That character insulted my sister

but it can't produce:

That ugly character insulted my sister.

We need to make provision so that it can. To do so, we will introduce
a couple of new concepts, and also a new rewrite of *NP*.

The two new concepts are those of the *matrix sentence* and the
constituent sentence, terms widely used by transformationalists. As
the terms indicate, a matrix sentence is one within which something
else (in this case the constituent sentence) "originates or takes form
or develops." (Check "matrix" in your dictionary.) Thus in this sentence:

The girl I loved had red hair

the matrix sentence is

The girl had red hair

and *I loved* is a constituent sentence embedded within it. You will no doubt recognize these as the traditional *dependent clause* and *independent clause* and may wonder why the transformationalist uses different terms. He is not merely being perverse, but feels that *matrix* and *constituent* are more descriptive and more precise. For sometimes, as we will see, the constituent doesn't appear as a sentence in the final product but is merely a fragment, a remnant, of what had originally been a constituent sentence.

As for the rewrite of *NP*, we will now always write it *NP (+S)*. Thus our rewrite of *S* will be:

$$S \longrightarrow NP\ (+S)\ +\ VP$$

As you can see, this means that every noun phrase *may be* (the parentheses indicate that it doesn't have to be) followed by another *S*. If you're on your toes at the moment, you may be thinking: Suppose we choose to include that optional *S*—then do we rewrite it the same way, again including an optional *S*?" The answer is, yes we do. This is what the transformationalist calls a *recursive* rule, which means that it can be applied again and again and again, theoretically without limit. Thus if we were to rewrite the string above, including the optional *S*, it would become:

$$NP + [NP\ (+S) + VP] + VP$$

The section set off in brackets is merely the original optional *S* rewritten—and now we have another optional *S* to rewrite in the same way if we choose. The effect is rather like those pictures that used to fascinate many of us when we were children: you have a picture of a boy holding a picture of himself, which picture is of the boy holding a picture of himself, and *that* picture is of the boy holding a picture of himself, until the thing diminishes to the point where it gets lost.

Like most explanations, this one would go much better with an illustration. Suppose we had a string which would produce the sentence

That dog bit my uncle.

Without actually reproducing the string, just for purposes of an example, let's write it like this:

that + dog + bit + my + uncle

Our *NP* is *that + dog,* of course. Now suppose additionally that we had had the optional *S* following the *NP:*

that + dog (+S) + bit + my + uncle.

Let us suppose further that we had selected the optional *S* and had developed it like this:

that + dog (that + dog + is + vicious) + bit + my + uncle

(We retain the parentheses merely to set off clearly the part of the string we're talking about.)

It would be very easy now to write a rule which would stipulate that whenever the embedded sentence is like the one we have here *(NP + be + Adj)* and when the *NP* of the embedded, or constituent sentence, is identical to that of the matrix sentence—the situation that obtains here—we can transform the matrix sentence into:

$$D + Adj + N \ldots .$$

which would give us:

that + vicious + dog + bit + my + uncle

Of course this rule needs stating more precisely, but in essence that's how it works. Note that the recursive feature of the optional *S* (the ability to apply it X number of times) would enable us to produce:

That big, ugly, vicious brown dog bit my uncle.

The rule can be stated more precisely as this:

$$D + \text{N-}matrix + \begin{Bmatrix} \emptyset_1 \\ Z_1 \end{Bmatrix} (+D + \text{N-}const + \begin{Bmatrix} \emptyset_1 \\ Z_1 \end{Bmatrix} + be, + Adj) \Longrightarrow$$

$$D + Adj + \text{N-}matrix + \begin{Bmatrix} \emptyset_1 \\ Z_1 \end{Bmatrix}$$

Applies only when $\text{N-}matrix + \begin{Bmatrix} \emptyset_1 \\ Z_1 \end{Bmatrix} = \text{N-}const \begin{Bmatrix} +\emptyset_1 \\ Z_1 \end{Bmatrix}$

That is to say, wherever the first situation obtains it can be transformed into the second. You might discover, if you experiment with this rule, that some kinds of adjectives won't work. We don't want *the boy is asleep,* for instance, to transform into **the asleep boy.* This merely means that we would have to modify our rule to prevent such un-English results, but we won't attempt that here.

We have now accounted for the construction of one of the sentences cited as unsolved problems on p. 224:

My *fat* sister married his *fat* brother.

We see that underlying the matrix sentence are two constituent sentences:

My sister (my + sister + is + fat) married his brother (his + brother + is + fat)

To produce the final sentence the adjective transformation *(T-Adj)* is merely applied in each of the two situations where it fits.

This still leaves us two other constructions unaccounted for:

The girls in the dorm are lovely.

His father, a judge, is an alcoholic.

These are produced by transformations very similar to *T-Adj* which we were just looking at. The first one grows out of a string like this:

The girls (the girls are in the dorm) are lovely

We simply write a rule that says when the *NP* of the constituent sentence is identical to that of the matrix sentence, and when it is followed by *Adv-P*, the *NP* and the *be* of the constituent sentence may be dropped, leaving simply *Adv-P*. Of course *Adv-P* may be a single word or it may be a P-group:

The girls *there* are lovely.

The girls upstairs are lovely.

The girls *in the boat* are lovely.

This rule, too, is recursive:

The girls *upstairs in the dorm* are lovely.

The rule, which we could call *T-Adv-P* since it locates adverbs of place, looks like this:

$$\text{D} + \text{N-matrix} + \begin{Bmatrix} \emptyset_1 \\ Z_1 \end{Bmatrix} \left(+ \text{D} + \text{N-const} + \begin{Bmatrix} \emptyset_1 \\ Z_1 \end{Bmatrix} + be + \text{Adv-P} \right) \Longrightarrow$$

$$\text{D} + \text{N-matrix} + \begin{Bmatrix} \emptyset_1 \\ Z_1 \end{Bmatrix} + \text{Adv-P}$$

Applies when: $\text{D} + \text{N-matrix} + \begin{Bmatrix} \emptyset_1 \\ Z_1 \end{Bmatrix} = \text{D} + \text{N-const} + \begin{Bmatrix} \emptyset_1 \\ Z_1 \end{Bmatrix}$

I'm sure that by this time you can see how we are going to go about creating a rule to produce the so-called "noun in apposition":

His father, a judge, is an alcoholic.

We will simply stipulate that when the embedded, or constituent, sentence is of the type *NP + be + NP*, and when its first *NP* is identical to that of the matrix sentence, we can drop out the first *NP* and the *be* of the constituent sentence, leaving only the second *NP*, which must be set off in the final sentence by double-bar junctures or, in writing, by commas. Fully stated, in symbols, the rule would look like this:

$$\text{D} + \text{N-matrix} + \begin{Bmatrix} \emptyset_1 \\ Z_1 \end{Bmatrix} \; (+ \text{D} + \text{N-const} + \begin{Bmatrix} \emptyset_1 \\ Z_1 \end{Bmatrix} + be + \text{NP}) \Longrightarrow$$

$$\text{D} + \text{N-matrix} + \begin{Bmatrix} \emptyset_1 \\ Z_1 \end{Bmatrix} + , + \text{NP} + ,$$

$$\text{Applies when: D} + \text{N-matrix} + \begin{Bmatrix} \emptyset_1 \\ Z_1 \end{Bmatrix} = \text{D} + \text{N-const} + \begin{Bmatrix} \emptyset_1 \\ Z_1 \end{Bmatrix}$$

We could call this rule *T-app*, for "appositive transform." Incidentally, we could simplify the mechanics of writing out the rule somewhat if we would use a symbol like $N°$ which would stand for the required "number" on the noun. Then we would have to have in our P-rules a rewrite like this:

$$N° \longrightarrow \begin{Bmatrix} \emptyset_1 \\ Z_1 \end{Bmatrix}$$

Though this would give us one more P-rule it would nevertheless be a simplification, for we wouldn't have to write out the clumsy $\begin{Bmatrix} \emptyset_1 \\ Z_1 \end{Bmatrix}$ in every string but could use the simpler $N°$ until we were ready to rewrite it, at which time we would make the required choice between $\emptyset_1$ and Z_1. The transformationalist is always looking for simplifications like this, and many of them look at first glance like complications rather than otherwise. But generally they result in simplifying things.

Well, we're all through listing and describing rules. There are, of course, many, many more needed to make a grammar capable of turning out anything like the complexity of English, and if you are interested in pursuing the matter further you will find much more information in the transformational grammars listed in the bibliography in the back of this book, but for our purposes we have looked at enough rules. We are not setting out to create a transformational grammar, or at least not more than a very sketchy one so that we can get an idea of how such grammars work. And that much, I think, we have achieved. To wrap things up, sort of, let's give our rules one more workout as we create a fairly elaborate sentence. We'll choose our options, where we have them, and apply the T-rules, so that we produce this sentence:

Can that dull clod, my roommate, have been dating my faithful fiancee?

Before we start on this exercise it would be well to point out that it is, in a way, a "perversion," or at least a "manipulation," of the grammar. In theory the grammar as it stands, a set of rules, actually *is* all of the sentences it is capable of producing. That is, if all the possible choices could somehow be selected simultaneously and instantaneously, we would miraculously have before our eyes, bang, all at once, *all* of the sentences the grammar could produce, and if the grammar was a complete one we would have all the possible sentences of English. Put another way, all of the sentences are already there, symbolically, in the rules. Now, to make the grammar turn out just one specific sentence, by foreseeing as we apply the rules what the outcome of each is to be, is a matter of hit and miss, of trial and error. The grammar can be *made* to operate this way—to analyze and show the underlying structure of given sentences—but this isn't the way it is intended to operate. We must remember as we work out our problem sentence that any time we make a choice aimed at producing our desired result there are "X" number of other possible choices which would create different results. In a figure of speech, one linguist says that a transformational-generative grammar is like a powerful diesel engine: great for driving a truck but impractical when put on a bicycle. In a nutshell, then, a grammar of this kind is intended to elucidate *a language,* not analyze individual sentences, though because we can understand the grammar we can force it to do this latter chore too. We can even get machines to do it—if they have the rules properly programmed into them.

With that understood, let's set about manipulating the grammar so that it produces our target sentence. We start, as always, with *S:*

1. $S \longrightarrow NP (+ S) + VP$
2. $D + N + \emptyset_1 (+ S) + VP$
3. $D + N + \emptyset_1 (+ S) + Aux + MV$
4. $D + N + \emptyset_1 (+ S) + Aux + Verb$
5. $D + N + \emptyset_1 (+ S) + Aux + V_t + NP (+ S)$
6. $D + N + \emptyset_1 (+ S) + Aux + V_t + D + N + \emptyset_1 (+ S)$
7. $D + N + \emptyset_1 (+ S) + C + M + have + en + be + ing + V_t + D + N + \emptyset_1 (+ S)$

8. D + N + $\emptyset_1$ (+ S) + s + M + have + en + be + ing + V_t + D + N + $\emptyset_1$ (+ S)

9. Dem + N + $\emptyset_1$ (+ S) + s + M + have + en + be + ing + V_t + D + N + $\emptyset_1$ (+ S)

10. Dem + N + $\emptyset_1$ (+ S) + s + M + have + en + be + ing + V_t + Pos + N + $\emptyset_1$ (+ S)

11. that + N + $\emptyset_1$ (+ S) + s + M + have + en + be + ing + V_t + Pos + N + $\emptyset_1$ (+ S)

12. that + clod + $\emptyset_1$ (+ S) + s + M + have + en + be + ing + V_t + Pos + N + $\emptyset_1$ (+ S)

13. that + clod + $\emptyset_1$ (+ S) + s + can + have + en + be + ing V_t + Pos + N + $\emptyset_1$ (+ S)

14. that + clod + $\emptyset_1$ (+ S) + s + can + have + en + be + ing + date + Pos + N + $\emptyset_1$ (+ S)

15. that + clod + $\emptyset_1$ (+ S) + s + can + have + en + be + ing + date + my + N + $\emptyset_1$ (+ S)

16. that + clod + $\emptyset_1$ (+ S) + s + can + have + en + be + ing + date + my + fiancee + $\emptyset_1$ (+ S)

At this point we have worked out a terminal string, except for the embedded *S's*, that you can see would ultimately produce:

> That clod can have been dating my fiancee.

However, our target sentence is a question, so we will have to apply *T-q,* and we will also have to take care of the constituent sentences if we are to develop the result we want. First, we'll apply *T-q.* You will remember (or you can look back at p. 226) that *T-q* says that the elements of the first *NP* and the first two elements of *Aux* (if it has two, which is the case here) are to be reversed. Our first *NP,* as it stands now, is:

> that + clod + $\emptyset_1$ (+ S)

The first two elements of *Aux* (step 16) are *s + can.* Reversing them we get a string like this:

17. s + can + that + clod + $\emptyset_1$ (+ S) + have + en + be + ing + date + my + fiancee + $\emptyset_1$ (+ S)

We now have to direct our attention to the constituent sentences. If you will glance back at our target sentence you will see that there are going to have to be three of them: one to produce the adjective "dull," one to produce the appositive, "my roommate," and one to

produce the adjective "faithful." Looking at our string (step 17) you
will note that S is always to be rewritten as *NP (+ S) + VP,* so that
every time we rewrite an embedded S we can, if we wish, get another
one. This recursive feature of the rewrite guarantees that there will
be no shortage of constituent sentences. We can have as many as we
want.

   To keep these S's distinct from one another we'll mark them
with little superscript letters. Thus the first one in the string (step
17) we will call S^a. Also, to keep the steps in developing these
constituent sentences separate from those in the matrix string that
we have worked out up to step 17 so far, we'll designate the steps of
the constituent sentences with letters too. The first of the constituent sentences, S^a:

   1a. $S^a \longrightarrow$ NP (+ S) + VP
   2a. D + N + $\emptyset_1$ (+ S) + VP

The embedded S in this constituent sentence we are going to need
(for our *T-app*), so we'll retain it; and when, later, we go to develop
it in its turn we'll designate it S^b.

   3a. D + N + $\emptyset_1$ (+ S) + Aux + MV
   4a. D + N + $\emptyset_1$ (+ S) + Aux + be + Pred
   5a. D + N + $\emptyset_1$ (+ S) + Aux + be + Adj
   6a. D + N + $\emptyset_1$ (+ S) + C + be + Adj
   7a. D + N + $\emptyset_1$ (+ S) + s + be + Adj
   8a. Dem + N + $\emptyset_1$ (+ S) + s + be + Adj
   9a. that + N + $\emptyset_1$ (+ S) + s + be + Adj
  10a. that + clod + $\emptyset_1$ (+ S) + s + be + Adj
  11a. that + clod + $\emptyset_1$ (+ S) + s + be + dull

This, clearly, is the terminal string for S^a, except for the development of the embedded sentence, which we will now designate as S^b
and proceed to work out:

   1b. $S^b \longrightarrow$ NP (+ S) + VP
   2b. D + N + $\emptyset_1$ (+ S) + VP
   3b. D + N + $\emptyset_1$ + VP

Here we elect to drop the embedded S in 2b, to which you might
respond, "Thank heaven!" But remember, there is no reason we
would have to drop it if the grammar was working freely instead of
being manipulated toward a specific sentence, and theoretically we
could have a zillion repetitions of the embedded S. To continue:

4b. $D + N + \emptyset_1 + Aux + MV$

5b. $D + N + \emptyset_1 + Aux + be + Pred$

6b. $D + N + \emptyset_1 + Aux + be + NP \;(+ S)$

7b. $D + N + \emptyset_1 + Aux + be + NP$

Again we elected to drop an optional *S*.

8b. $D + N + \emptyset_1 + Aux + be + D + N + \emptyset_1$

9b. $D + N + \emptyset_1 + C + be + D + N + \emptyset_1$

10b. $D + N + \emptyset_1 + s + be + D + N + \emptyset_1$

11b. $Dem + N + \emptyset_1 + s + be + D + N + \emptyset_1$

12b. $Dem + N + \emptyset_1 + s + be + my + N + \emptyset_1$

13b. $that + N + \emptyset_1 + s + be + my + N + \emptyset_1$

14b. $that + clod + \emptyset_1 + s + be + my + N + \emptyset_1$

15b. $that + clod + \emptyset_1 + s + be + my + roommate + \emptyset_1$

And this is the terminal string for S^b.

However, we still have a constituent sentence to develop. If you look back at the string of the matrix sentence the way it stood at step 17, you'll see that at the very end of it is an optional *S*. We are going to call this one S^c and will proceed forthwith to work it out:

1c. $S^c \longrightarrow NP \;(+ S) + VP$

2c. $NP + VP$

Again we have chosen not to develop an optional *S*.

3c. $D + N + \emptyset_1 + VP$

4c. $D + N + \emptyset_1 + Aux + MV$

5c. $D + N + \emptyset_1 + Aux + be + Pred$

6c. $D + N + \emptyset_1 + Aux + be + Adj$

7c. $D + N + \emptyset_1 + C + be + Adj$

8c. $D + N + \emptyset_1 + s + be + Adj$

9c. $Pos + N + \emptyset_1 + s + be + Adj$

10c. $my + N + \emptyset_1 + s + be + Adj$

11c. $my + fiancée + \emptyset_1 + s + be + Adj$

12c. $my + fiancée + \emptyset_1 + s + be + faithful$

This is the terminal string for S^c.

At this point we have worked out the terminal strings for the matrix sentence and also for all three of the constituent sentences we are going to need to arrive at our target sentence. We'll now put them all together in one long string which we will call Step 18, since step 17 was where we left off our developing the matrix sentence in order to work out the constituent sentences. To make the constituent sentence strings stand out more sharply we'll keep them enclosed in parentheses, though they are no longer optional since we have committed ourselves to including them.

18. s + can + that + clod + $\emptyset_1$ (that + clod + s + be + dull) (that + clod + s + be + my + roommate + $\emptyset_1$) + have + en + be + ing + date + my + fiancée (my + fiancée + $\emptyset_1$ + s + be + faithful)

As we look at this we immediately see that, concerning the first embedded sentence, we have exactly the situation to which the *T-Adj* transform applies. (See p. 233 for rule.) We apply *T-Adj*:

19. s + can + that + dull + clod + $\emptyset_1$ (that + clod + $\emptyset_1$ + s + be + my + roommate + $\emptyset_1$) + have + en + be + ing + date + my + fiancée + $\emptyset_1$ (my + fiancee + $\emptyset_1$ + s + be + faithful)

Looking at the string again we find, relevant to the first of the two constituent sentences which remain, that there obtain exactly the conditions under which *T-app* applies (see p. 235 above). So we apply that T-rule:

20. s + can + that + dull + clod + $\emptyset_1$ + , + my + roommate + $\emptyset_1$ + , + have + en + be + ing + date + my + fiancée + $\emptyset_1$ (my + fiancée + $\emptyset_1$ + s + be + faithful)

Now we have only one embedded constituent sentence string left, and as we look at it we see that again it is such that *T-adj* applies, and we apply it:

21. s + can + that + dull + clod + $\emptyset_1$ + , + my + roommate + $\emptyset_1$ + , + have + en + be + ing + date + my + faithful + fiancée + $\emptyset_1$

We have now applied all the rules except the final one, the flip-flop. In order to apply it, we first mark off our *Af*'s and *v*'s:

> Af——v
22. s + can + that + dull + clod + $\emptyset_1$ + , + my + roommate + $\emptyset_1$
>   v   Af—v   Af——v
> + , + have + en + be + ing + date + my + faithful + fiancée
> + $\emptyset_1$

We make the reversals which the flip-flop rule instructs us to make:

23. can + s + that + dull + clod + $\emptyset_1$ + , + my + roommate + $\emptyset_1$
+ , + have + be + en + date + ing + my + faithful + fiancée +
$\emptyset_1$

You have enough experience with these strings by this time to see immediately how this one is going to develop with the application of M-rules, and it is, of course, going to produce our target sentence. *can + s* will clearly give us "can"; *be + en* will produce "been"; and *date + ing* will come out "dating." Our string will then work out to:

Can that dull clod, my roommate, have been dating my faithful fiancée?

Certainly this is not one of the language's more memorable sentences, especially to have cost so much sweat to churn it out the way we did, but equally certainly it is recognizable English. It is plain, then, that following only the relative handful of rules we have in our Third Model Grammar will enable us to produce a tremendous number of sentences, and sentences of quite a number of different kinds.

However, as you can see, with all its potentialities this grammar of ours is still pretty primitive. It has, for instance, these glaring inadequacies:

1. We still have not provided for sentences with subjects in the first or second person. Certainly a grammar that can't create such sentences is not much of a representative of English, especially when you consider the terrific percentage of sentences in the normal give and take of conversation that have either "I" or "you" as subject. It would be easy to devise a rule to fix this.

2. Though we observed earlier that there are different classes of nouns, and that they operate differently with different kinds of determiners, we still have made no provision for controlling this. Thus our grammar could as easily ask for "a water" as "some water," for "some pencil" as for "a pencil." We would need to make some rules of the sort that are called "context sensitive" so that in one situation a given class of determiner would be used and in a different situation a different class. Such rules are available, and are not difficult, but we won't go into them here. (They are something like our rule for the rewrite of *C.*)

3. Our rewrite of the postdeterminer *(Post-D)* allows for a choice of only one item, whereas it should allow for two or

in some cases all three. Also, our rules shouldn't permit the selection of both *Pre-Art* and *Pre-D* as they do at present.

4. Our grammar has no provision for a linking verb with a noun complement, as in "That girl became my wife."
5. Our grammar can construct "Most of the boys met yesterday." It can, however, also construct *"Most of the boy met yesterday." Again a context-sensitive rule is needed.
6. We need, of course, many more transformations. We need to add *T-wh,* so we can create questions with "who," "what," "where," "when," etc. We need a transform which will turn a statement into a command. We need a transform permitting conjunctions, so that we can hook patterns together, have double subjects, double predicates, etc. We need many, many others. We need also rules stipulating that some transforms can be applied only after certain others, in order to avoid creating some impossible constructions. In short, our grammar is truly as we have said, only a sample. We were not being modest.

However, even with all these shortcomings, and many others not cited, we still have a grammar capable of producing a tremendous number of sentences and, really, of a considerable variety of types. We have made considerable progress—and especially with various modifications we could introduce—toward creating a language-producing machine.

We now have to turn to a question which you might well have had in the back of your mind, and perhaps in the very forefront of your mind, for quite some time: "So what?" Or, rephrased, "What good is it?" Or, again, and as many students put it, "Why do we have to read this stuff?" These are always good questions and worthy of answers, even though sometimes we teachers are inclined to be impatient with them. Let's see what we can do about offering some answers.

As partial answer to the question "What good is it?" I would suggest that if the meaning here is to be taken as "What practical utility has it?" the answer might well be in turn another question: "What practical utility have most of the things we include in a liberal education?" I'm serious. Take biology, for example. Unless we are studying to be medical doctors or nurses, biology is likely to be of little real *use.* But we study it because we are curious about ourselves and other creatures, how we are put together and how we function. Again, what *good* is a course in the history of the Renaissance, or in the literature of nineteenth century America? It would be hard to prove to me, certainly, that these subjects have any real usefulness. But I would argue all day that they have a place in a liberal education, and that what we call a "well-rounded," "educated" person is quite likely to have a lively interest in such things. Similarly with an analysis of our language, including transformational-generative grammar. Since language is, as we have seen, one of the most characteristic and intimate of human activities, since it is so inescapable a part of us, we have (and should have) a natural curiosity about it. (It goes without saying that naturally we will have this curiosity in varying degrees. Not everyone is equally enthusiastic about biology or philosophy, either.)

There is, however, another answer to "What good is it?" It is proving of tremendous actual value—and of even more tremendous potential value—in such far-out things as machine translation of languages. Imagine, for instance, that a language—let's say English—could be broken down into a "computer language." Imagine further that "Language X" could also be broken down into this same computer language. Then we could have an article in Language X fed into one end of the machine, through the computer language, and an English translation would come out the other end, as it were.

Nor is this fantastic. It's actually being done today, though with varying degrees of success and not, of course, with all languages. As you might guess, the machines handle technical language best, like that in scientific articles. This is primarily because such language characteristically uses few idioms. We could define an idiom as a construction having a meaning for native speakers quite different from what the normal, or literal, meaning of the words in that construction would lead one to expect. Thus, pity the poor machine coming on a construction like "He kicked the bucket." How would it be expected to know that this is a breezy way of saying "He died"? And so, translated into another language, which would very likely not have the same idiom, we would get the unintended picture of a man literally kicking, with his foot, a real bucket, thus reducing death to incomprehensible burlesque. But, as we say, scientific, technical writing employs relatively little idiom, so that machine translation is even today being used with considerable success.

Another very practical use of transformational grammar is in teaching English to speakers of other languages, or of what we might call "standard English" to speakers of what are sometimes called "non-standard dialects." Of course, the foreigners are not taught the symbols and the ways of manipulating them, such as we have just been looking at. That might well discourage anybody from even attempting to learn English. But consider with me briefly—very briefly—the principal problems of teaching English as a second language (or ESL as it's called in the trade). What the naive learner of a second language always thinks he needs to learn is the *words* of the language he wants to acquire. He is wrong. Of course eventually he is going to have to have a vocabulary in the "target" language, as we call the one he is trying to learn. But *first* he needs to learn the basic structures. Sentence patterns. Something to put the words into. And he is going to have to master these patterns so that he can use them habitually, without thinking about them, the way you do when you talk. (When was the last time you worried about whether the indirect object should precede or follow the direct object?) Suppose we have some six (or however many) kernel sentence patterns in English. Surely through adequate drill (i.e., repetition) we could get the foreigner to master these patterns. Then through more drill, and more drill, and still more drill, we get him to master the way these kernel sentences are transformed into other structures. In this way he can master what you somehow did when you were yet an infant, and he speaks English, as you did when you attended school that first long-ago day. Thus we see that the theory of transformational grammar underlies a great deal of all modern teaching of English to speakers of other languages.

But beyond this mere "practicality" of transformational-generative grammar there is, it seems to me, the marvelous insight it gives us into what language is and how it operates. Don't you find it amazing, upon reflection, that it is possible to take this language which we use all day every day, unceasingly and unthinkingly, as naturally as breathing, and break it down into something that can be presented as a handful of almost mathematically precise formulas? The language turns out to be explainable in terms of only a few rules which operate as regularly as clockwork. System, order, neatness, precision: these things appear to govern where superficially all seemed chaos. Instead of "rules" with exceptions, and exceptions to those exceptions, as in older analyses, here we have only several dozen rules, of quite a different kind, which are perfectly explicit and which operate without exceptions.

We have observed before that whatever the secret to how we learn a language might prove to be, it *has* to be something simple, for as we also observed—matter-of-factly rather than snootily—we all know some very stupid people who speak their language with unthinking fluency. As a matter of fact, in the bilingual community where I live there are many people not too "b-r-i-g-h-t" who speak *two* languages easily and fluently. I don't think that any transformational-generative grammarian would insist that as infants we went through the process of creating terminal strings, flip-flopping them, applying morphophonemic rules, and all that. On the other hand, the very precision and regularity of this grammar suggests that it is very likely that perhaps we went through something like it, minus the apparatus of symbols, formal rules for applying them, and rewrites by the score. After all, it stands to reason, doesn't it, that if a child learns that

Jerry wrote the theme

transforms into

The theme was written by Jerry

and that

Mother baked the pie

transforms into

The pie was baked by mother

he is going to learn the T-passive (without the label and the symbols) so that he can use it himself? And as a matter of fact we learn this particular transform so well that we vastly overuse it in our writing, most of us, to the point where it lacks life and sparkle. Things get done, all right, but nobody ever does them.

Transformational-generative grammar seems to make it clear that as we learned our language what we really learned was only a few simple formulas (which we never dreamed of stating *as* formulas) and the ways of transforming them into other sentences based on other formulas. It's an intriguing line of speculation, and to me seems incontrovertibly on the right track.

On campuses all over the country today, people—especially linguists and computer-technician types—are having fun with transformational-generative grammar, as well as trying to accomplish serious ends with it. They are programming computers to turn out free compositions, the best and most fun of which are modern poetry. The attention of the general public was perhaps first drawn to this sport in an article in *Horizon* magazine[5] which included samples of machine-produced poems. In fact, the editor played a trick on the reader, so that he read and judged the poems first and only *then* was

---

5. Vol. IV, No. 5, May, 1962, pp. 96-99.

given an explanation of how they were written. (The "poet" in the lab where the *Horizon* poems were written was a computer named "Auto-Beatnik" by its "teachers.") It was low down of me, I admit, but I gave a handful of these poems to a faculty colleague who is a critic—and a very good poet—himself. He praised them highly, citing their "vigor," their "fresh imagination," and their "sensitive feel for words." Then I clued him in. He didn't get as mad as you might expect. He only hopped up and down and cussed, poetically, for five or ten minutes. Anyhow, he was right the first time. The poems do appear to have vigor, fresh imagination, and a sensitive feel for words. Let's take a look at some computer-produced poetry and then consider briefly how one goes about getting a computer to write such stuff. And we *can* be brief, for you already understand all the principles involved. Here are a few poems we have cranked out by computer on my campus:

SURF

A moon seeks the obscure rocking bomb.
Our dirty surf mocks our happy slow moon.
Who is not and haunts the huge demon.
A sticky smoky surf is like a ringed land.

SHADOWS

Sea tilts the hollow joyous girl.
A spider views her parched bright plain.
The cotton equips the snake,
Their grey ascetic stick is not a shadows.

PILL

A blue spy drains their tired hill.
Their thin gay nose carries my minor pill.
The pill pinches and idles his lively scar.
Who erases and wrongs a pooped scar?
Who equals and builds the feline hill?
An angel chokes and trusts her golden beast.
Their stony torrid pad numbs the pill.
Who anchors the angels?
Who passes our bright spy?
The dizzy bright angels see their sooty spy.
His machine excites that brown pitted angel.
Who is that cat?
The spy catches and stills her angels.

A pill drains and bursts the crazy pill.
Their dismal mundane angels desert a spy.
A hollow shiny wine smells a pill.
His glassy frigid fence like a warm hill.
Who pays the angels?
Our old scar turns sleepy scar and cool wind.
His absurd quiet pill equals the sharp rainbow.

MAN

That doll scorns my flower.
The dark man steals a wiry doll.
Their glossy doll haunts dreary bear and
    aged doll.
My beat bomb wounds the leaden bomb and a
    rusty face.
Who is like and blasts the wild doll?
Her hostile women trap a fast man.
Her A-bomb cuts a cool hungry bomb.
My pink doll equips a horned bead.

WOOD

Golden book chokes the arid subway.
An end dreads their wood.
Our land visits a sleepy obese road.
Their hot road chokes opulent wood and the
    wormy train.

Here is just one more:

YOUTH

And who forgot an astral flower?
The pain strikes his youth.
The golden arctic lamp bores a wry realm.
Who is near and fans the fast pencil?
Their rubber pain mocks a little lamp.
A lamp seeks a lamp.
The realm goads their youth.
The vacant realm idles the magenta realm and
    my lethal lamp.
Who steers and rejects the soaked youth?
A cotton feeds and steals the realm.
A lamp evades droopy savage lamp.
Her sky lowers and kills the mouth.

Well! What do you think? Of course it's uneven, and some of it is a little rough, but aren't some of the lines splendid? How could you beat:

> Our old scar turns sleepy scar and cool wind.
> His absurd quiet pill equals the sharp rainbow.

We could improve these poems quite a bit by not having every line a complete sentence, and perhaps by including a few more sentence patterns, but generally, don't they strike you as similar to much handwritten (or "human-written") poetry being turned out today? (Whether you like this kind of stuff is a different question, and is perhaps irrelevant at the moment.)

Let's consider a little more about how it's done. First, obviously, you are going to have to give the machine a vocabulary, and you are going to have to sort out the vocabulary into the various form classes and function words, with sub-classes where appropriate. Visualize the words as being stored in boxes. You would have a box full of demonstratives (labelled *Dem*), you would have another box containing transitive verbs (V_t), you would have one with nouns, one with adjectives, and so on. Then you simply instruct the machine in which order to select from which box—perhaps with formulas very like those we were using a little while ago—and let'er rip.

You could let the machine have a completely free choice in its selections from the boxes, but it might produce better results if you restrict it somewhat. That is, if the same noun crops up now and then, and the same verb, it gives the poem more of an illusion of being *about* something, so instead of letting it operate entirely according to the laws of chance you load it a bit, like the one-armed bandits in Las Vegas. You can instruct the machine: You get completely free pick of what noun you select first, but whatever one it is you are going to have to use it again four times out of every ten nouns." It was an instruction like this which made "pill" crop up so often in the poem with that title.

Suppose we have the machine set up to follow this pattern:

$$\text{Dem} + N + \emptyset_1 + s + V_t + \text{Pos} + N + \emptyset_1$$

And suppose it goes though its rewrites until it produces this terminal string:

$$\text{that} + \text{doll} + \emptyset_1 + s + \text{scorn} + \text{my} + \text{flower} + \emptyset_1$$

You can easily see how this is going to become, with the flip-flop and M-rules:

> That doll scorns my flower.

This is, of course, the first line of the poem "Man" above.

Some process akin to this, varying only according to the final sentence pattern desired, underlies every line of those poems. Lest you think this incredible, let me remind you of two things: 1. the computer works with lightning speed and does not labor through rewrites like you and me, and 2. the computer doesn't get tired. For instance, the computer on my campus "reads" magnetic tape at 75 inches per second—and furthermore reads six tracks on the tape simultaneously. It can complete 200,000 cycles (operations) per second. When it comes time for it to make its print-out it handles lines up to 135 characters in length—considerably longer than the average typewriter line—and prints them at the rate of 1000 lines a minute. So you see that handling these rewrites, tedious though it may be for us humans, is a snap for the computer.

With the sample grammars we have been experimenting with we couldn't produce these poems. Too many of them involve exactly the kinds of shortcomings we have already noted in our model grammars. But it wouldn't take many refinements, really, to enable us to produce sentences of that complexity. I'm not sure we even want to. What's more important is that you understand the principles involved. And, I think, surely you do.

You might be interested to learn that the immediate-constituent grammar and the transformational-generative grammar that we have examined by no means exhaust the kinds of modern grammars. There is tagmemic grammar, stratificational grammar, algebraic grammar, slot-and-filler grammar, and others. All of them are devoted to trying to explain the syntax of English. Though they are interesting, we are not going to examine them here, but mention them merely to show that the work of analyzing English goes on.

Before we finally drop the subject of transformational-generative grammar and bring this rather long chapter to an end, you might like a peek at its Achilles heel, which we've kept decently covered so far. You will recall that the goal of such a grammar is to produce acceptable English sentences (all possible sentences, in a complete grammar) and no unacceptable ones. But how do we tell which is which? Aha! Here's a problem. Once again we have to rely on the intuition, the "feel for the language," of the native speaker. And it quickly becomes apparent that not all native speakers are in unanimous agreement about all constructions. Of course, most constructions we will agree on: they're either acceptable or not. But there is a borderline area where some will feel a construction is good English and others will disagree. I remember disagreeing with an example in a popular textbook. It says that while "Herbert never stayed home" is grammatical, *"Herbert stayed never home" and *"Herbert stayed home never" are both ungrammatical. I wonder about this last one. It seems to me it is an acceptable English construction, or at least it might well be under certain circumstances:

> Mary stayed home all the time. Charlie stayed home some of the time. Herbert stayed home never.

I'm not even going to *insist* that "Herbert stayed home never" is an acceptable English construction. All I need do to make my point is suggest that I might, in disagreement with the text, think it is. Where is the Supreme Court to which we appeal for a judgment in the matter? Who is to decide what is an acceptable construction and what is not?

Thus, after all this hoopla about a "scientific grammar" we find that, fascinating and enlightening though it may be, it rests ultimately on the foundation of the native speaker's intuitive feel for his language. It may be analogous to Euclidian geometry: if you accept the base axioms all the rest of it proceeds flawlessly. But if some wise guy, like Einstein, challenges the axioms, then the whole system crumbles—and a new one is developed. We might say, then, that transformational-generative grammar is just as good as its basic assumption: that a native speaker of language knows what is grammatical and what is not grammatical in his own language.

On the other hand, we could insist that these differences in judgment as to what is and what is not acceptable are not really very important. That is, we could construct a grammar which would be perfectly accurate for the English of *one* speaker, and if it did not describe in all respects the language of some other speaker, this is simply because in actual fact they use the language differently (see discussion of "idiolects" in chapter following). Perhaps then all anyone could ever hope to do is develop a grammar which would be accurate for most features of English as used by most of the speakers of English (or, more narrowly, for most of the features of a dialect of English as used by most of the speakers of that dialect). The only way we could have a single grammar—transformational or otherwise— which would describe exactly and in all respects the English of every speaker of the language would be for all of us to speak it identically— and that, as we will see, isn't about to happen.

SUGGESTED READINGS

Eschliman, Herbert R., Jones, Robert C., and Burkett, Tommy R. *Generative English Handbook* ("Rules of Grammar," part 1). Belmont, California: Wadsworth Publishing Co., 1966.

Gleason, H.A. Jr. *An Introduction to Descriptive Linguistics*, rev. ed. ("Transformations," chapter 12). New York: Holt, Rinehart & Winston, 1961.

Roberts, Paul. *English Sentences* ("Transformation" and "Questions and Related Structures," chapters 10 and 32). New York: Harcourt, Brace and World, 1962.

CHAPTER 8

WHAT IS "ENGLISH," ANYHOW?

Having looked at "grammar" somewhat, according to our own definitions of the term, it is no doubt only fair that we direct our attention to the meaning popularly given it, as when we say of a person who says "I don't want none a them" that he uses "bad grammar." Of course, we have noted that the linguist never uses the term "grammar" in this sense, but we can be big about it and bow to the voice of the people for a while. In any event, no matter what we might want to call *he don't* vs. *he doesn't*—grammar or usage or dialect or whatever—the fact remains that there are varying ways of saying "the same thing" and that we should consider them and what they imply about our language.

Let's begin by a moment's reconsideration of Snangti, the previously-undiscovered language which we imagined, way back in Chapter I, that we had discovered on some remote Pacific isle. We found that, at first, the language sounded to us like an assortment of grunts and barbaric sounds, because it was unlike English and therefore somewhat ridiculous. But we struggled with it until we mastered it, and we even provided it with a writing system and a statement of its grammar. Now as we revisit that island and re-examine the language we discover a peculiar thing: not all the speakers of Snangti speak it in the same way. The tribal chieftains and the medicine men—the island big shots—use certain sounds and expressions which are not used by the lowly hewers of wood and drawers of water. And vice versa. We find, too, that there are certain expressions fairly common among the men which the women never, never use, and would be highly embarrassed to be caught using. In some other ways, too, the speech of the women differs from that of the men, for they use certain turns of speech which seem to be reserved for them. At least, the men never use them.

We find, further, that the island is a pretty good-sized one and that there are noticeable differences between the language spoken in its northern regions and in its southern parts. There are also a few isolated pockets, valleys sort of, where the language of the natives is quite strikingly different from that on the rest of the island.

One day, as we are contemplating this variety of ways of speaking Snangti, perhaps wondering how to incorporate it into our "grammar," we happen to ask ourselves: "Which manner of speaking Snangti is correct?"—and even as we ask the question it strikes us as ludicrous, for *all* the varieties of it seem pretty outlandish. What difference, after all, does it make whether a person says /ŋæt/ or /ŋæk/ when he's referring to coconut milk? However, we are conscientious researchers and want to get to the bottom of this matter, we hunt up a few of our old native informant friends—and we learn some pretty surprising things.

We find, for instance, that coconut milk is /ŋæt/ to all the high brass on the island. Most of the rest say /ŋæk/, but they are kind of sheepish about it when asked and readily admit that /ŋæt/ is somehow "better." Still they carelessly persist in their "sloppy" pronunciation, perhaps because it is somehow more comfortable for them. We find many instances like this. Also, we discover that the people in the north of the island are aware of the speech differences of those in the south, and vice versa, and they view each other's speech with tolerant amusement, sometimes imitating the foreign sounds with much hilarity. We, of course, are able to view this kind of sport with detachment because we recognize that both brands are ridiculous.

Enough of our make-believe language. Let's direct our view toward our own language. And what do we find but that everything we've observed about Snangti is perfectly true of English! Precisely and exactly, except for the detail that we say neither /ŋæt/ nor /ŋæk/ for coconut milk. We find that there are many varieties of English—in fact, and to be technical, there are as many varieties as there are speakers, for no two people will use the language identically in all respects. What the linguist calls an individual's speech is an "idiolect." Your own English speech, then, is your idiolect, and it is as individual as your fingerprints.

Idiolects cluster into bunches, though, and we want to consider some of them. For instance, you know perfectly well that the people around Atlanta, Georgia, don't talk like the people who live in New

York City, and neither talks like the person from Chicago or Dallas. We observe that English is spoken differently in England, too, and in Australia. The individuals in Atlanta may all have different idiolects, but they have enough in common so that a person from there is readily identifiable. We say he speaks a "dialect." Nor is this to say that the Atlantan is somehow peculiar, for *everybody* speaks a dialect, the Chicagoan as surely as the Bostonian, the Briton as much as the Australian. The trouble is that as we contemplate our own particular variety of English it is so thoroughly familiar, so comfortable and so somehow "right" that it seems incredible that anyone could consider it a dialect—which seems to imply that there's something strange about it. It all boils down to the old gag among linguists: "*I* speak English; everyone else speaks a dialect." (One of my colleagues recently informed a student, haughtily, that *she* spoke "Standard American English.")

All anyone need do to convince himself that English is spoken in different ways all over the United States is go around the country with his ears open—and he will probably hear all dialects except his own. Do "pin" and "pen" sound the same to you? Do you pronounce "Jim" and "gem" alike? If so, you're from somewhere south of the Mason-Dixon line. And let no Yankee convince you that your inability to differentiate words like these is a "defect" in your speech. It is simply a characteristic of the Southern dialects that /i/ and /e/ before a nasal are both pronounced /i/, so that instead of /pin/ and /pen/ you get /pin/ for both. However, if you come from a part of the country with this dialectal feature you probably make some distinctions that other areas don't make. For instance, you very likely pronounce "merry," "marry," and "Mary" all differently— /mérɨ/, /mǽrɨ/, and /méyrɨ/—while some one like me, raised in Montana, pronounces them all exactly alike: (mérɨ/. When I was a youngster we used to have a feeble, kid-type joke: "No wonder I'm a little hoarse this morning—I have a little cold." "Cold" was pronounced like "colt," but the pun was already set up by the fact that in that part of the country "hoarse" and "horse" are pronounced exactly alike: /hɔrs/, or more likely /hohrs/. This pun would be impossible in the South, where they "quite sensibly" keep the two differentiated: "horse" /hɔhrs/ and "hoarse" /hohrs/. In the far Northwest the distinction made elsewhere between "cot" /kat/ and "caught" /kɔt/ gets lost, both of them coming out /kat/. In my own family we have frequent mixups because we have two friends, a Mr. Barnes and a Mr. Bonds, and I never can tell which one my wife, raised in Georgia, is referring to. She pronounces both names the same: /bahnz/. It would help if they didn't both have the same first name, George /j̈ohj̈/.

All of this is probably no news: we know that English is spoken differently in different geographical areas, and we are accustomed to referring to those different varieties of the language as dialects. What might come as a bit of a surprise is how very many of these dialects there are. We are likely to say that so and so speaks with "a Southern accent" or "a New England accent," implying that there is *a* Southern accent and that there is *a* New England accent. Actually this is wrong on two counts.

In the first place, there is not a Southern accent but a number of them. People in Virginia, North Carolina, Alabama and Texas don't all speak alike: in fact, all their speech is quite different. There are differences within states, too. The same is true in New England—and elsewhere in the English speaking world, for that matter.

Secondly, referring to a Southern (or New England) "accent," as we do, seems to imply that it's all a matter of phonology, whereas actually some of the most interesting and spectacular, dialectal differences are in vocabulary. For instance, do you eat "pot cheese," "Dutch cheese," "smearcase," or "cottage cheese"? Do you fry eggs in a "skillet," a "spider," a "fry pan," or a "frying pan"? What do you call a small, flowing body of water? A "creek"? (If so, do you say /kriyk/ or /krik/?) A "stream"? A "brook"? A "run"? A "branch"? And how about the long, slender insect with gauzy wings that you see hovering and darting over small ponds in the summer? Do you call it a "dragon fly"? A "darning needle"? A "snake doctor"? A "mosquito hawk"? Something else?

There are quite literally thousands of these vocabulary variations as we go from one to another part of the country (thousands more if we take on the entire English-speaking world), and obviously they contribute as much to the various dialects as do differences in pronunciation. A vast project studying both phonological and vocabulary dialectal variations has been under way for a number of years. It is *The Linguistic Atlas of the United States and Canada.* Some parts of it already have been published; others are in various stages of progress. If your library has any published parts of it, you would no doubt enjoy examining them—and you would reap one of the rewards of having learned a little about phonetics.

However, when linguists use the term "dialect" they do not always have in mind this sort of geographical variation. Often they seem to indicate just what the man in the street—or the teacher in the classroom—is thinking of when he uses the term "grammar." The linguist will refer to what he calls "social dialects," by which he means the varieties of language used by people in different social levels. Thus "I don't want none a them" is characteristic of one social level; "I don't want any of those" of another.

How does this strike your knowledge of the realities of language use? *Do* the people in the different echelons of our society use language alike, or are there differences which we associate with certain classes of people? Who would most likely say "I ain't never gonna do that no more"?—a mechanic or a doctor of medicine? A preacher or a plumber? A registered nurse or a scrubwoman? There is no doubt in your mind, of course, for it is a truth we all know that these social differences in language usage exist. It really doesn't matter very much whether we want to refer to these different "levels" of language use as "social dialects," with the linguist, or call them matters of "usage," or, for that matter, go along with the traditionalist and consider them matters of grammar—though I prefer not to think of them as "grammar," reserving that word for the meanings we have already assigned it. What does matter is that we recognize that these differences exist, and that they are important. They are important because they play a large and significant role in the way we judge one another. When you meet a person for the first time you are busily trying to get a line on him, to peg him and put him in the proper pigeonhole. You observe his (or, of course, her) clothes, his manners, his cleanliness, and so on. And above all, you listen to him talk.

Suppose this new man you've just met is wearing soiled blue jeans, a ragged T-shirt and worn sneakers. He needs a haircut, his fingernails are dirty, and he is unshaven. In the first few minutes that you've known him he says "I seen him when he done it," "He don't read so good," and "I ain't had no dealings with them people." Would you be surprised to learn that he's one of the leading bankers of your community? You bet you would! In fact, you probably wouldn't believe it, and neither would I.

But suppose he had been wearing a neat, dark business suit, with button down collar and conservative tie. He is clean, well-groomed and attractive. And, again, in the first few minutes of your acquaintance he says "I seen him when he done it," "He don't read so good," and "I ain't had no dealings with them people." Now would you *still* be surprised to learn that he's one of the top financial men in town? Sure. Because language is one of the *key* items we use in sizing people up, and we're not used to having the leaders of our society talk like that. Similarly, we would be somewhat surprised to come across a half-drunken, unshaven, chewing-tobacco-stained wretch begging handouts in a very "refined" or "elegant" kind of English. Nor would this be snobbery. It's just one of the facts of life, sad or otherwise: we are typed by the language we use.

Let us imagine that we can somehow divide all the people in the country into three groups on strictly non-linguistic factors. We'll call them Groups I, II, and III, and we'll sort them out like this:

To get into Group I, a man (or woman) has to be a college graduate, has to be a professional man (i.e., medical doctor, lawyer, clergyman, etc.), has to be earning at least $15,000 a year (which rules out teachers), and if in the service has to be a commissioned officer with the rank of captain (Army or Marine) or higher.

For eligibility in Group II, a man would have to have begun high school but not graduated, he would have to be a "white collar" worker or clerk (shop foreman, shoe salesman, or something similar), he would have to earn between $6,000 and $9,000 a year, and if he's in the military would have to be a non-commissioned officer, say one of the grades of sergeant.

For inclusion in Group III, a man could have no formal education beyond the fourth grade, he would have to be a day laborer—a pick and shovel type—and he would have to earn less than $3,500 a year. If in the service, he would have to be a plain private, though perhaps we could permit the exalted rank of p.f.c.

Now, we sort people into these three groups. Wait a minute, you object. Wouldn't there be an awful lot of people who wouldn't fit into one of these groups? Of course there would be—and those people we would ignore. What we would finally have, and I'm sure you would agree, would be three widely different groups. If you met a person from Group I, you wouldn't likely guess that he belonged in Group III, would you? Notice, too, that these people have been sorted into these groups without any attention being paid to the way they use language. Our criteria for selection were strictly non-linguistic.[1]

After having sorted our people out in the fashion just described, we would turn our attention to the English they use. And we would find, as you full well know, that some very sharp differences exist.

---

1. What is being described here as an imaginary venture, is, of course, patterned after the research done by Charles Fries and associates, published as *American English Grammar* by Appleton, Century, Crofts in 1940. Fries and his colleagues had available to them a large body of written material—letters, in fact. They hunted up the writers and categorized them on a plan similar to the one we've been "making up." *Then* they looked at their use of English. The results were often surprising and always informative. You might like to look up Fries' book.

Which group would you think most likely to say "I ain't seen him in a week"? Which would be most likely to say "She looked badly"? (As for this one, I don't know, but I'd bet on Group II. A Group I speaker might more likely remember and use the "correct" form; a Group III speaker would say what comes naturally, which would incline more to omitting the "-ly" morpheme from adverbs than adding it where it didn't belong; but the Group II speaker, remembering having been criticized in school for constructions like "The boy came quick," would be the likely candidate to overcompensate in an effort at "correctness" and add the "-ly" where it shouldn't go. *The New Yorker* magazine used to run a feature in which it quoted and made fun of over-elegant people who used "whom" where it didn't belong. It's my hunch that many of these poor ridiculed people were Group II's, though it's certainly likely also that many of them were Group I's who had been betrayed by the general unnaturalness of the who-whom distinction.)

We don't have to beat this point to death. It's something you know as well as anybody, from your own day-to-day observation of people and the way they talk. However, we might pause a moment to draw a moral from it: The school child hopes—or at least his parents hope for him—that he will some day take his place in Group I. Certainly the college or university student, by his very presence in his chosen institution has implicitly declared his intention of being a Group I type of person. It behooves the child, then, and the university student as well, to learn to be comfortable and at home with the kind of English used by the people in Group I, if he doesn't already use it. And this is the real, and the important, reason why generations of dedicated schoolteachers have so earnestly preached against usages like "I ain't never seen it."

I can't resist adding, however, that in my opinion many teachers handle this problem badly, however sound their motives. The usual approach is to tell the student that "I ain't seen him yet" is "wrong," "bad English," "ignorant" etc. Yet think for a moment. Where did little Johnny learn these constructions? Probably at home, that's where, and he is likely, first, to be surprised that there's anything wrong with them (and more than a little disbelieving) and, second, he's likely to resent the implication that his parents are wrong and ignorant. He might even like his parents better than he does his schoolteacher. It would seem preferable to somehow lead little Johnny to see that there are different *kinds* of English, and that some are appropriate for one kind of situation and some for another, and that the smart lad is the one who learns to use more than one kind. With a little encouragement, like the right kind of assignments, Johnny could quickly find this out for himself, which would certainly be more convincing than just having teacher tell him.

Further, a study of Groups I, II, and III, such as we were just hypothesizing would reveal some surprising things about who says what. (As did the Fries study, already mentioned.) For instance, who says things like "With whom did you go to the party?" Practically nobody, that's whom. Not Group III, nor Group II, nor even Group I. We all say "Who did you go to the party with?" And on top of that, we say it: /húwjə/. Such a study would reveal that nobody ever wants "a cup of coffee," in four distinct words, but "a cuppa coffee" /əkˆəpəkɔ́fɨ/, and that this is not "sloppiness" of pronunciation but is standard American English. In fact, if there is sloppiness here it's in the way the spelling system inadequately represents what it is we really do say.

This matter of the several social echelons using different kinds of English is what the linguist has in mind as he refers to "social dialects." We might like to think of our democracy as "classless," but the reality would seem to be otherwise, and even the way we speak our language indicates it.

However, it isn't with his recognition of "classes" that the linguist infuriates the purist, but with his insistence that one "class dialect," as he also calls social dialects, is as "good" as another. The linguist is not a fool. He knows perfectly well the social implications of a Group III utterance. But what he insists on is that "We ain't got none of them" communicates good like a denial should, and he dismisses the idea of "correctness" or "incorrectness" as irrelevant to his purposes. He is as interested in the grammar of one dialect as another.

Someone created a brilliant analogy to demonstrate the linguist's attitude toward correctness, and if I could remember who it was I'd give him credit. He said something like this: Imagine a bunch of students who have trapped a rat in a cage, and they take it in to their biology professor and ask him if it's a correct rat. The professor would consider the question totally irrelevant. He would be prepared to look the rat over and comment on its sex, its apparent age, the fact that it was somewhat undernourished, whether it was this type of rat or that—but the question whether it was a "correct" rat would stop him cold.

And so it is with the linguist. Bring him a sample utterance and he can find a great deal to say about it: whether it is a kernel sentence or a transform, and if the latter how it got to its present state; what its immediate constituents are, and so on. But "correctness" no more concerns him than it does his colleague in biology. He would insist, that is, that the difference in the way people view "He isn't going" versus "He ain't going" is a *social* matter rather than a linguistic one. (Please note, this is not to say that it's unimportant.)

Oddly enough, what we might call the grammar of Group III English is in some ways more complex than that of what is often called "standard English," that of Group I. Consider the pair we just cited: "He isn't going" and "He ain't going." As we know, underlying "He isn't going" would be a string like this:

$$He + s + be + ing + go$$

We convert this to a negative simply by adding *n't* where *T-not* instructs us to, and it flip-flops so that in the final version we merely have added *n't* to *is,* producing a negative.

But look at what the "ain't" speaker has to go through. Like his fellow, he starts with the same affirmative: "He is going." But for him, "is" has two allomorphs: /iz/ and /ey/. He uses the /iz/ for the affirmative statement, but when he wants to make a negative he shifts to the /ey/ and adds his *n't* morpheme to that, producing, of course, /eynt/. Thus in this little feature he has a more complicated structure than so-called "standard English." Certainly to call "he ain't" *ungrammatical* is to be unaware (or ignorant, if you wish) of the grammar that underlies it. Obviously, "he ain't" is governed by grammatical rules just as much as "he isn't," though the rules are different.

So far we've considered varieties of English—"dialects" we've called them—which differ according to the speaker's geographical background and his social "class." It should be obvious that these work together, and that any individual speaker will reveal the effects of both. That is, a Group III speaker in Mobile, Alabama, will not talk like a Group III speaker in Missoula, Montana, nor will he talk like a Group I speaker in his own home town. Phonologically his speech will be like that of his Group I fellow townsman, but it will have a different grammar. His grammar might resemble in many ways that of his Group III fellow citizen in Missoula, but the sound system would be very different from his.

There are other kinds of differences in the language we use. There are those based on the speaker's sex, for instance, Consider these sentences:

> I bought a darling pair of slacks this afternoon.
> Man, that was damn fine lunch.

Would we have much doubt in deciding which was more likely spoken by a man? Which by a woman?

You will recall that way back in Chapter I we noted that language is always changing, that this is as true of English as of any other language, and that the changes in English can be demonstrated historically. In fact, we demonstrated some of them. But it is a mistake to think that these changes are sudden developments. English did not remain Old English until Chaucer's time and then suddenly convert itself into Middle English. Rather, the changes occurred gradually and steadily. They are still going on, so that in our American society today there are notable differences in the language of older and younger people. These differences are most noticeable in vocabulary, but they undoubtedly are developing in the phonology too. For instance, I have noticed, I think, a change in the dipthong /ey/ as it occurs in "O.K." I, and people of my advanced years, all say /ow+key/, whereas everywhere I go—all over the United States—I hear young people saying /ow+kay/, or something pretty close to it. Perhaps this is the foreshadowing of some sort of general change, perhaps not. If we could all come back in another 100 years we'd know for sure.

As for vocabulary, we have already noted the constant addition of new words, and new meanings for old words, as new developments in our society create need for them. Unheard of, at least in their present sense, only a few years ago were words like *stereo, to orbit, to blast off, TV, Molotov cocktail, tap* (as on a telephone, either noun or verb), *air-to-air missiles, swing-wing* (airplane), *variable geometry* (fighter planes), *drag strip, SAM's* (surface-to-air missiles), *honkies, a trip* (resulting from use of drugs)—and all of these I picked up from this morning's paper. A little effort could easily turn up thousands of similar words, but with some exceptions, like *trip,* they are as likely to be used by older people as by younger so they don't reflect the generation gap.

The differences which do make up this gap are, it seems to me, primarily of two kinds: slang, and the "acceptability-level" of words known to both old and young but used by one age group and frowned upon, or at least not used, by the other.

Slang resembles some other features of language in that though we all know what it is, it isn't necessarily easy to define. A quick check of three late-model dictionaires and several language-reference books turns up a number of different definitions, no two exactly agreeing and yet all having certain essentials in common. All agree basically that, as Webster's III puts it, slang is a "non-standard vocabulary . . . composed typically of coinages, freshly made-up words, or arbitrarily changed words, clipped or shortened forms, extravagant, forced, or facetious figures of speech, or verbal novelties usually experiencing quick popularity and relatively rapid decline into disuse." Another characteristic of slang, mentioned, among the reference books I happened to check, only by Fowler's *Modern English Usage*[2] is that it results from "the favourite game among the young and lively of playing with words and renaming things and actions; some invent new words, or mutilate or misapply the old, for the pleasure of novelty, and others catch up such words for the pleasure of being in the fashion." Thus we see several attributes of slang: 1) it is, typically, deliberately invented by some unsung hero, 2) it is ephemeral, transient, 3) it is associated particularly with the young, and 4) it is a "non-standard" use of language, which is to say that however much fun it might be, and however witty and fresh you might think a slang construction to be, it is very likely going to be sadly out of place in a formal context such as a term paper.

This tells us, or should tell us, several things about slang. For one thing, and contrary to the ideas some of us might have picked up in school, there is nothing inherently wrong with it. It's good clean fun and it hurts nobody—but it is more appropriate to some situations than to others. Picture yourself reading to your classmates in sociology a paper which describes the activities of some middle-aged ladies who through idleness and boredom play bridge every afternoon and sometimes become intemperate. Which of the following would you more likely say?

> These matrons, with their children raised and gone away, and their husbands engaged in their offices, idled away the time playing cards and consuming alcohol, in which they frequently overindulged to the point of intoxication.

> Their house apes had blown the pad, their better halves were digging up scratch, so these old bags got stoned out of their minds every pm over the pasteboards.

The point is clear enough. But there is another point to be made: some of this slang just displayed—perhaps all of it—will sound strained, artificial, or—worst of all—*dated* to you. Some of it is of my generation rather than yours, and even that which is hot stuff at this moment is likely to be old hat by the time you read it. As Bergen and Cornelia Evans point out in *A Dictionary of Contemporary*

---

2. Second Edition, Revised and Edited by Sir Ernest Gowers, Oxford, 1965.

American Usage. "Slang ages quickly and nothing so stamps a total lack of force or originality upon a man or woman as the steady use of outmoded slang." This fact alone, perhaps, renders slang unsuitable for print, for what is fresh today as you write it will very likely be stale, and maybe even unintelligible, when someone reads it tomorrow.

It is also true, as most writers on the topic point out, that some slang words catch on and find a permanent home in the standard vocabulary. Some remain hovering just beneath the level of total respectability, like *guys* for "men" and *bucks* for "dollars." Some become so thoroughly standard that we are surprised to find they ever were regarded as slang, such as *mob* (for *mobile vulgus*) against which Jonathan Swift fulminated, and *bus* (for *omnibus*) which Bergen Evans says was written as '*bus* in this country as late as 1923. The status of still other words is hotly debated by the purists—and largely ignored by the general public, so that their permanence and ultimate respectability is assured. An example is *kids,* meaning children. I remember being bawled out as a kid for using the word in that sense. I was informed quite firmly that "kids" were young goats and that I had therefore committed a grievous impropriety and had perhaps been insulting to boot. If you hear it said of some woman that she has wonderfully-trained kids, do you assume that she is the owner of a marvellously accomplished bunch of young goats? "Kid" meaning "child" goes back to 1599 according to the *Oxford English Dictionary,* which marks the word as "slang" ("Originally low slang") but points out that its stock is going up. (The volume of the *OED* which contains "kid," by the way, was published in 1901.)

Slang keeps bubbling up, and while much of it seems rather pointless, beyond providing a few kicks to its users, some of it fills a need by saying something more neatly, more concisely, than has previously been possible. Two recent examples occur to me. The other day a student told me that he had "totalled" his new Pontiac. I had never heard the word used this way before but its meaning was immediately clear: he had not merely wrecked it but made a total wreck of it. What a neat way of expressing this thought. He totalled it. I predict a great future for this word.

Another student was griping mildly to me that though he has attained the grand age of 21, his youthful appearance causes the bartenders in the local beer joints to make him produce his draft card whenever he asks for a glass of suds. "They carded me three times last week," he said. Presto, a new verb, and a perfectly intelligible one. (Not all writers on language would label these two new word-uses as quite properly "slang," for some hold that in order to qualify, a word or expression must be used with an attempt at wit or cleverness, and "totalled" and "carded" might merely be utilitarian. But who is to say whether or not the first user of either of these words felt he was being witty?)

We observed a few lines back that a second difference in language among the generations was the "acceptability-level" of certain words. We need to explain that a bit.

Fashions in what society considers proper fluctuate wildly. A number of words Chaucer used in the *The Canterbury Tales,* one of the great masterpieces of the language, couldn't possibly be printed today in a book like this one, and though they have only very recently again been permissible in contemporary fiction, they have also helped set off controversy about the "degeneracy" of the modern novel. In contrast, our Victorian forbears were "proper" in public to a degree that seems fantastic to us today. "Legs" were unmentionable, for instance. The decent word for them, especially on ladies, was "limbs," but it was no doubt preferable not to have to mention them at all. It was during this era that the "breast" of chicken became "white meat," to avoid any unpleasant suggestivity in mixed company. At about the turn of the century Owen Wister wrote a story entitled "Skip to my Loo," set in Texas, in which much is made of the disapprobation of the local people for names like "boar," "stallion," "rooster," and "bull," euphemisms being employed in their stead. I myself have heard an old timer refer to a bull as a "he cow." (Incidentally, dancing was frowned on as quite sinful by the people in this story, though they enjoyed a game set to music, remarkably like dancing, which was called Skip to my Loo, and hence the name of the story.) I remember that during my boyhood something of this attitude lingered on in the more primitive backwaters of the West, where I was raised, and I was punished once for using the word "belly" and again for calling my younger brother a "liar." In this latter instance it wasn't my attitude toward my brother that was considered wrong—calling him a "story teller" would have been all right—but the coarse, bald, ugly word "liar" itself.

If these examples seem funny to you, it is only because as time passes some words gain in respectability and others lose. I doubt that anyone would boggle over the word "rooster," though the equally innocent "bitch" is distasteful in many circles. Words that had nothing wrong with them fall into disuse. "Trousers" occurs to me as an example. I doubt if any man under fifty in this country would buy a pair of trousers. He would buy a pair of pants, or even more likely among young people, slacks. Another example, offered by Bergen Evans, is the word "fetch," which he cites as a perfectly respectable word that has become mildly offensive to younger people, perhaps because of its use in training dogs. On the other hand, some words considered in poor taste by older folks have lost their stigma to younger people. I recall being shaken ("shook," if you prefer) a couple of years ago when I was addressed shortly before finals by a sweet young girl in one of my classes. She certainly looked decent, good middle-class background, well-groomed and all that. What she said was, "I simply don't know what I'll do if I screw up your final." I don't remember what I answered, if anything. I was shocked. I tottered back to my office to check out the expression in the then-brand-new Webster's III, and found that my reaction had dated me. There the expression is labelled simply "slang."

More recently I have had other similar experiences, both occasioned by co-eds like the first one. One girl I overheard saying of a quiz she obviously considered unfair, "Boy, he really shafted me on that one." And the other, referring to a lecture which she apparently held in low esteem, called it "a lot of crap." Both of these words, in these senses, are labelled "slang" by the latest Webster's. I'll tell you one thing: I'd have been jumped on, but good, had I used such words as a boy. I still feel just a little uncomfortable with those words (very much *aware* of them maybe) and would probably refrain from using them in mixed company. Which serves merely to make the point we've been belaboring: people of different age levels differ in the language they use and the way they use it. Quite obviously today's undergraduates regard these words as quite routinely and satisfactorily expressive of certain concepts, and the dictionary accurately reports this fact. (Webster's also labels "bitch" as slang, both as noun—meaning "complaint"—and as verb, "to complain, grouse.")

One lesson to be drawn from the above is that if you are interested in language, if you have to work with it (and what college student doesn't?), you need a *modern* dictionary. As you can see, the one your father used in *his* college days is seriously outdated. Not only will it not have words for many recent things and concepts which you will need to know about, but it will be misleading in its information on usage-levels and propriety. You are not going to school in his day nor are you using his language. Further, your dictionary should not only be up-to-date, but it should be sizeable enough to be useful for college and university-level work. The kind the drugstore might give you as a bonus for buying a whole case of toothpaste is likely to be of very slight value.

Another way that the English you use varies spectacularly from that of other people, in vocabulary at least, depends upon what you know and are interested in. Almost every different field has its specialized vocabulary, usually called "jargon" or "shop talk" by language students. Do you know the context in which the following terms would be used together and have a sensible relation?

flare pattern
screen
button hook
blitz
slant
red dog
audibles
pocket
belly series
naked reverse

If you do, you clearly know something about football. If you don't understand the game, these terms might well be gibberish to you. Now consider these:

baste
bias trim
back rib
presser foot
appliqúe
darts
plackets
batiste
nainsook
gusset

Know anything about sewing? If so, these terms were familiar. If not, they didn't mean much. Now try these:

gripes
painter
toggle
chocks
falls
two-blocked
davit

chafing pad
strongback
handy-billy

If you knew those, you've probably been a sailor—and without experience at sea you're very unlikely to have known them.

There are a couple of points we can draw from this little exercise. For one, since your experience and your knowledge are probably not exactly like anyone else's, your English vocabulary won't be exactly the same either—further support for the idiolect idea mentioned earlier. What do you know about that your best friend doesn't? Are you interested in photography and he's not? *(Focal length, emulsions, half-frames)* Guns? *(Sear, handload, wadcutter)* Music? *(Adagio, harmonics, vibrato)* And so on through countless specialized areas of human activity. Each carries vocabulary with it. A second thing we deduce from this exercise is that as we learn more and know more, our vocabularies expand. The way to a large vocabulary is to learn about many different things, not to memorize five arbitrarily-selected words a day. This is why, of course, vocabulary tests are pretty good indicators, not of intelligence, but of intellectual activity, of how inquiring and busy a person's mind has been. And a third thing we can learn from this discussion—a humbling thing, perhaps—is that nobody, but *nobody,* knows "the vocabulary" of English.

We've been discussing the way language use varies among individuals, whether because of geography, age, sex, social class, or particular specialized interests. It is also true that the way we use language varies constantly for each of us depending on the situation in which we happen to be using it. We need not make a great deal of this point, for surely you already recognize it. The easy, informal English you use at the lunch table with your family or friends is not what you use when you are being interviewed by the dean, nor is the language you'd use with the dean exactly what you'd select in making a speech before your church group or to the interfraternity council. Quite a few women students have pointed out to me that a serious weakness of J.D. Salinger's *The Catcher in the Rye* is that boys don't really use the vile language employed by Holden Caulfield in that book. I happen to be in a position to know something about this and I can testify that boys do, indeed, use such language. In fact, Salinger has artistically used only enough profanity and obscenity to suggest the monotonous vulgarities which characterize the speech of many teenage boys. Interestingly enough, I have never heard men students raise this objection to the novel. The girls' criticisms, then, are really a tribute to the average boy's control over his vocabulary. Around girls he simply doesn't talk the way he does when he's talking to other boys.

Look over the following samples of language and consider where they might have been spoken:

> It is my privilege to introduce to you this evening Dr. Reginald Smith, world-renowned authority on . . .

> Sir, I'd like to introduce Dr. Smith. Dr. Smith, Dr. Henry. Dr. Smith is an expert in . . .

> Hi, Sid. Say, I'd like you to meet Reginald Smith. Dr. Smith, that is. Reg, this is Sidney Spector. Reg is a great authority on . . .

> C'mere, Joe. Meet Reg Smith. Reg is an ol' buddy of mine from way back. He knows a whale of a lot about . . .

> Oh, *hello* there! I'd like you to meet one of my dearest friends, Reginald Smith. Reggie, Dr. Henry. Reggie has been simply *every*where and has just *scads* of information about . . .

Alas, we are never to know what Dr. Smith is expert in. But we can tell quite a bit about the situations in which the lines above might have been uttered, can't we? And wouldn't it be ludicrous for the language appropriate for one situation to be introduced into another?

There is still another difference in the way we use language, and this occurs when we shut our mouths and pick up a pen, but since that will be dealt with at some length in the next chapter we'll just observe for now that we don't write the way we speak. Nor, for that matter, do we always write the same. There are significant language differences between the history paper you turned in last week and the letters you write to your own true love. At least there should be, or you're going to have either a stunned history professor or a girl who thinks you've finally blown your mind.

Having observed all these differences in the way we use English, we are perhaps left with one nagging question, a persistent remainder of our schooldays: What is "good" English? How do we recognize it? How can we be sure we are using it? What *is* good English?

It doesn't help to dismiss the question airily and to say, as one book title had it: *Leave Your Language Alone!*[3] For we have been indoctrinated, all of us, into thinking that it makes a great deal of

---

3. When this book was reprinted it bore a different title, indicating that perhaps its author had second thoughts.

difference what kind of language we use—and all our experience tells us it is largely true! As we have seen, we are judged by the language we use, just as we judge others, and however regrettable this fact may be, it's still a fact. So we had better use "good English" insofar as we are able, if we can only discover what it is.

In the first place, we need to recognize that there are some differences in English that are irrelevant. If you live in Savannah you will, and should, talk like a Georgian. You'd be a real fool to try to remodel your speech so that you sounded like a native of somewhere else. And so would you be wherever you live, Milwaukee, San Francisco, Boston, Seattle or Dallas. Anywhere. Even Brooklyn, that butt of TV and movie "humor." No geographical dialect is recognized as superior to any other—except that of course the people who live in a given area are inclined to think the speech of that area is somehow "natural" and others sound peculiar. It was this which moved the East Texas woman to remark, shortly after Lyndon Johnson became President, that it certainly was nice to have someone in the White House who didn't talk funny. When I was a schoolboy in Montana I once had a teacher who informed my class that the best English in the United States was spoken in Boston. I suppose I believed her, then. I don't know, but I can imagine why she thought that. Perhaps she came from there. Or, more probably, it was a hangover from the 19th century when Boston—with Longfellow, Emerson, Holmes, and all the other "Brahmins"—so dominated American culture that Bostonians called their city "The Hub" without much argument from their fellow citizens. It isn't the case any more, if it ever really was, that the dialect of Boston is "the best" American English. What makes a dialect superior, when that occurs, is that the speakers of it are regarded as especially prestigious, as is the case with the so-called "Received Standard" dialect in England. In the rest of the English-speaking world, and most especially in this country, no such situation exists.

Certain other dialectal differences are irrelevant too. If you're female you would naturally expect to talk like a woman. Just so, if you're 19 years old you would naturally use the language of your own generation. Just as naturally, you will find older people objecting to it. (This has been going on for centuries, and probably in all languages.) Since students are frequently under the thumbs of older people, it is sometimes good politics to bow (temporarily, of course) to their pronouncements about what is and is not "correct," but the smart student will recognize politics as politics, not to be confused with gospel. It follows, too, that the perceptive 60-year old will refrain from trying to talk like a teenager. The effort will be phony and its product will be appreciated as such.

All this adds up to advice: be natural.

But it doesn't answer the question, "What if my natural English is lousy?" The only thing that could produce a verdict like this, from you or anyone else, would be your employment of usages from a social dialect that is felt to be lacking in prestige. If you use the language of what a few pages back we were calling Group III you will find your professors, and maybe even your fellow students, criticizing you—and quite properly, for you are now in a Group I situation. The remedy is extremely simple: Learn to use Group I language.

So the question becomes, "How do we determine what is and what is not Group I language?"

The typical American procedure, inculcated by the schools for many generations, is to appeal to authority. Characteristically when we are confronted with a disputed usage or pronunciation we appeal to "the dictionary" or "the rules of grammar." It is true that nine times out of ten a language dispute can be settled on the testimony of such authority, but this is as likely as not because the disputants are naive. Certainly you and I know better. As for "the dictionary," there is not one but many, and they differ. I remember one class that got into an argument over the status of the word "jalopy." I sugested that they look it up in their dictionaries. There happened to be three different dictionaries owned by various class members: *Webster's New World, Webster's Collegiate,* and *The American College Dictionary,* all good ones. As luck would have it, one dictionary indicated the word was standard English, one labelled it "colloquial," and the third called it "slang." So which is it? (Or rather, since that was a few years ago, which *was* it?) The appeal to "the dictionary" hadn't helped much. We would clearly be confronted by another question: "Which dictionary is the best?" The answer would certainly have to be something like "The one that gives the best description of English as used by educated Americans"—and in order to judge this matter we'd have to know, ourselves, how educated Americans really use their language. So we're right back where we started.

The fact is that few people really *read* their dictionaries and try to comprehend what a dictionary maker, or lexicographer, sets out to do. If they did, they would always find in the front matter a statement something like this: "the standard of English pronunciation . . . is the usage that now prevails among the educated and cultured people to whom the language is vernacular." This happens to come from Webster's II, but it is repeated in Webster's III, and you can check any good, standard dictionary and find similar statements, not only about pronunciation but also about definitions, usage labels, and so on. In other words, the lexicographer is a *reporter*. He and his staff survey the language and the way it's being used (and sometimes the way it has been used) and report their findings in their dictionary. This can be a tremendous undertaking. Webster's III was some twenty-five years in the making and cost some $3.5 million. The great *Oxford English Dictionary* was begun in 1858 and the final volume was published in 1921. And *then* a Supplement was necessary, published in 1933, to pick up loose ends. Naturally, a vast effort by a scholarly staff is likely to produce a better end result than a slipshod job done by hucksters after a fast buck, but in the last analysis the validity of the dictionary, regardless of the effort and expense put into it, depends upon the accuracy and completeness with which it presents the facts of the language. The final determiners of the language, then, are the people who use it, whether they like the honor or not. Many don't. They want someone to dictate "correctness." But this seems to be a practical impossibility, running counter to the facts of language life. (It is true that the publication and sale of dictionaries is a highly competitive business, and that sometimes the sales departments of publishing houses make statements which the firm's scholars would disown, such as advertising a dictionary as "the ultimate authority," an obvious pandering to the American yearning for such an authority and the misconception that somewhere, somehow there has to be one.)

After the lexicographer has ascertained the facts, as best he can, then he has the problem of how to present them, what to say about them. What does the user of the dictionary probably want to know? What does he need to know? What can be omitted? For as even the editors of the vast *OED* were constrained to point out, limitations of space make it impossible to include everything. (It is inaccurate and even silly to call any dictionary "unabridged," therefore.) Does the reader need elaborate usage guides? The editors of the recent Webster's III decided that he didn't, and thereby received a great deal of criticism from people who felt that the dictionary had abandoned a responsibility. Much appeared in the press, for instance, over that dictionary's entry at *ain't*. Here is what it says as to the usage of this word: "Though disapproved by many and more common in less educated speech, used orally in most parts of the U.S. by many cultivated speakers especially in the phrase *ain't I*." Contrast this with the treatment given the word by *The Random House Dictionary of the English Language:* "Nonstandard in U.S. except in some dialects; informal in Brit." Then under the heading *usage,* it adds:

> *Ain't* is so traditionally and widely regarded as a nonstandard form that it should be shunned by all who prefer to avoid being considered illiterate. *Ain't* occurs occasionally in the informal speech of some educated users, especially in self-consciously or folksy or humorous contexts *(Ain't it the truth! She ain't what she used to be!),* but it is completely unacceptable in formal writing and speech. Although the expression *ain't I?* is perhaps defensible—and is considered more logical than *aren't I?* and more euphonious than *amn't I?*—the well-advised person will avoid any use of *ain't.*

Well, which do you like? Certainly the palm for being concise must go to Webster's III, that for fullness to *Random House.* Do you think the information in Webster's III is enough? Do you think it is accurate? Do you know any people you would consider educated who use *ain't?* What does the fuller discussion achieve in the *Random House Dictionary?* Finally, since the *RHD* was published later than Webster's III, do you think the fuller explanation might be a commercial ploy, an effort to appeal to those who were dissatisfied with Webster's III?

Both of these dictionaries are excellent, though *RHD* has about half the linage of *Webster's III,* and both are what we might call "general" dictionaries of the language. In an effort to meet the popular demand for authority in disputed matters, some writers have created more specialized "dictionaries" which are concerned only with usage. These are such works as Bergen and Cornelia Evans' *A Dictionary of Contemporary American Usage* and Fowler's *Modern English Usage,* both mentioned earlier. There are others, such as Margaret Nicholson's *A Dictionary of American English Usage,* which is an Americanization of Fowler's book. Books like these are often very interesting and even useful, but they very frequently are in disagreement with each other. And what does the seeker after authority do in such a case? As the old expression has it, he pays his money and he takes his choice. His only possible recourse is to measure what the authorities say against his own knowledge of his own language, and this is not a very satisfactory way of "appealing to authority."

As for any attempt to appeal to the "rules of grammar," we have spent quite a bit of time in this book considering grammar, and we know enough to beware of any unsophisticated attempt to call upon its "rules." Whose grammar are we going to consult? How good a description of the language is it? Is it really accurate? Does it give the facts as they actually are? Whose language does it describe? (Group I's? Group II's? Group III's? All of them?) What if we find, as frequently happens, that two grammars differ on a given point? Where do we find the referee? And how far can we trust him?

The truth is becoming more and more obvious: you must be your own authority. There is no getting around this. You can go to the dictionary, to the reference books, for advice, and probably most of the time you will feel that, after all, the lexicographer has dedicated his career to language matters and you can trust him. You and I don't have the time or the money—or the interest—to hire huge staffs of people and direct their research on linguistic problems, so most of the time we'll accept the judgment of those who do. But occasionally we'll run across something that makes us say, "Awwwww, come on!" And this is when we must exercise our inalienable right to rise superior to all the "authorities." For we do have eyes and ears, this is our language, we are aware of how people say and write things, and we do *not* have to accept what others tell us, except as we see fit.

Consider all the recent pother over "like" used to mean "as" or "as if," like in:

> Winston tastes good like a cigarette should.
> She drooped like she was tired.

The *Random House Dictionary* labels these uses flatly "non-standard." Webster's III gives both meanings of "like" ("as" and "as if") without comment, citing their use by such authorities as Art Linkletter and the *St. Petersburg (Fla.) Independent*. Fowler says of "like" for "as" that this misuse, "if it is a misuse at all," is used by "most" people daily in conversation but that in "good writing this particular *like* is rare." He adds that "like" used for "as if" is colloquial in the U.S. and grates on British ears. Nicholson, in her Americanization of Fowler, drops this last crack. Bergen Evans says, "Some people believe that it is a mistake to use *like* in this way. But they are in a minority." He is talking about "like" used for "as." When he comes to "like" for "as if" he says, "At one time *like* could be used to mean *as if* . . . " and concludes that "The construction is generally frowned upon, but it is more acceptable in the southern states than it is in other parts of this country."

On top of all this authority, I know this: I constantly observe "like" used in both these senses in my reading. The usage has become so widespread that it occurs more often than the "standard." Writers use it like they had a compulsion.

So what do you do with "like"? Use it when you want to and don't worry much about it. Wouldn't this be something to lose sleep over? And how in the world could you possibly bow to the "authorities" when they offer such a spread of advice? I feel that if someone jumps me for my "ignorant" use of "like" for "as" or "as if" (either one) I will challenge him. He produces an authority. I produce a counter-authority, and insist that my authority could lick his authority. He considers me an upstart. I consider him a stuffed shirt. This kind of "scholarly debate" could, and does, get childish, and has in almost this bald a form disgraced the pages of many journals dealing with language matters. It would be better for us to keep our cool and save our emotions for where they might be more fittingly exercised.

(*Important note:* If one of my teachers insisted that "like" employed to mean "as" or "as if" is ignorant, I would avoid it in his class. "Winston tastes good as a cigarette should." It's tough to win an argument when your opponent is also the judge.)

It's clear, then, that you must be the final authority in usage matters. But we still haven't answered the question we set out with: How do we tell what is "good English?"

It has been described quite simply, and I think precisely, as "effective English that does not call unfavorable attention to itself." If we could be assured of using the language so as to meet these simple standards all the time, we'd probably be happy. It seems a simple enough thing to ask for. And yet in practice it isn't always easy.

Note that the first thing stipulated is that the language be "effective." This implies simply, what we certainly concede, that the most usual purpose of language is communication and that language that fails to communicate well is bad, no matter how in accordance with somebody's "rules" it might be. It is true that in some artistic uses, as in poetry, perhaps, what the speaker (or writer) is trying to communicate may not be simply information but an emotion, a feeling about something, and his language might not have immediate and obvious clarity. Nevertheless it can be effective or ineffective measured against what it's trying to do. However, in our everyday use of language we are not often attempting anything so subtle, but are rather trying to convey an idea, to give information, or perhaps persuade someone to do something. If the message is transmitted easily and clearly, the language is effective; if it gets messed up somehow, the language certainly leaves something to be desired. First of all, language must get the job done. Without that it's just noise.

The idea that good English "does not call unfavorable attention to itself" carries with it a couple of implications. First, it suggests that language can call *favorable* attention upon itself, and indeed it can. We have all heard brilliant speakers whose appeal is largely based on a marvellous facility with language. Always the perfect word, the precise figure of speech, the sparkling pun. Many writers, too, owe their success not so much to what they have to say as to the artful way they manage to say it. Most of us can't hope to achieve that kind of brilliance. (Perhaps, if the truth be told, it's because we're not willing to work hard enough at it.) But we should at least have a reasonable hope, with only moderate effort, of whipping our language into such shape that it doesn't attract *un*favorable attention.

The phrase suggests secondly what we have already considered a bit, that language can have appropriateness or inappropriateness. It is appropriate (or it fails to be) in three different ways, principally. We have already touched on these, but let's consider them systematically.

Your language should be appropriate to you. Just as you select clothes suitable to your age, sex, personality, tastes, and so on, so should you adapt your language. It has to be suitable to you, not to someone else. Otherwise it will be fake, it will be detected as such, and you yourself will be regarded as a fraud. Polonius' platitude has relevance here: "This above all—to thine own self be true. . . . "

Second, your language needs to be appropriate to your listener. If you're whispering in your girl's ear, your words should not sound like an oration. If you're talking to a class of Sunday school children, the language suitable to your research paper in Biblical history would hardly be fitting. If the language is going to communicate, it must be within the understanding of your listener, and at the same time must strike him as appropriate. If you are talking on a technical subject with a person who understands the subject, go ahead and be technical. If you get quite elementary he's likely to be offended. On the other hand, if you're talking about the same subject to someone ignorant of it, you obviously have to water it down to his level. Sometimes it takes a nice tact to strike the balance between being true to yourself and appropriate to your audience. For instance, you're a college person and if not yet "well educated" at least you're on the road toward it. So suppose you get a job where you have to deal with uneducated laborers. It is necessary to *communicate* with them. At the same time, you must remain appropriate to yourself. If you try deliberately adopting Group III language, or what you consider to be Group III language, they will know you're talking down to them and they will resent it. They don't expect *you* to talk that way and you shouldn't. You'd be lucky if you didn't get a bust in the eye.

Finally, your language should be appropriate to the situation in which you find yourself. As illustration, picture yourself and three or four of your good friends having a bull session in the dorm. Now picture the same group engaged in a discussion of some topic in a seminar. You're the same person, and so are your listeners the same, but the language suitable for the situation would have changed quite a bit.

If you can manage to make your language effective, and if you can keep it appropriate to yourself, your listener, and the situation you find yourself in, you won't have to worry much about it calling unfavorable attention to itself, and you won't have to worry at all about "good English." It will be good.

CHAPTER 9

LITTLE SQUIGGLES ON PAPER

Way back on page 1 we observed that most of us chatter away unceasingly from morning to night, day in and day out. The production of language is one of your principal activities. So much do we lean on this constant verbal exchange with our fellows that one of the harshest punishments that can be dealt even a hardened criminal is solitary confinement. Traditionally this deprivation of companionship, which is basically nothing more than taking away the right to talk to someone, is considered an extreme measure. However, perhaps an equally effective punishment, if it wouldn't be too cruel, would be this: award a writing assignment.

For the average person, nothing dries up the flow of words more effectively than the simple act of picking up a pen. Sit before a typewriter and verbal paralysis sets in. The same student who has been regaling his companions at lunch with an account of some hilarious things that happened to him and his family on a recent vacation trip will be struck dumb if his English teacher asks him to write on "My Vacation Trip." You know this is so, very possibly from remembered personal experience. Perhaps even from a recent experience, for the anguish of writing doesn't diminish much as one becomes a university freshman confronting the traditional themes, or even an upperclassman with a term paper to produce. Even admitting that something like "My Vacation Trip" may be a less than inspiring subject to be asked to write on, one still has to wonder why it is that many "unattractive" topics are so easy to talk about with friends and such unadulterated misery to say anything about on paper.

As a matter of plain fact, no topic, except possibly sex, is interesting to read about until some writer has *made* it interesting. You have read and enjoyed many little pieces on subjects essentially trivial which were entertaining because some writer had made them entertaining. Unfortunately the converse is also true: many a fascinating subject has been rendered dull by an inept author. (On second thought, I'll take back my exemption of sex from this general principle. I've read some boring articles on that subject too. Haven't you?) Therefore, though we have to concede that frequently teachers offer their students some pretty trite topics to write about, we can't entirely agree with the student complaint that "Nobody can write on a subject like that." Somebody can, with a little imagination and some expenditure of effort.

The trouble with us when we make such complaints (and I most certainly include myself) is that we don't really want to write the blasted assignment anyhow. Let's face it, openly and honestly: writing is a pain in the neck. Writing is hard work, especially decent writing, and none of us really relish hard work. Particularly do we dislike having it imposed on us. That makes it almost unbearable. Even if the writing is something we have assigned ourselves, it isn't easy. In a volume entitled *Writers at Work,* edited by Malcolm Cowley, there are published interviews with many top writers wherein these writers are led to talk at length on their profession. They all have different techniques, of course, they go about writing in different ways, and they achieve different results, but there is one thing that they all agree on without exception: writing is hard work. On my campus recently there was an NDEA Institute in English in which the participants were forty grade school and junior high school English teachers. Those who laid out the Institute program thought that since these people spent much time teaching composition it wouldn't hurt them to do quite a bit of writing, polishing up their own techniques somewhat. You might be interested to know that these teachers dreaded their composition assignments, and groused and complained much as their own students undoubtedly do. When it came right down to producing prose, they too indicated that they found it hard work.

Why is it that writing is so difficult? Further, is there anything that can be done about it? Understanding a few of the reasons that cause trouble might help alleviate some of it. But it is to be feared that nothing will ever make it really easy, especially if one wants to write well. It's not too difficult to churn out a sloppy piece, but as Thomas Moore put it, "Easy writing's curst hard reading."

One reason many of us have trouble putting words on paper is that we don't do enough of it. Writing is a skill, and like other skills it must be used to keep the rust off it. More than that, it must be used to be developed to any significant degree in the first place. Compare the sad fix of the weekend golfer. He's nuts about the game, but the poor guy has to earn a living and his job keeps him pretty well tied down, so his opportunity for daily practice with his clubs is nil. No doubt, too, he has a wife and family, a house to keep up, and other responsibilities which eat up one day of his two-day weekend. So on his one free day each week he tears out to the course, meets the others in his foursome, gets the bets all arranged, tees off—and shoots 112 and hates himself all the next week. In the evenings he will pore over volumes from his extensive shelf of how-to-do-it golf books by Mr. Palmer, Mr. Snead, Mr. Nicklaus and countless others, looking for some tip, some secret, that will enable him to cream the competition next week. And next week, of course, the same disastrous performance is repeated. Will he ever get any better? Certainly there's no reason to be optimistic, is there? And yet golf isn't all that hard. The one thing that could possibly help, that would certainly help, this pathetic fellow is the one thing he sadly believes he hasn't the time and the money to do: take a series of weekly lessons from a pro and put in an hour's practice every day on what the pro is trying to teach him.

The ironic thing about watching an expert perform is that he makes it look so easy. Watch a pro hit a golf ball. Watch an Olympic diving champion perform off the high board, or one of our beautiful young lady champion figure skaters twinkling on the ice. Observe the grace of a major league shortstop scooping up a hot ground ball, or a pro football halfback dancing away from tacklers. Or, for that matter, read a page of Steinbeck or Hemingway. Doesn't it look easy? But what we don't see, of course, and what we don't appreciate, except abstractly, is the thousands of hours of hard, sweaty, purposeful practice which makes the performance possible. Of course there is such a thing as ability. You and I might practice until we wore our fingers down to the knuckles and never be able to play a cello like Pablo Casals nor a piano like Van Cliburn. Neither, for that matter, can practice guarantee that we'll be able to write like James Thurber or Truman Capote. But suppose we're not aiming at being a top professional, but rather just want the competence to do a good workmanlike job, one that will command anybody's respect. Surely practice, earnest practice with some coaching, can guarantee that.

Have you read Ben Franklin's *Autobiography*? (If not, you should.) If you have, you will recall Franklin's account of how he taught himself to write; how, as he put it, "I acquired what little ability I have in that way." He had been involved in an argument with a young friend (over the propriety of "educating the female sex in learning, and their abilities for study") when the friend moved away and the argument had to be continued by correspondence. Franklin became convinced that often his friend won points not by better logic but simply through superior ability with the pen. So he set out to do something about it. He took issues of *The Spectator*, which was then current stuff, and made sketchy outlines of some of the articles. Then, after leaving his outlines on the shelf for a time, so the authors' wording would have fallen out of his mind, he would attempt rewriting the pieces so that he could compare his version with the original. With that lack of false modesty which makes the *Autobiography* so human, he writes that "I sometimes had the pleasure of fancying that, in certain particulars of small import, I had been lucky enough to improve" on the original. He had two other devices he used in his practice. One was to turn the *Spectator* article into verse, because he felt that the need to find words which would fit the meter and rhyme would force the expansion of his vocabulary. Also, he would sometimes jumble the arrangement of points in his outline so that he would have to re-order them as he tried to re-create the original, thus gaining practice arranging them into "the best order" before "compleating" the paper. All of this kind of practice makes tremendous sense, of course, but it requires dedication and self-discipline far beyond what most of us possess. What makes the performance almost incredible is that Franklin was a thirteen year old boy when he did this, and further, he worked on his writing in the evenings after having put in a full day as apprentice in his brother's print shop. Of course, he was one in a million, or better one in many million, but nevertheless, the principles of his self-imposed regimen have applicability to us lesser beings.

Another thing that makes writing agonizing for most of us is the way it is "taught" in the schools. Generally the process is one of the teacher's giving the class a topic or topics to write on, collecting the completed papers, and eagerly pouncing on each error with her flashing red pencil. The papers are then given back to the students, who are supposed to contemplate their sins and resolve to commit them no more. Actually this isn't what happens. As poor Johnny looks at his paper, which seems to have broken out with measles, a great feeling of hopelessness wells up within him. "What's the use?" he groans to himself. "I'll never learn to do this stuff." Perhaps he's right, but there is one thing he's a cinch to learn, and that is a thorough detestation of having to put pen to paper. If you have a puppy and every time he performs a certain act you smack him one or otherwise make his life unpleasant, what happens? Either he quits doing whatever it is or, if he can't stop it, or doesn't understand, he becomes neurotic. Thus it is with numberless Johnny's and Susie's in our classrooms. What they are really being taught is to hate writing.

Often enough, too, Johnny's paper really has much that is good about it. Perhaps it has a fresh, lively point of view toward some commonplace event, perhaps he has really put his heart into baring his feelings about someone or in expressing his secret ambitions. This makes it all the harder to take getting blasted by a judge interested only in ruthlessly tracking down misplaced commas, aberrant spellings and "errors in agreement." This is teaching writing? Not really. It is, rather, suppressing harshly whatever creative urge a youngster might bring with him to his writing assignment. Donald J. Lloyd in an article entitled "Our National Mania for Correctness" surveys the sorry state of writing in America today and, by implication at least, attributes it to these comma hounds. His thesis is that every time we take up a pen we can visualize someone getting ready to be nastily critical about the "mistakes" we are certain to commit, so we are reduced to a losing struggle with our own language—the same language we use so freely, and often so beautifully, in our daily speech. He's right. Very largely we are "psyched" into writing badly.

As we observed earlier, writing is basically a different *kind* of language use from speech. No one remembers learning to talk. Learning to speak comes easily and naturally, to everyone. But we have to be taught to write. And oh, what a struggle it is!

A clue to one of the fundamental differences between writing and speech is found in the way linguists sort out sentences into the different kinds, principally "declarative," "interrogative." and "imperative" (also called "request" and "command") sentences. As usual, traditional grammar proceeds by first understanding the sentence and then affixing a label to it. Thus the student is taught that if the sentence asks a question he is to call it "interrogative," but he hasn't really learned anything beyond a new name. He already knows the sentence asks a question—that's how he knows what label to apply—but how does he know it? That's something more basic, and traditional school-grammar ignores it. As Fries pointed out, essentially what the traditional approach teaches the student is that a sentence that asks a question is a sentence that asks a question. And isn't that quite an accomplishment? The linguist sorts out these sentences according to what kind of response is expected. Thus to sentences like "What time is it?" "Do you like shrimp?" and "Watcha doin' tonight, babe?" the expected response is a verbal answer. We can say, then, that a sentence to which the expected response is a reply in words is a question. Similarly, if you tell someone "Go wash my socks" the expected response is an action, and we can say that sentences of this kind are to be called requests, or commands. (Note that the person spoken to might well say, "Go wash them yourself," but we are talking about the normal or *expected* response.)

Now we come to the kind of sentence we call "declarative," the ordinary statement. What kind of response does it elicit? It isn't just silence, as you might first guess. It's a series of spoken "signals" which seem to mean something like "I'm listening. Please go on." What the signals are is a steady stream of little utterances like "Uh huh," "Yes," "That's right," "You don't say," "Hmmm," and so on. We depend on those signals as we speak to assure us that we're getting through to our listener. Of course, we also observe his expression, but we need the spoken signals, and they're always there. You can test this out for yourself. Next time some friend is telling you something on the phone don't make these signals. Don't make a sound. Pretty soon he's sure to come back with something like "Hello, you still there?" Something important was missing, you see. So we say that a statement, a simple declarative sentence, calls forth these "attention signals."

We rely on these signals, all of us, to make certain that we are really communicating. This is one reason that so many have trouble addressing large groups, like presenting a talk to the class. The familiar kind of signal is missing and we have to learn to look for others. There *is* a kind of response from audiences, and part of becoming an experienced speaker is learning how to detect it and use it, but it is different from that of ordinary conversation.

In writing, obviously, there is no response whatsoever. Just the writer, a writing instrument and a horribly blank piece of paper, miserably alone together. Language, which has always been a two way proposition, has suddenly become a strictly one way street, and it's disturbing. This is one of the very basic differences between speech and writing, this absence of response signals, and one which is probably insufficiently appreciated. There doesn't seem to be a great deal one can do about it, either, though sometimes it does help when one is writing to try to visualize and write to a specific reader. Perhaps attempting this helps the writer to "hear" the missing responses. Anyhow, maybe just knowing that part of the terror of writing is caused by the absence of these little signals will somehow help a little.

Of course as we write we are, perhaps inescapably, afflicted by the "national mania" for correctness. We do, after all, want our writing to escape "drawing unfavorable attention to itself" and hence to us. So we are concerned about such mechanical things as punctuation and spelling, worries we naturally never have in speech. But isn't it amazing that we have all mastered the subtleties of English intonation patterns only to be thrown by punctuation, which is much simpler? There are reasons for this, naturally. One is that when we were children learning our language we did a great deal of practicing and experimenting with intonation patterns. We dedicated a great many of our waking hours exactly to this, playing with the patterns, altering them, making games of them. And we have used them every day since. In contrast, we have paid hardly any attention to punctuation, spending relatively few hours with it. Another reason we have difficulty with punctuation we already know: our punctuation system is inadequate. It can't come anywhere near representing the range of our intonation patterns. You put a question mark on the end of a question. What inflection does it have? Falling? Rising? Is it *really* a question or only a rhetorical one? Does it ask for information or indicate skepticism? We might say that the question mark is a sort of generalization, giving the reader a mere hint that he is to apply one of quite a variety of possible intonations. What assurance does the writer have that the reader will "hear" the intonation he intended? None.

Still another reason we have difficulty with punctuation is that the "rules" are not really "rules" at all but attempts to describe usage, and usage varies. This is especially true with some of the trickier marks like the comma and the hyphen. If one were to go to work on a newspaper or magazine, or in a publishing house, one of the first things he would be confronted with would be the "stylebook," in which problems of usage, including punctuation, are dealt with. You would conform to its dictates or soon be job-hunting again. These stylebooks differ, of course. For instance, in my own city the morning paper doesn't use "Mr." in attributing quotes.

"Murder should not be tolerated," Smith said.

But in the afternoon paper it's different:

"Murder should not be tolerated," Mr. Smith said.

(However, should Smith be convicted of a crime or otherwise indicate that he is not a desirable citizen, he loses his Mr.) They punctuate differently, too. In the morning paper you might live at 6127 Pennsylvania Ave. In the afternoon paper, however, you would live at 6127 Pennsylvania ave. Which is "correct"? The question is not answerable. If we were to rephrase it we'd be getting closer to making sense: "Which is in accord with general practice?" Or, "Which way do the majority of newspapers do it?" This we could answer, with some research.

I remember a few years ago I was reading *Sports Illustrated* and came across a sentence something like this:

The fight took place in Shelby, Montana in the summer of . . .

I immediately noticed the absence of the comma after "Montana" and figured it was a typo. However, elsewhere in the magazine I found the same thing. So I leafed through the whole issue, and a couple of others too, and found that the magazine was consistent. That comma was always missing. So was the one following the year in a construction like this: It was on May 5, 1969 that the record was broken.

It occurred to me that *Sports Illustrated* is one of the magazines of the Henry Luce chain so I thought I'd check some of the others. Sure enough, *Time* omits those commas and so does *Life*. In my school days I had been given the distinct impression that leaving out those commas was sure indication of ignorance and a bar to a successful life. And here were three of our large-circulation magazines whose editors (or publisher) obviously thought those commas were less than vital. Who is "right"? Again, not too profitable a question.

Some years ago, when a student in one of my courses got interested in punctuation and how it is practiced, he made a list of some ten situations in which there seems to be a bit of a problem and then investigated a dozen different magazines to see how each handled it. Magazines such as *Time, Newsweek, The New Yorker, Harper's, The Atlantic, The Saturday Evening Post, Seventeen*. Would you be surprised to learn that he discovered no unanimity on any of the problems, and in fact not even general agreement? I trust not. You see, part of the problem we have with punctuation, you and I, is that there really are no well-established standards to follow, and most especially not where the issue is at all "controversial."

As for spelling, that old bugaboo, the time we spend worrying about minor spelling slips is out of all proportion to their value. Yet spelling "correctness" is socially of extreme importance. No matter how beautifully or elegantly we write, if we misspell a few words, those who know how to spell them will ignore all our glittering

virtues and look upon us as dolts. This is an unhappy fact with which
we must live. One might maintain that it shouldn't matter how we
spell, as long as it can be read, and once upon a wonderful time it
didn't. But with the "Augustan" era's craze for order there came an
insistence on orthodoxy in spelling. The feeling was that there *ought*
to be a right way, and the opportune appearance of some of the early
great dictionaries provided a standard which was promptly seized.
The schools took it up. Millions upon millions of spelling books were
sold. The spelling bee became an institution. Kids *had* to learn to
spell. And in the process of all this, spelling somehow became equa-
ted with intelligence, one of our more outstanding distortions of
value. Thorstein Veblen, the great American economist, and satirist,
had some acid things to observe about our foolish worship of correct
spelling. His book *The Theory of the Leisure Class* has as a basic
thesis that those of the leisure class must, if they are to be recognized
and looked up to by their lesser fellows, ostentatiously waste both
time and money, and in all ways possible, simply to show that they
are of such stature that they can. The time wasted on learning to
spell conventionally, he says, is a good example:

> English orthography satisifies all the requirements of the canons of repu-
> tability under the law of conspicuous waste. It is archaic, cumbrous, and
> ineffective; its acquisition consumes much time and effort; failure to acquire
> it is easy of detection. Therefore it is the first and readiest test of repu-
> tability in learning, and conformity to its ritual is indispensable to a blame-
> less scholastic life.[1]

However much we may agree with Veblen, it will do us little good to
rail against the obtuseness of our society in this matter, for it is our
society, we're part of it, and we're stuck with it. We have to conform—unless, of course, we want to reject society altogether. It may
well be that, as the late Edgar Sturtevant only half facetiously suggested, the way to cure our problems with English spelling would be
"the complete cessation of the teaching of spelling." He adds:

> This would shorten the school course by a year or two, adding that much to
> the useful life of every child, and saving considerable sums of money now
> wasted.[2]

But he also adds, wistfully it seems to me, that "vested interests"
would doubtless block such a progressive step. No doubt he's right,
and no doubt, either, that the "vested interests" are Veblen's leisure

1. Thorstein, Veblen, *The Theory of the Leisure Class* (New York: Random House, Inc.,
1934).

2. E.H. Sturtevant, Introduction to Linquistic Science (New Haven: Yale University Press,
1947).

class, anxious to prop up their self-esteem by looking down upon those who lack their ability at this trivial trick. However, as we said, there's no use fussing about it. That's the situation and we might as well face it. So, if you're a bad speller, what to do about it?

My advice might shock you. It is to find someone who is a good speller and have him read everything important that you write—letters applying for jobs, English themes, term papers, letters to the editor, anything that you want to make a good impression. (Except love letters, of course. But then if your sweetheart really loves you, maybe spelling errors will be forgiven.) If you can't get a friend to do this service for you, hire somebody. If necessary, marry a good speller. But be sure that everything you write that you care about is checked over for spelling. This is the single most practical thing you can do about a really bad spelling problem. I say you might find this advice shocking because it seems to run counter to all we've been told about doing our work "independently." Don't cheat, we've been told. But this is not cheating. It's simple common sense. We'll have more to say about this kind of "outside help" later on.

You should, of course, make every effort on your own to improve your spelling. Try to learn—simply memorize—the words that you *know* you have trouble with. And cultivate the acquaintance of your dictionary. These are standard bits of advice, but they're not really very helpful unless your spelling is already "fair." If it is frankly bad, you've probably been trying both these ideas without much success. The difficulty with memorizing your "trouble" words is that there are so many of them, and you've already been trying to learn them. Perhaps like some of my students you can spell them all right when challenged, but then you go right ahead and get them wrong again on your next writing assignment. As for the dictionary bit, the rub here is that you naturally look up a word like "aphro-disiac," should you have occasion to use it, but you confidently go ahead and spell "quite" when you mean "quiet" and "dinning room" when you mean "dining room." You don't look up these simple words, and they're the ones you trip over. Unless, of course, you look up every word you write. A young friend of mine completed a 350 word theme for an English assignment and, perhaps exaggerating, told his father, "Dad, I looked up every one of those 350 words in my dictionary." This kid had flunked freshman English twice and he was taking no chances. But this seems to me a foolish and excessively time-consuming way to go about tackling the problem. If there ever is any pleasure at all in doing a writing assignment well, as some teachers assure us there is, this hardly seems the way to discover it.

How much simpler it would be to consult a *living* "dictionary"—someone who doesn't have trouble with spelling—and ask him to check your paper. Essentially it's the same thing.

Not only are mechanical matters like punctuation and spelling a problem in writing but there are differences in the grammar, especially in the kinds of sentence patterns that are employed. For instance, introductory phrase or clause modifiers, considered by many teachers one of the marks of "mature" writing, are not very common in speech:

> Muttering angrily to myself all the while, I wrote the stupid paper.

> Because I was literate, I was exempted from freshman English.

In fact, elaborately embedded constructions of all kinds occur much more frequently on paper than in the mouth. They enable us to achieve in writing a kind of conciseness that is not normal to speech, and that sounds odd and stilted when occasionally people do produce it orally. One of my colleagues who has mastered this skill is widely regarded as rather pompous. His friends fail to envy his articulateness. "He talks like a book," they say. Right. That's exactly the difficulty. In his speech he over-uses patterns more common to writing. Incidentally, this basic difference between written and spoken language is one reason so many of us have trouble reading aloud and making it sound natural. We're trying to give normal intonation to patterns we don't normally speak.

Another illustration of the differences between speech and writing occurs when we print casual speech verbatim. It looks terrible. It's full of interrupted sentences, statements that don't end but just trail off, long strings of sentences linked with conjunctions, backing-ups and retracings, and all kinds of "errors." When Dwight Eisenhower was President, some reporters used to delight the Democrats by printing his press interviews word for word, including all the *uh's* and *ah's*. This was good clean fun, the Democrats figured, and clearly demonstrated what an incompetent we had in the White House. He couldn't even speak decent English. However, when John F. Kennedy succeeded to the Presidency some reporters continued the practice, with about the same results. His spoken English looked bad in print, too. There was one difference, however: the Democrats no longer thought it was quite so funny. Actually, the grammar of speech is much more complicated than that of writing. Written English is neater, tighter, more compact. Speech sprawls. And so we see another reason that so many of us had so much trouble, and maybe still have, with writing: it involves, in a very real sense, learning a new grammar, or at least a grammar with many new features. Many students never master it. In fact, many elementary-level teachers, perhaps unaware of the nature of the problem, fail to point out that "We would usually say it this way, but we write it like this," and fail also to proceed from there to give concentrated practice on patterns peculiar to written English.

Writing does have one advantage over speaking, one which we don't often take enough advantage of. When one says something, it's said. But when one writes something it's still there to be tinkered with. The writer can scratch it out and do it over, he can puzzle out alternate and more effective ways of saying it, he can move words and phrases around in the sentence—in short, he can revise to his heart's content. Most of us have hearts that get contented too soon, but nevertheless the possibility, the opportunity, of revision is always there. This is one of the biggest differences between professional writers and the rest of us. They revise. They cut and hack. They rewrite. They polish. Most of us, unhappily, somehow slop a sentence onto the page and then sit back and admire it. In a published interview, Hemingway said that he rewrote the final page of *A Farewell to Arms* thirty-nine times before he was satisfied with it. The interviewer asked him what technical problem had stumped him. "Getting the words right," said Mr. Hemingway. Tom Lea, the author of *The Brave Bulls,* estimated that he wrote over 40,000 words before he got the first chapter of that novel the way he wanted it. The chapter as it stands in the novel is something under 2,000 apparently simple words, and it's beautiful. James Thurber said of a 20,000 word short story of his that he rewrote it fifteen complete times and that "there must have been close to 240,000 words in all the manuscripts put together, and I must have spent two thousand hours working at it." He also said that it almost always took him at least seven drafts to turn out anything he was satisfied with.

Now do we begin to understand why most writing lacks the sparkle, the life—and the deceptive ease—of the professionals? Are we ever that ruthless with what we put on paper? Hardly. Yet, as I say, the opportunity is always there. Be assured that there is nothing illegal about rewriting, or revising, or correcting. It's done extensively by the very best of writers.

We'll concede, then, what we could have taken for granted in the first place: writing is difficult. So is there anything practical we can do about it?

We've already mentioned a couple of things that would help, though they have the drawback that they require a measure of self discipline: practice and revision. Implicit, too, in the discussion above was the suggestion that a writer make himself sensitive to such mechanical matters as punctuation and spelling. As he reads, he should notice how punctuation is handled. Also, he should try to implant in his mind what correctly-spelled words look like. I'm not sure if this will be any help, to be honest. I've given up trying to teach spelling, after what feels like fifty years of failure. But I am convinced that good spellers never really "learn" how to spell. Not consciously, that is, except for the few problem words that each of us has. Good spellers seem to have a visual memory and they just know by looking at a word whether or not it's wrong, just as if someone saw a person with three eyes he would have an instinctive feeling that there was something not quite right about him. Anyhow, for bad spellers it might be worth a try to attempt to cultivate an interest in words and what they look like. The student who writes "gril" for "girl"—and don't laugh, it often happens—simply isn't *looking* at what he's doing.

One thing that would greatly help the writing of most students, and often especially those who starred in English, would be a deliberate, coldblooded effort to write simply. Try to say things in a straightforward and direct manner. I wouldn't want to give you the idea that it's necessarily easy, but every step taken in this direction will give your writing extra force. It's the short words that have power. It's the short sentences that snap. Look at how beautifully simple are the writings of so many of the masters. Read Ben Franklin or David Hume, and consider how much better writers they were than their pompous contemporary, the learned Dr. Samuel Johnson. Read the speeches of Lincoln. Read the *Bible.* Or, coming down to date, read some of the prose of Carl Sandburg. Try his autobiographical *Always the Young Strangers* and pay particular attention to the simplicity of his language, if you can avoid getting caught up in the beauty of it.

Paradoxical as it may sound after the comments earlier in this chapter about what a chore writing is, most of us try too hard. We get snarled in tremendous, complicated sentences with modifiers hanging all over them. We try to bowl the reader over with the magnificence of our vocabulary. We try to dazzle him with images. All the time we're really working against ourselves. True, some of us have been taught this "style." We've been told that we should write a higher proportion of "complex" sentences. We've been made to underline all the figures of speech in poems, with the instruction, expressed or implied, that we should include loads of similes, metaphors and whatnots in our own writing. We have been put through vocabulary drills, having to memorize ten esoteric words diurnally and being constrained to demonstrate the effective utilization of each with contextual propriety. So we get the natural idea that all this kind of stuff is what makes good writing. Wrong. Somerset Maugham, who knew a little something about writing, said that he set for himself three goals. The first two were *simplicity* and *clarity*. The third was *euphony*, which means that he thought writing ought to sound good. This is desirable, too, but the first two are vital.

Always some student hearing this advice for the first time will ask, because it seems contrary to all that he thinks he has been taught, something like, "Well, then, what's all this noise about building up a big vocabulary? What good is it if we're not supposed to use it?" A reasonable question, certainly. It might be answered with an analogy. Suppose you have a fancy car with 475 horses. Does this mean that you have to floorboard it all the time? Of course not. All that power-potential simply means that at normal speed you operate more efficiently, more comfortably. In an emergency the reserve is there. So it is with anyone's vocabulary. There are times when you want the big, flashy word, times when nothing else will do. It's nice to have it in a pinch. Further, if you know ten or a dozen words expressing more or less the same concept your chance of getting exactly the one needed is obviously greater than if you only know two or three. You cruise more smoothly. Doesn't that make sense? Somewhat the same principle applies to the ability to handle long, complex sentences. It's a useful skill to have in your repertoire, but it should be used sparingly.

What's involved in all this is the principle of "appropriateness" which we were discussing in the last chapter. It applies to writing as well as speech. What is written needs to be appropriate to the writer and to the reader, and also to the situation, which as often as not will mean the subject. Most of the things people write about are really quite simple, and they should be written about in simple language. If you live in a house, say so. There is no need to reside in a domicile. There are millions of domicile residers in this country, and they're all bad writers. They're pretentious, and the reader gets enough of them very quickly.

Here is an excerpt from a typical piece by a married student who seems to have a gripe:

> My "better half" was exceedingly dissatisfied with the palatial quarters which our kind institution of higher learning condescended to provide us—at an exorbitant monthly cash expenditure. The "powers that be" in the business office evidenced enthusiastic concern relative to collecting this tribute, however they were not equally efficacious *re* the details like maintenance of paint and the insurance of adequately functioning plumbing . . .

A reasonable critique of this could run for pages, but essentially— it's flatulent. The attempt at sarcasm is obscured by the miasma of words. Even the meaning tends to get lost. Above all, who could read much stuff like this? Nobody really can. English teachers have to read lots of it, which is why they always justifiably consider themselves underpaid. As for mistakes, there aren't any "bad" ones except for the comma after "tribute" which is our old nemesis the comma splice (alias comma blunder, etc.), and the author was trapped into this partly by his predilection for big words. Had he used "but" instead of the more stuffy "however" his punctuation would have been okay. The main trouble, obviously, is inappropriateness of language. He's writing about something simple. Why all the fancy words? How about something like this:

> My wife was disappointed in our high-priced married-student housing. The university was prompt about collecting the rent but slovenly about upkeep. The paint was dingy and the plumbing continually got stopped up.

This is not rich, beautiful prose, but it's an infinite improvement over the first version. At least it is simple language about a simple subject. Try making your own writing thus simple and direct, and see if you are not more pleased with it.

One of the big problems a student writer faces is simply getting words on paper, and particularly getting started. It is all too easy to sit and agonize over a blank page, pondering and rejecting one possible beginning after another. He gets up and paces about the room, he explores the refrigerator, he thinks of phone calls he has to make, he sharpens all his pencils, he curses and fumes at the stupid necessity of writing the paper in the first place—and he sits and stares, sits and stares. It's tough to get started. One wise old head once said "Don't worry about a decent beginning. Get something down. Anything. It's extremely difficult to revise a paper that hasn't been written." He has something there. Write it any old way, but write it. You can always change it later, and probably will have to no matter how much you sweat it. Nine times out of ten the first paragraph is no good anyhow. This was forcibly described by James Thurber, reminiscing in *The Thurber Album* about a tough-as-a-boot newspaper editor he once worked for:

"Write a flowery introduction in the first paragraph," he told one cub reporter. "In the second paragraph, tell who, when, where, what, and how. Then, in as few paragraphs as possible, relate the most important details. Write an equally flourishing conclusion. Spend the next five minutes finding the sharpest pair of shears in the office, and cut off the first and last paragraphs. You'll have a helluva good news story."[3]

Perhaps we are not interested in news stories, but this is good advice for *any* writing. When a writer has something to say, he should start saying it, and when he gets through, stop. Fancy introductions and conclusions are generally a waste of time, most especially on a short piece, where they are like a thick bread sandwich with no filler. Very often when one looks back at some composition he's struggled with, he'll find that the thing really begins with the second paragraph and that the ornate beginning is an excrescence. Probably, too, at the end he didn't stop soon enough. At least those things are forever happening to me.

One useful trick in getting started was passed on to me years ago and many students have since found it useful. It is a way to help answer the question "What in the world do I have to say about *that?*" which students often ask, disgustedly, as they shake heads at an assigned topic. This gimmick consists of writing down a list of questions that the writer would like answered if he were reading, instead of writing, an article on the subject. For instance, suppose the writing assignment is to write on this moldy old subject: "Should Intercollegiate Football be Abolished?" A typical freshman theme topic, as you will recognize. However, the principles to be discussed here apply as well to a term paper in an advanced course. One finds he doesn't have any profound convictions on the proposition one way or the other. So he jots down a list of questions, which might look something like this:

1. Why did the old guy assign this topic?
2. Are there good things about college football?
3. If so, how many of them can I list? And can I offer evidence that they are indeed good or must I rely on assertions?
4. Ditto for the bad things.
5. Do the students have strong feelings on this? (Ask a dozen or so.)
6. How about the athletes themselves? What do they think? (Ask some. If they are pro-football, as probable, why? Mere self-interest? Other reasons?)

---

3. James Thurber, *The Thurber Album* (New York: Simon and Schuster, Inc., 1952).

7. Who supports intercollegiate football?
8. What is the attitude of the faculty toward it? (Don't guess. Ask some of them.)
9. How much time is a football player called upon to devote to football?
10. How does football compare with other sports, like tennis and golf, in the university's attitude toward it? In the attitude of the student body? Of the players?
11. Is there anything to say about different *kinds* of college football? That is, the Notre Dame-Michigan State game is one thing—but might not East Chalkboard Teachers vs. Old Slipstick Tech be something else?
12. How about post-season games?
13. Is it "intercollegiate" or is it really *pro*?

And so on. It shouldn't be hard to extend this list, but it shouldn't be necessary. In writing a thoughtful, detailed answer to almost any one of these questions anyone should have plenty of material for a theme. And the paper will have an "angle." It will be oriented toward saying something specific about a topic instead of being the assortment of dreary generalizations that English instructors have come to expect, and dread, and get. The writer might want to take more than one of the questions and answer them together—some of them seem to combine neatly. This question device may very likely be useful in getting started; getting ideas unstuck.

Some teachers think the outline very useful. Some, indeed, feel it essential and require it. Others have less confidence in it. A student, naturally, is bound by his instructor's wishes in this matter, but as an advanced student confronted by a term paper, say, or for writing one might want to do on his own, he is his own boss, so let's consider the proposition briefly. Let's discuss it first in terms of something other than writing. Suppose a man is faced with the necessity of making an office-type desk with just his own hands and an assortment of tools. You know, the standard type desk with three drawers in each pedestal and a tray drawer in the middle. What would be the first step? No, not quit. Let's assume this problem is real. The first thing to do would be to obtain or draw up a fairly detailed set of plans, and a man would have to do that to know what material to buy. A desk is a pretty complicated thing to build, after all, and one needs to know ahead of time what he is about to get involved in. Now let's imagine the desk all built, and another little job of carpentry to do. This time he needs to build a little three-legged stool. Does he need fancy drawings? Probably not. He just goes ahead and builds it. In other words, as the job gets more complicated our writer needs more elaborate guidelines. For a simple project, he doesn't need so many.

It seems to me that this parallels the relation of the outline to a job of writing. In planning a 100-150 page paper, like a master's thesis, the writer probably will need a pretty careful set of "drawings," but for a 500 word report, like the three-legged stool, he'll need less. In fact, he probably won't need to make a formal outline on paper at all, but could carry the plan in his head. Note, though, that as he sets about building the stool he should have some sort of plan, even if it's only a mental picture of what he wants the final product to look like. He's not working with no direction at all. So it is with the short paper. The writer must have some idea of what it's going to be like before he plunges into it, or he will likely turn out a shapeless monstrosity. It's the fact that it's only a little job that enables one to dispense with a formal written outline. This is what permits the typical student practice, when outlines are required to be submitted with the freshman theme, of writing the theme first and then writing the outline. If the student has really planned his composition in his head, the instructor will be none the wiser. However, this isn't really "fooling" the old boy because in his mind the really important thing is that the final paper have a readily-apparent organization, and he views the outline as merely a means to that end. If the paper is well written and well ordered, I'm sure the instructor could care less whether the student wrote the outline first or last. In fact, if his paper *is* well-constructed, he planned it, whether in his head or in black and white, so he's really done all that anyone could ask. Logically ordered papers don't just happen. In writing, as in so many other areas, it's the results that count.

If the assignment is a "research" paper, whether for a freshman course or a term paper for an advanced-level course, it helps tremendously in the final writing if the student has done a bang-up job on the research. For one thing, it is a very common experience for all of us to get really caught up in a topic as we begin to become expert on it and the resultant enthusiasm and the calm confidence springing from knowing what we're talking about, is highly likely to be reflected in the final product. This, as Hamlet said in another context, is a consummation devoutly to be wished. Further, even a difficult job of writing becomes somewhat easier if the writer really knows his subject.

Another tip that should help with writing assignments is to do them as soon as possible. No doubt this is against all human nature.

We all procrastinate, especially if the job to be done is distasteful. But if one does his paper right away he gains several advantages. For one thing, he can let it set a while and then come back to it. This gives him a big bulge on his rewriting because he can look at his words a little more objectively, almost as though someone else had written them. He'll do a much more effective job of evaluating his own stuff when his words are not fresh in his mind.

A second and very important advantage one gains by not putting it off is that he has time to get a friend, or friends, to help edit it. This is important. But he must be sure to get a friend who is "good in English." Even if he himself is "good in English," he should get someone to read the essay anyhow. It's always possible to make a blunder that the writer doesn't catch in a dozen re-readings of his own paper, but which another reader might well see right off. Why let that "other reader" be the instructor? He should get an editor.

I know that some might feel this is "cheating," that one is not "doing his own work." But they are wrong. As a matter of fact, they don't "do their own work" either, if they think this is an example of such crime. Not if they're smart, they don't. What does your instructor do when he's about to mail off an article to a professional journal? He gets a colleague to read it. He gets three or four if he can. He doesn't want some stupid mistake to appear in print with his name over it and I don't blame him.

Now certainly, one has to write his own paper. It would be serious cheating to get someone else to do it, and it would be *serious* because the one really getting cheated would be the would be writer. Presumably a student is in the class to learn a skill, writing, which will be one of the most useful anyone could possibly acquire. And he won't learn anything if he doesn't try. But granted this, it is still the part of wisdom to have someone else "read copy." The kind of person needed is, first of all, someone who knows decent writing when he sees it—and bad writing when he sees that. But of equal importance, someone who will tell you when he finds something objectionable. This is not the time for a kind and admiring friend. It's time for a critic.

Only a very naive person believes that what he reads in print is the author's unassisted work. First, the writer's work is scanned as we have seen by as many knowledgeable friends as he can corral to do the chore for him. Then the publisher will assign an editor, or editors, to work it over. True, changes are usually made with the author's concurrence, but not always. For instance, if a professor has written an article for a quarterly and his footnotes don't conform to the style used by that publication, they will be altered for him, perhaps with a tart note from the editor such as I actually saw once: "Why don't you *read* our journal?" In short, what anyone reads in print is certainly going to be the work of a number of hands, though of course the prime role is the author's. (The principal exception to this would appear to be college "humor" magazines, whose authors and editors feel their words are sacrosanct and protest any suggested editing as a violation of their academic freedom. This may be partly why such magazines are so generally sorry.)

Therefore, when an important paper is to be turned in, the author shouldn't be proud. He should get himself an editor. But in order to do this, in order to give his editor time to be helpful, he can't yank the last page out of his typewriter five minutes before the paper is due. He must do it early. It doesn't cost any more sweat in the long run, and the results are better.

This chapter has sketched a few suggestions which may be an aid to better writing. They can't help doing so, if they are applied. But there is no magic formula, no "Five Easy Steps" kind of thing. Writing will remain what it has been: work. Good luck with it.

SUGGESTED READINGS

The suggestions listed here are compiled with no unifying thought in mind except the idea that you might enjoy reading some thoughts on writing not by teachers or theoreticians but by people who made (or make) their living at it.

Writers at work. Subtitled "The *Paris Review* Interviews" and edited by Malcolm Cowley, this book was published in 1958 and contains interviews with sixteen top modern writers on the subject of their craft. The interview with Ernest Hemingway was too late to be included in the volume. However, it was reprinted in *Horizon* magazine, Vol. I, no. 3, January, 1959.

Somerset Maugham, *The Summing Up,* N.Y. Literary Guild, 1938. In this volume the old pro looks back over what was already a long and distinguished career.

Erskine Caldwell, *Call It Experience.* Subtitled "The Years of Learning How to Write," this book was originally published by Little, Brown & Co. My copy is a reprinting by Signet Books, Number Ks344.

Kenneth Roberts, *I Wanted to Write,* Doubleday, 1949. In this book the fine historical novelist (*Oliver Wiswell, Northwest Passage*) tells how he lives and works.

Benjamin Franklin, *The Autobiography.* No matter what edition you happen to get hold of, the parts dealing with his teaching himself to write will be in the first 25-30 pages. You might well want to read on, however.

Frank Gelett Burgess, "Short Words Are Words of Might." In this well-written article Burgess never uses a word of more than one syllable—that is, if you concede that "rhythm" could be considered a one syllable word. Often reprinted, my copy of it is in *Weigh the Word,* itself an interesting anthology of articles on language, edited by Charles B. Jennings, Nancy Kind and Marjorie Stevenson and published by Harper in 1957.

Paul Roberts, "How to Say Nothing in Five Hundred Words." This is chapter 27 in Roberts' *Understanding English,* Harpers, 1958. Though Roberts is not a professional writer in the sense those cited above are, he is nevertheless, in my opinion, the top writer among American scholars, as well as a very prolific one. This "How To Say Nothing" etc. has some very good tips in it for students plagued with theme writing assignments.

John Ciardi, "What Every Writer Must Learn," *Saturday Review,* Dec. 15, 1956. Poet and poetry editor of *The Saturday Review,* Ciardi in this article offers some thoughts on what differentiates good writing from pedestrian stuff, and though he is talking about literature, it seems to me that what he says has much application to our workaday writing chores too.

SELECTED BIBLIOGRAPHY

Perhaps "Bibliography" is too pretentious a label for the following list of books which is offered in the hope that some readers of this book would like to read further and deeper in some of the areas it touched on. This list is in no sense a comprehensive bibliography of books on modern language study, which would run for many pages, but simply a listing of some books which should be enjoyable (and/or useful) to the student. It is not intended to be an "annotated" list, but most of the books are commented on.

Alexander, Henry. *The Story of our Language.* Dolphin Books C383. Garden City N.Y.: Doubleday & Co. This little book is a history of the language written for the nonspecialist.

Allen, Harold B. *Applied English Linguistics.* New York: Appleton-Century-Crofts. An anthology of useful articles on linguistics, this book exists in two different editions.

Anderson, Wallace L. and Norman C. Stageberg, eds. *Introductory Readings on Language.* New York: Holt, Rinehart & Winston, 1966. Widely used as a freshman reader, this is a large collection of articles dealing with many different aspects of language.

Bach, Emmon. *An Introduction to Transformational Grammars.* New York: Holt, Rinehart & Winston, 1964. This is not a book for idle-hour reading.

Bailey, Dudley, ed. *Introductory Language Essays.* New York: W.W. Norton, and Co., 1965. Another assortment of articles on different aspects of language. Not too difficult.

Baugh, Albert C. *A History of the English Language.* New York: Appleton-Century, 1957. In spite of many later studies, this one is still perhaps "standard" history.

Bloomfield, Leonard. *Language.* New York: Holt, Rinehart & Winston, 1961. One of the basic books. Clearly written and therefore easy reading.

Bloomfield, Morton W. and Leonard Newmark. *A Linguistic Introduction to the History of English.* New York: Alfred A. Knopf, 1963.

Buchanan, Cynthia. *A Programed Introduction to Linguistics.* Boston: D.C. Heath & Co., 1965. In spite of its title, this self-teaching book deals only with phonetics and phonemics.

Chomsky, Noam. *Syntactic Structures.* Mouton and Co. S-Gravenhage, (U.S. edition, New York: Humanities Press). I include this book because it is the source of transformational grammar. It is difficult reading.

Curme, George O. *Parts of Speech and Accidence.* New York: D.C. Heath & Co., 1935.

——————. *Syntax.* New York: D.C. Heath and Co., 1931. Both of these books of Curme's represent the best of the traditional approach.

Dineen, Francis P., S.J. *An Introduction to General Linguistics.* New York: Holt, Rinehart & Winston, 1966. Among other things, this book gives a clear account of the development of language study.

Evans, Bergen and Cornelia Evans. *A Dictionary of Contemporary American Usage.* New York: Random House, 1957. This work has much information and is written in a lively style.

Francis, W. Nelson. *The Structure of American English.* New York: Ronald Press, 1958. Has much useful information, though nothing on transformational grammar.

Fries, Charles C. *American English Grammar.* New York: Appleton-Century-Crofts, 1940. A pioneering study in determining the English that Americans actually use.

——————. *The Structure of English.* New York: Harcourt Brace World, 1952. Also a pioneering study, like the one just cited, this book was the trail blazer for "structural linguistics."

Gleason, H.A., Jr. *An Introduction to Descriptive Linguistics,* revised edition. New York: Holt, Rinehart & Winston, 1961. Not easy reading, but clear—and rewarding.

——————. *Linguistics and English Grammar.* New York: Holt, Rinehart & Winston, 1965. This very useful book has one of the best accounts of "school grammar" available anywhere. It also has a fine section on the relation between linguistics and literature.

Hall, Robert A., Jr. *Leave Your Language Alone!* Linguistica. This very lively and readable book is less inflammatory than its title suggests. It was republished under the title *Linguistics and Your Language*, New York: Doubleday.

Hill, Archibald A. *An Introduction to Linguistic Structures.* New York: Harcourt Brace & World, 1958. A valuable book, but not armchair reading.

Hockett, Charles F. *A Course in Modern Linguistics.* New York: The Macmillan Co. The same comment as for Hill's book above is applicable here.

Hughes, John P. *The Science of Language.* New York: Random House, 1961. Less difficult than the Hill or Hockett Books, it is also less rewarding.

Johnson's Dictionary, a modern selection by E.L. McAdam, Jr. Pantheon Books. I include this one just because it's so much fun to dip around in it.

Koutsoudas, Andreas. *Writing Transformational Grammars: An Introduction.* New York: McGraw-Hill, 1966. This you might call an advanced-level book. However, it has many interesting problems for the reader to work out (answers provided) and is a very profitable book for the serious student.

Laird, Charlton. *The Miracle of Language.* New York: Fawcett. (Originally published by World Publishing Co.) Written for non-specialists, this is one of the brightest books available.

Long, Ralph B. *The Sentence and its Parts.* Chicago: University of Chicago Press, 1961. Long is one of the best of the modern traditionalists. Unlike many, he is thoroughly familiar with the findings of modern linguists, and hesitates not at all in disagreeing with them.

Roberts, Paul. *English Sentences.* New York: Harcourt, Brace & World, 1962.

——————————. *English Syntax.* New York: Harcourt, Brace & World, 1964. This self-teaching book is straight transformational grammar.

——————————. *Patterns of English.* New York: Harcourt, Brace & World, 1956. This lively book, written as a high school text, is one of the clearest presentations of the IC approach, which Roberts calls "pattern parts."

——————————. *Understanding English.* New York: Harper & Row, 1958. Surely one of the sprightliest English texts ever written, this book has much good information in it, though it is somewhat dated (1958) and is written for the freshman level.

——————————. *Understanding Grammar.* New York: Harper & Row, 1954. This book presents Roberts as a traditionalist, before he began looking for new and better ways of trying to describe language.

Sledd, James. *A Short Introduction to English Grammar.* Glenview, Ill.: Scott, Foresman and Co., 1959. This is the book, mentioned in the text, which presents us with nominals, adjectivals, etc.

——————————, and Wilma R. Ebbitt, eds. *Dictionaries and That Dictionary.* Glenview, Ill.: Scott, Foresman and Co., 1959. This anthology is a compilation of articles pro and con Webster's III, printed during the uproar which followed the publication of that dictionary.

Thomas, Charles Kenneth. *The Phonetics of American English*, 2nd ed. New York: Ronald Press, 1958.

Whorf, Benjamin Lee. *Language, Thought and Reality.* Cambridge: M.I.T. Press, 1956. One of the early anthropological linguists, Whorf was one of the most stimulating thinkers, and writers, on the nature of language.

INDEX